Interme
Language Practice
with key

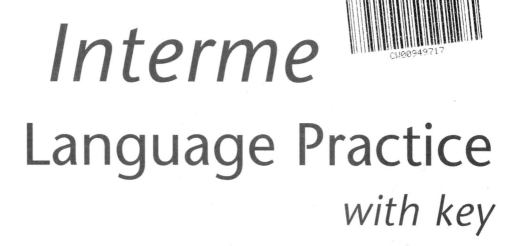

Michael Vince
with Paul Emmerson

English Grammar and
Vocabulary

MACMILLAN

Macmillan Education
Between Towns Road, Oxford OX4 3PP
A division of Macmillan Publishers Limited
Companies and representatives throughout the world

ISBN 1 405 00767 2 without key
ISBN 1 405 00768 0 with key

First published 1998
This edition published 2003

Design by Mike Brain Graphic Design Limited
Layout and composition by Mike Brain Graphic Design Limited
Cover design by Oliver Design

Illustrations by:
Ed McLachlan pp 57, 85, 174, 198; Janek Matysiak pp 224, 259;
Julian Mosedale pp 18, 33, 105, 119, 178; Martin Shovel pp 22, 49,
54, 65, 132, 155, 164, 188, 193, 217, 226, 229, 238, 241, 262, 271.

Photographs by:
Eyewire, Photodisc and Oliver Design.

The author would like to thank the many schools and teachers who
have commented on these materials. Also special thanks to
Paul Emmerson and Sarah Curtis.

Printed and bound in the UK
by Scotprint, Haddington

2007 2006 2005
10 9 8 7 6 5 4

Contents

Vocabulary

Introduction

Understanding grammar words

1 **Match the examples (a–n) with the grammar words (1–14).**

a) *a/an, the* ...12....

b) *at, to, for* ....

c) *do, have* ....

d) *can, must* ....

e) *If you do that, I'll* ....

f) *she, someone, myself* ....

g) *all, some, both, either* ....

h) *past simple, present perfect* ....

i) *What's your name? Where do you live?* ....

j) *happy, important, good* ....

k) *slowly, carefully, well* ....

l) **get up** *in the morning,* **look up** *a word* ....

m) *The letter* **that arrived this morning** *is for you.* ....

n) **It is made** *of wood. The book* **was written** *in 2001.* ....

1 verb tenses
2 auxiliary verbs
3 modal auxiliaries
4 prepositions
5 questions
6 adjectives
7 adverbs

8 conditional sentence
9 passive voice
10 pronouns
11 phrasal verbs
12 articles
13 determiners
14 relative clause

2 **Match the tenses in *italics* (a–h) with their names (1–8).**

a) Helen *is leaving* first thing in the morning. .....2....

b) *I've been studying* English for two years. ....

c) If I *had* a helicopter, I'd get to school more easily! ....

d) I *get up* at 7.30 every day. ....

e) Next year I*'ll be taking* my final exams at university. ....

f) By the time we got to the station, the train *had left*. ....

g) I*'ve lived* in Athens all my life. ....

h) While I *was walking* along the street a dog ran in front of a car. ....

1 present simple
2 present continuous
3 present perfect
4 present perfect continuous

5 past simple
6 past continuous
7 past perfect
8 future continuous

Thinking about language in context

3 For each situation (a–d) <u>underline</u> the best expression. The other alternatives may be wrong in grammar, or too informal/impolite for the situation, or too formal/polite for the situation.

a) It's your birthday on Saturday. Invite a friend to your party.
   1 I'll have a party on Saturday. You will come.
   2 I'm having a party on Saturday. Do you want to come?
   3 I have a party on Saturday. Are you coming?

b) You are on the bus. Ask a stranger to open the window.
   1 Could you open the window, please?
   2 Open the window.
   3 Excuse me, but do you think you could possibly open the window?

c) You arrive late for class and apologize to your teacher.
   1 I'm late, I apologize.
   2 Sorry I'm late.
   3 Please accept my most sincere apologies.

d) You are a witness to a minor accident. Explain what you saw to a policeman.
   1 This car comes down the road and hits a tree, bang!
   2 A car had come down the road and had hit a tree.
   3 A car came down the road and hit a tree.

Other ways of learning

4 Which ways of learning English do you use? What could you start doing now?

a) Reading for pleasure.
b) Translating.
c) Making lists of words, or problem points, in a notebook.
d) Using a dictionary.
e) Listening to songs.
f) Keeping a diary.
g) Reviewing your written work.
h) Looking at English-language internet sites.
i) Watching television, watching films or listening to the radio.
j) Using a self-study grammar/vocabulary book.

Which English?

English is a world language, and the English spoken in the USA or Australia differs from the English spoken in Britain. There are also differences between speakers from Scotland, Ireland and England, and between different parts of the same country. This book uses what is generally called Standard British English. References are also made to some differences in American English.

Present time 1

Explanations

Present simple:
form

■ The present simple is formed with the bare infinitive form of the verb. We add *s* in the third person singular *he/she/it*.

> *I like*   *You like*   *He/She/It likes*   *We like*   *They like*

Some verbs are irregular: *have, be*

> *I have*   *You have*   *He/She has*   *We have*   *They have*
> *I am*   *You are*   *He/She is*   *We are*   *They are*

■ Spelling problems

Verbs ending in *o, s, ch, sh, x* add *-es* for the third person singular.

> *He goes*   *She misses*   *She watches*   *He wishes*   *He relaxes*

■ Questions

Yes/No questions are formed with *do* and the bare infinitive form of the verb. The third person singular uses *does*.

> **Do** *you like Italian food?*   **Does** *she like Italian food?*

We also use *do/does* when we form questions with *when, what, why, where, how* etc.

> **What do** *you want?*   **Where does** *she live?*

■ Negatives

Negatives are formed with *do not* and the bare infinitive form of the verb. The third person singular uses *does not*.

> *I* **do not** *like that.*   *She* **does not** *like that.*

In speech and informal writing, *do not* becomes *don't*, and *does not* becomes *doesn't*.

> *I* **don't** *like that.*   *She* **doesn't** *like that.*

Present simple:
meaning

■ We use the present simple to describe:
Habitual actions.

> *I usually* **get up** *at 7.30.*

Actions and situations that are generally or usually true

> *Liz* **plays** *in the school basketball team.*
> *We* **like** *ice-cream.*

Facts which are always true.

> *The sun* **rises** *in the east.*

■ The present simple also has some future meanings.

Present simple: pronunciation	Verbs which end in /z/, /dz/, /s/, /sh/, /tsh/ and /ks/ make an extra syllable in the third person, pronounced /ɪz/.

watches   misses   relaxes

After /f/, /k/, /p/, /t/, third person sound is /s/.   *hits* /hɪts/

Other third person /s/ are pronounced as /z/.   *sees* /si:z/

Does is normally pronounced /dʌz/

Present continuous: form

■ The present continuous is formed with the auxiliary verb *be* and the *-ing* form of the main verb.

*I **am relaxing**.   You **are relaxing**.   He/She **is relaxing**.*
*We **are relaxing**.   They **are relaxing***

■ Spelling problems
Verbs ending *-e* drop the *-e* when they add *-ing*.

*like **liking**   decide **deciding**   write **writing***

Verbs with one syllable, ending in one vowel and one consonant, double the consonant when they add *-ing*.

*sit **sitting**   swim **swimming**   dig **digging***

Verbs ending *-ie* change *-ie* to *-y*.

*lie **lying**   tie **tying**   die **dying***

■ Contractions
In speech and informal writing, the verb be is contracted:

I'm writing.   You're writing.   He's/She's writing.
We're writing.   They're writing.

■ Questions
Yes/No questions are formed by inverting the subject and the auxiliary *be*.

Am I writing?   Are you writing?   Is he/she writing?
Are we writing?   Are they writing?

Wh- questions follow the same pattern.

What are you writing?   Why are we writing?

■ Negatives
Negatives are formed with the verb *be* + *not*. This is contracted in speech and informal writing.

I'm not writing.   He's not writing.   They're not writing.

Present continuous: meaning

■ We use the present continuous to describe:
Actions in progress at the present moment.

*Sorry, I can't speak to you, **I'm washing** my hair.*

Actions happening 'around now', even though not at the moment of speaking.

I'm reading The Lord of the Rings.

■ The present continuous also has some future meanings.

→ SEE ALSO

Grammar 3: Present time 2
Grammar 8: Future 1
Grammar 9: Future 2

Practice

1 <u>Underline</u> the correct phrase in each sentence.

a) What time *go you*/<u>*do you go*</u> to bed on Saturdays?
b) Why *are you waiting/do you waiting* outside the door?
c) Don't ask Tim. He *doesn't know/not knows* the answer.
d) *I having/I'm having* my lunch at the moment.
e) When *you leave/do you leave* the house in the morning?
f) I don't understand. What *is happening/is happen*?
g) Excuse me, *does you know/do you know* the time?
h) This is a great party. *I'm having/Am I having* a lovely time.

2 Read the answers and then complete the questions.

a) Where *does Sue live?*
Sue? She lives at the end of Axwell Road.
b) Do ....
Jim? No, I don't know him.
c) What ....
At the moment? I'm doing my homework.
d) Are ....
Here? No, I'm sitting over there.
e) Do ....
Here? No, we change trains at the next station.
f) Why ....
I'm wearing two pullovers because I feel cold!

3 Rewrite each sentence so that the verb in *italics* is a negative contraction.

a) Naomi and Bill *are watching* television.
  Naomi and Bill aren't watching television.

b) Peter *likes* chocolate cake.
  ....

c) *I'm using* this pencil at the moment.
  ....

d) The children *are having* lunch in the kitchen.
  ....

e) I *get up* early on Saturday.
  ....

f) Elena *is writing* a novel.
  ....

4   Complete each sentence with a present simple or present continuous form, using the words in **bold**.

a)   ......*Do you like*... cheese sandwiches?
  you like

b)   What time .... ?
  the sun rise

c)   What .... at the moment?
  you read

d)   Sorry, I can't talk. .... a bath.
  I have

e)   We .... at school.
  not watch videos

f)   Look out of the window! ....
  it snow

g)   This is an examination! Why .... ?
  you talk

h)   Ann .... to school by bus every day.
  go

i)   .... a uniform at your school?
  you wear

j)   Pat has got an interesting hobby. .... a boat.
  she build

5   Choose the correct spelling from each pair of words.

a)   writing/writting
b)   diging/digging
c)   takeing/taking
d)   deciding/decideing
e)   swiming/swimming
f)   having/haveing
g)   lying/lieing
h)   readding/reading
i)   using/useing
j)   waiting/waitting
k)   washeing/washing
l)   riding/rideing
m)   flyeing/flying
n)   studing/studying
o)   going/goeing

Present time 2

Explanations

Present simple: frequency adverbs

■ Frequency adverbs are often used with the present simple. They explain how often someone does an action, or something happens.

always	✓✓✓✓	I **always** get up at 7.00.
often	✓✓✓	Pat **often** goes to football matches.
usually	✓✓✓	It **usually** rains when I go on holiday!
sometimes	✓✓	We **sometimes** eat pizza for lunch.
rarely	✓	Jane **rarely** listens to jazz.
never	–	My bus **never** arrives on time.

■ Note in the above examples that the frequency adverb comes before the verb. With the verb *be* the adverb comes after.

   *Jim **is usually** late.*

■ Other frequency adverbs are: *frequently* (✓✓✓), *normally* (✓✓✓), *occasionally* (✓✓), *seldom* (✓), *hardly ever* (✓).

State verbs and action verbs

■ A state is when something stays the same. An action is when something happens. State verbs are not usually used in any continuous form.

   I know what you mean.   (NOT ~~I am knowing what you're meaning~~.)

Examples of state verbs are:
- senses: *appear, hear, look like, see, taste*
- feeling: *like, hate, love, prefer, want, wish*
- thinking: *agree, believe, forget, know, think, understand*
- possession: *belong to, contain, have, own*
- being: *be, exist*
- other: *cost, depend on, mean, need*

■ Some of the verbs in the previous list can have a 'state' meaning and an 'action' meaning. Examples include *be, have, taste, think.*

   I have *two sisters.*   (permanent state)
   I'm having *problems with this computer.*   (temporary action)

■ Sometimes state verbs can describe temporary feelings.

   How are you getting on at your new school?
   I hate/I'm hating *it!*

Present simple or continuous?	Compare:	
	Present simple	Present continuous
	permanent	temporary
	habits and routines	in progress now
	facts that are always true	events happening at the moment
	general situations	a particular situation

> *I **live** in Budapest.* (all the time)
> *I'm **living** in Budapest.* (for a few months)
> *This plane **lands** in Frankfurt.* (routine)
> *We're **landing**.* (in progress now)

Present continuous: future meanings

- The present continuous can be used to describe a fixed future arrangement. There is usually a future time expression.
  > *Paul **is leaving** early tomorrow morning.*
  > *My parents **are buying** me a mountain bike for my birthday.*

  This usage is common when we describe social arrangements.
  > *Are you **doing** anything on Saturday? **We're going skating**.*

Other problems

- *feel*

  There is almost no difference of meaning between the simple and continuous.
  > *I **feel** awful!*   *I'm **feeling** awful!*
  > *How **do you feel** now?*   *How **are you feeling** now?*

- Present continuous or present perfect continuous?
  > *Sue **is staying** with Jill.*
  > (in progress now, and will continue)
  > *Sue **has been staying** with Jill since March.*
  > (in progress up to now, and may or may not continue)

- Present continuous with *always*

  We can use *always* with the present continuous when we are exaggerating or complaining. We emphasize *always* in speech in this case.
  > *You're **always** forgetting your keys!*

- Present simple in narratives

  In speech we can use the present simple to make a story or joke appear more immediate and interesting, even though the events were in the past. This is also used in written summaries such as plots of television series.
  > *A man **walks** into a bar and **asks** for a glass of water. The barman says ...*
  > *The story so far: Michael **meets** Susan in the library and **tells** her about the missing earrings ...*

 SEE ALSO

Grammar 4: Past time 1
Grammar 5: Past time 2
Grammar 6: Present perfect 1
Grammar 8: Future 1

Practice

1 <u>Underline</u> the correct sentence for each situation.

a) You want to invite a friend to your party on Friday. You say:
   1 I have a party on Friday. Do you want to come?
   2 <u>I'm having a party on Friday. Do you want to come?</u>

b) You find a wallet on your desk and ask the people nearby:
   1 Who does this wallet belong to?
   2 Who is this wallet belonging to?

c) A friend invites you to a snack bar at lunch time. You say:
   1 Thanks, but I always go home.
   2 Thanks, but I'm always going home.

d) A friend opens the door and says: What are you doing? You reply:
   1 I work as a secretary.
   2 I'm repairing the computer.

e) You haven't decided yet about buying a new bike. You say:
   1 I think about it.
   2 I'm thinking about it.

f) A friend asks: Do you like lemon tea? You reply:
   1 I prefer tea with milk.
   2 I'm preferring tea with milk.

g) A friend asks you if you have finished the book she lent you. You say:
   1 Sorry, I still read it.
   2 Sorry, I'm still reading it.

h) It's a hot day, but a friend has a heavy coat on. You ask:
   1 Why do you wear a heavy coat?
   2 Why are you wearing a heavy coat?

2 <u>Underline</u> the correct word or phrase in each sentence.

a) That can't be right! *I don't believe/I'm not believing* it!
b) Caroline can't swim today. She *has/is having* a cold.
c) See you in the morning. I *leave/I'm leaving* now.
d) What *do you do/are you doing*? If you drop it, it will explode!
e) Stop doing that, Bill! *You're/You're being* very silly.
f) *I drive/I'm driving*! You can sit in the back with Martin.
g) *What do we eat/are we eating* this evening? I'm really hungry!
h) You're a great cook! This cake *tastes/is tasting* wonderful.
i) Where *do you go/are you going*? I haven't finished speaking to you!
j) Chemistry is hard. *I don't understand/I'm not understanding* it.

3 **Put each verb in brackets into the present simple or present continuous.**

a) Ugh, don't show me that picture! I (hate) ......*hate*........................ mice!

b) Who (you, go) .... to the match on Saturday with?

c) In the winter, what (you, wear) .... ?

d) I can't stand horror films. I (think) .... they're silly!

e) Diana (not, usually, sit) .... next to Ellen.

f) Why (you, look at) .... me like that?

g) Excuse me. (this bus, stop) .... outside the station?

h) I (not take) .... the bus to school today.

4 **Match each sentence (a–h) with a suitable response (1–8).**

a) What do you usually do on your birthday? .....*1*.....

b) Would you like to meet again on Saturday? ....

c) What do you usually do when there is an earthquake? ....

d) Have you finished your homework? ....

e) What are you doing? ....

f) What are you doing on Friday? ....

g) Are you in the school basketball team? ....

h) What do you do? ....

1 I have a party.
2 I lie under the table.
3 I work in a travel agency.
4 Yes, we play every Friday.
5 I'm still doing it.
6 It's hot in here. I'm opening some windows.
7 I'm going back to Canada tomorrow.
8 I'm having a party.

5 **Put each verb in brackets into the present simple or present continuous.**

a) What (usually, you, do) *do..you..usually..do.* at the weekend?

b) Don't worry about the cat. It (only eat) .... once a day.

c) I can't work out the answer. (you, know) .... what it is?

d) What's the matter? Why (you, stare) .... at me like that?

e) (you, speak) .... English? I'm looking for a hotel.

f) Elena (stay) .... with me while her house is being decorated.

g) You should go on a diet. (you, put) .... on weight.

h) (they, speak) .... French or German? I can't tell the difference.

Past time 1

Explanations

Past simple: form

■ Regular verbs

Past simple regular verbs add -*ed* to the bare infinitive. Verbs ending in -*e* simply add -*d*.

> I **enjoyed** *the film.*   I **loved** *the music.*

All persons have the same form.

■ Spelling problems

Verbs ending in consonant + -*y* change -*y* to -*ie*.

> *try* **tried**   *cry* **cried**

Verbs ending with one vowel and one consonant double the final consonant.

> *regret* **regretted**   *fit* **fitted**

■ Irregular verbs

The most common irregular verbs are listed on page 277. It is necessary to learn these forms.

> *eat* **ate**   *drink* **drank**   *wake* **woke**

■ Questions

Questions are formed with *did* and the bare infinitive.

> **Did you enjoy** *the film?*   **Did you drink** *all the milk?*
> *What* **did you do** *yesterday?*   *Why* **did she leave?**

■ Negatives

Negatives are formed with *did not* and the bare infinitive. This is contracted to *didn't* in speech and informal writing.

> *The coat* **didn't fit** *me.*   *Carol* **didn't eat** *very much.*

Past simple: meaning

■ The past simple is used to describe actions and states in a completed period of time. We know when the action happened, so a definite time expression can be used.

> I **enjoyed** *the film we saw* **last night**.
> *We* **listened** *to some new CDs* **yesterday afternoon**.

■ The past simple is also used to describe habitual actions in the past.

> *Every day we* **got up** *early and* **went** *to the beach.*

Past continuous: form

- The past continuous is formed with the past of the auxiliary verb *be* and the *-ing* form of the main verb.

    *I **was sitting** by the door.*   *You **were laughing**.*   *He/She **was driving**.*
    *We **were crying**.*   *They **were eating**.*

- Questions
    Yes/No questions are formed by inverting the subject and the auxiliary verb *be*.

    ***Was I** sleeping?*   ***Were you** waiting?*   ***Was he/she** driving?*
    ***Were we** writing?*   ***Were they** leaving?*

    Wh- questions follow the same pattern.

    ***What were you** writing?*   ***Why were they** waiting?*

- Negatives
    Negatives are formed with the verb auxiliary verb *be + not*. This is contracted in speech and informal writing.

    *I **wasn't** listening.*   *He **wasn't** playing.*   *They **weren't** looking.*

Past continuous: meaning

- The past continuous is used to describe a situation in progress in the past. This is often contrasted with a sudden event in the past simple.

Background situation	Sudden event
*I **was having** my lunch*	*when Ruth **phoned**.*
*While I **was waiting** for the bus,*	*I **met** Karen.*

- The past continuous can be used to describe several situations in progress, happening at the same time.

    *While James **was cooking**, David **was phoning** a friend.*
    *The airport was full of people. Some **were sleeping** on benches, some **were shopping**, others **were reading**. Everyone **was waiting** for news of the delayed plane.*

Time expressions

- With the past simple
    *I arrived here **two hours ago/in September/last week/at 6.00**.*
    *Helen lived in Madrid **for three years**.*

- With the past continuous
    We can use *when* or *while* with the past continuous to mean 'during the time that'.

    ***While** we were waiting for the train, it started to rain.*
    *I cut my finger **when** I was peeling the potatoes.*

    But if we mean 'at the time that' then we only use *when* with the past simple.

    *She was very happy **when she got** her exam results.*

> → SEE ALSO
>
> **Grammar 7:** Present perfect 2
> **Grammar 32:** Time expression

Practice

1 <u>Underline</u> the correct word or phrase in each sentence.

a) While I *washed/was washing* my hair, the phone *rang/ringed*.

b) How *did you felt/did you feel* yesterday afternoon?

c) When I *got/was getting* home I *received/was receiving* a phone call.

d) Last summer I *was going swimming/went swimming* every weekend.

e) When the dog *bit/was biting* Laura's leg, she *screamed/was screaming*.

f) We *sang/sung* some songs and then *ate/eat* some sandwiches.

g) When you *fell/felt* over the cliff, what *happened/was happening* next?

h) While Mary *washed-up/was washing-up*, she *broke/was breaking* a cup.

i) I didn't *see/saw* where the bus stop was, so I *was missing/missed* the bus.

j) What *did you do/were you doing* when I *phoned/was phoning* you last night?
   There was no reply.

2 Rewrite each sentence according to the instructions given.

a) I enjoyed the concert. (negative)   *..I didn't enjoy the concert...........*

b) You ate all the bread. (question)   ....

c) Did John spend a lot? (affirmative)   ....

d) I felt well yesterday. (negative)   ....

e) Anna didn't buy a car. (affirmative)   ....

f) They won the prize. (question)   ....

g) Paul doesn't speak Greek. (affirmative)   ....

h) I paid all the bills. (negative)   ....

3 Complete each sentence with a suitable time expression from the box. You can use an expression more than once.

ago	in	last week	at	when	~~while~~

a) A burglar broke into the house ....*while*...... we were watching television.

b) .... I met an old friend of mine in the city centre.

c) What were you doing .... the police officer knocked on the door?

d) Jan met Sarah .... half-past eight outside the cinema.

e) .... Dick was preparing lunch, he cut his finger badly.

f) I first came to this town more than twenty years ....

g) Jeff was studying to be a doctor .... he met Sally.

h) Tony bought his first motorbike .... 1992.

i) .... did you start playing basketball?

j) Most of the young people left this village a long time ....

4   Match each sentence (a–h) with a suitable response (1–8).

a) What was Katrina doing when you knocked on the door? ....*3*.....

b) How did Brenda spend her holiday? ....

c) What happened when the lights went out? ....

d) When did you meet Cathy? ....

e) What did Julie do when Tony called? ....

f) Did Suzannah hear what David said? ....

g) What did Lucy do when the bell rang at the end of the lesson? ....

h) Why did Alicia leave so early? ....

1 She went sailing most days, and sunbathed at the beach.

2 She put the phone down.

3 She was listening to the radio in the kitchen.

4 She went to meet her parents at a restaurant.

5 She came to my brother's birthday party.

6 While Tina was looking for a torch, they came back on.

7 She wasn't listening.

8 She put her books away and left.

5   Put each verb in brackets into either the past simple or past continuous.

a) When Harry (wake up) ......*woke up*........... , we (tell) ......*told*.................. him the news.

b) Everyone (wait) .... for the concert to begin when a message (arrive) ....

c) Charlotte (want) .... a relaxing holiday, so she (choose) .... to stay on a small island.

d) When Roberto (study) .... in America, his parents (phone) .... him every week.

e) I (find) .... my pen while I (look for) .... my bag.

f) Ann (watch) .... a film on television when Julie (arrive) ....

g) When the lights (go out) .... , I (lie) .... in bed reading.

h) When you (go) .... to the new Chinese restaurant, what (you eat) .... ?

Past time 2

Explanations

Past perfect: form

- The past perfect is formed with the auxiliary *had* and the past participle (third column in verb tables). The past participles of irregular verbs are listed on page 277.

    *I **had decided**.   She **had left**.   We **had eaten**.*

    In speech and informal writing these forms are contracted to:

    ***I'd** decided.   **She'd** left.   **We'd** eaten.*

- Questions and negatives

    Questions are formed by inverting the subject and *had*. Negatives are formed with *not* and contractions are used.

    ***Had** she **left**?*

    *She **had not left**.   She **hadn't left**.*

Past perfect: meaning

- The past perfect is used to show clearly that one past event happened before another past event. We use the past perfect for the earlier event.

    Sue left at 7.00.   We arrived at her house at 8.30.

    → *When we **arrived** at Sue's house, she **had left**.*

    It is not necessary to use the past perfect if we use *before* or *after* to make the time sequence clear, although many speakers do so to show a strong connection between the two events.

    *Sue **left** her house **before** we arrived.*

    OR *Sue **had left** her house **before** we arrived.*

    *We **arrived** at Sue's house **after** she left.*

    OR *We **arrived** at Sue's house **after** she **had left**.*

- Note that it is not necessary to use the past perfect just because an event happened a long time ago. We use past simple.

    *The Chinese **built** the Great Wall over two thousand years ago.*

Past perfect: common uses

- The past perfect is often used with verbs of thinking like *think, know, be sure, realize, remember, suspect, understand* etc.

    *I thought **I'd seen** the film before, but I hadn't.*

    *David knew **he'd seen** her somewhere before.*

    *Ellen was sure she **hadn't locked** the door.*

    *When I got home I realized **I'd lost** my wallet.*

    *The inspector suspected that the thief **had used** a special key.*

used to

- *Used to* describes a habit or state in the past. There is no present form. *Used to* suggests that the action or situation is no longer true and so makes a contrast with the present.

  *I **used to** have long hair when I was younger.*

  It is used for repeated actions and not for single events.

  *I **used to** play tennis, but now I play football.*

- Questions and negatives

  With questions and negatives *used to* becomes *use to.*

  ***Did you use to** have long hair when you were younger?*

  *I **didn't use to** play tennis, but now I play most weekends.*

- Pronunciation

  Used is pronounced /juːst/. This is different from the past tense of the verb *use*, pronounced /juzd/.

would

Would is used in the same way as *used to*, but it only describes repeated actions in the past, not states. It is more common in descriptive writing than in speech.

  *On winter days, we **would/used to** all sit around the fire and tell stories.*

  *I **used to own** a motorbike. (NOT I would own a motorbike.)*

Past perfect and past simple

- Study the situations and the example sentences:

  Situation 1: the film starts at 8.00, I arrive at 7.50.

  a) *I **arrived** at 7.50, just before the film **started**.*

  b) *When the film **started**, I **had** already **arrived** ten minutes before.*

  Situation 2: the film starts at 8.00, I arrive at 8.10.

  a) *The film **started** at 8.00, but I **arrived** ten minutes late.*

  b) *I **arrived** at 8.10, but the film **had** already **started**.*

  To describe these situations it is possible to use the past simple for both verbs, as in 1a) and 2a). It is also possible to put the event that happened first into the past perfect, as in 1b) and 2b).

  However, 1a) is more simple and much more likely than 1b). In 1b) we emphasize which event happened first (me arriving) – but arriving first is normal when we go to the cinema so we don't need to emphasize it.

  In situation 2 both a) and b) are possible. 2a) is simple and easy to use and understand. But 2b) helps the meaning by emphasizing which event happened first (the film starting).

Past forms used in conditionals

- Note that the past simple and past perfect are also used in conditional sentences (*If ...*). In these sentences they have a different meaning.

SEE ALSO

Grammar 13: Conditionals 1
Grammar 14: Conditionals 2

Practice

1 Underline the errors in these sentences. Rewrite each sentence.

a) When we had <u>ate</u> lunch, we <u>were sitting</u> in the garden.
   When we had eaten lunch, we sat in the garden.

b) While I looked for my keys, I remembered I left them at home.

c) Anna had used to play badminton when she had been at school.

d) When I got into bed, I was falling asleep immediately.

e) When I was finally finding the house, I was knocking at the door.

f) After Jill was giving Nick his books, she went home.

g) Maria would live in Sweden when she was a child.

h) I was using to get up early when I had gone sailing.

i) The Vikings had sailed to North America a thousand years ago.

j) Juliet was sure she was seeing the tall man before.

2 Underline the correct word or phrase in each sentence.

a) While I *had waited/<u>was waiting</u>/waited* at the bus stop, I *had noticed/was noticing/noticed* a new shop which *wasn't/hadn't been* in the street the day before.

b) I *had gone/went* out into the garden to fetch my bike, but *found/was finding* that someone *stole/had stolen* it.

c) When George *met/was meeting* Diane at the party, he *thought/was thinking* that he *saw/had seen/was seeing* her somewhere before.

d) Emily *got off/was getting off* the bus, and *walked/was walking* into the bank when she *realized/had realized/was realizing* that she *left/had left/was leaving* her handbag on the bus.

e) After I *was buying/had bought* my new computer, I discovered that I *wasn't having/didn't have* enough memory.

f) I went to the post office to ask about my package, but they *had said/said* that it still *hadn't arrived/didn't arrive*.

3 Put each verb given into the past simple, past continuous or past perfect. More than one answer may be possible.

The police suspected that Brian (a) ...*had broken*..... (break) the window at his house because he (b) .... (want) to make them think that a burglar (c) .... (steal) his valuable stamp collection. They (d) .... (think) that Brian (e) .... (do) this because he (f) .... (need) the money. However, they (g) .... (not know) that Brian (h) .... (fly) to Brazil the week before, and (i) .... (be) abroad when the burglary (j) .... (take place).

4 Complete each sentence, using *would* or *used to* and the verb in brackets. More than one answer may be possible.

a) Jack (have) ...*used to have*......... a beard but he shaved it off.

b) My mother (read) .... to me every night.

c) In the holidays we (meet) .... at the beach every morning.

d) I (not like) .... spinach, but now I do.

e) Helen (write) .... to me often, but now she phones.

f) Tina (live) .... in the house opposite.

g) When I was young, the summers (be) .... warmer.

h) Whenever our teacher let us leave early, we (cheer) .... !

5 For each question, complete the second sentence so that it means the same as the first, using no more than three words.

a) Michael took a deep breath and dived into the water.
   After Michael ....*had taken*............... a deep breath, he dived into the water.

b) Terry was fatter.
   Terry .... to be so thin.

c) Gary was sure his keys were not in his pocket.
   Gary was sure .... his keys.

d) When he was younger David played tennis.
   David .... tennis when he was younger.

e) Last summer, Julia got up early every morning.
   Last summer, Julia used to .... early every morning.

f) We missed the bus so we took a taxi.
   We took a taxi because .... the bus.

g) In those days, we spent the summer in the mountains.
   In those days, we .... the summer in the mountains.

6 Combine the two sentences to make one sentence. Use *when* and the past perfect.

a) I washed and got ready. I went out to meet my friends.
   When I'd washed and got ready, I went out to meet my friends.

b) I knew much more about the job. I visited their offices.
   ....
   ....

c) I looked at the new dress for ages. I asked how much it cost.
   ....
   ....

d) I felt much more independent. I passed my driving test.
   ....
   ....

e) Anne went on holiday. She saved enough money.
   ....
   ....

f) The team finally won the match. They ran round the pitch to celebrate.
   ....
   ....

Present perfect 1

Explanations

Present perfect: form

- The present perfect is formed with the present tense of the auxiliary verb *have* and the past participle (third column in verb tables). The past participles of irregular verbs are listed on page 277.

  *I **have decided** to leave tomorrow.* (regular)

  *She **has written** the email to Lucy.* (irregular)

  In speech and informal writing these forms are contracted to:

  I've decided. *She's written.*

- Questions and negatives

  Questions are formed by inverting the subject and *have*. Negatives are formed with *not* and contractions are used.

  ***Have you decided** yet?*

  *She **has not written** the email.* *She **hasn't written** the email.*

Present perfect: meaning

The present perfect describes past events which are connected to the present. There are a number of different uses:

- Experiences in our life up to now.

  ***Have you visited** any other countries?*

  *Yes, **I've been** to Italy and France.*

  There is no time expression because we are talking about a whole life experience, not individual events. If we wanted to say when the events happened we would use the past simple.

- An event in the past that has a result in the present.

  *Helen **has broken** her pencil.*

  ***I've hurt** my foot.*

  There is no time expression because when it happened is not important. Our attention is on the present (Where is the pencil sharpener? / I can't play football). If we wanted to say when the actions happened we would use the past simple.

- A situation that started in the past and continues until the present.

  ***I've lived here** for ten years.*

  ***I've often seen** Jim with his dog in the park.*

  Here there is a time expression, describing how long or how often something has happened.

■ Completion
We often use the present perfect when we describe how many things are completed so far.

I've read a hundred pages of this book.

An exact time is not mentioned.

Time expressions

■ *ever, never*
We use *ever* and *never* when we ask or talk about our experiences in life.

*Have you **ever** eaten Japanese food?*

*No, I've **never** eaten it.*

■ *yet, so far* and *already*
We use *yet* in questions and negative sentences. It has a similar meaning to *so far* (or 'up to now'), which is used in questions and positive sentences.

*Have you **finished** this book **yet**? No, I'm on page 56.*

*How many pages have you read? I've **read** 56 pages **so far**.*

We use *already* in positive sentences to describe an action which happened before.

When are you going to finish your letter?

*I've **already written** it.*

■ *just*
We use *just* when we describe a very recent event.

*Cathy **has just phoned** from the airport.*

■ Frequency adverbs: *always, often* etc.
Frequency adverbs that are used with the present simple can also be used with the present perfect.

*He **has always loved** you.*   (a state)

*We **have often visited** Spain.*   (a repeated event)

■ *for* and *since*
for describes the length of a time period.

*Tom **has worked** here **for three months**.*

since describes the point when the time period started.

*Tom **has worked** here **since July 10th**.*

 SEE ALSO

Grammar 3: Present time 2

21

Practice

1 **Put each verb into a form of the present perfect simple.**

a) What's the matter? (you cut) .....*Have you cut*......... yourself?

b) I (have) .... a headache ever since lunchtime.

c) Nadia (never see) .... any Chinese films.

d) Someone (steal) .... Mr Grant's bike.

e) The passengers are tired because they (not sleep) .... all night.

f) I'm afraid we (just break) .... your window. Sorry!

g) David (not win) .... a prize this time, I'm afraid.

h) (you ever eat) .... Spanish food? It's great!

2 **Complete what each speaker says.**

a)

We ....*'ve been married*...... for twenty-five wonderful years!

b)

I .... on holiday to Australia.

c)

I .... twenty-three letters!

d)

I .... a snail before!

e)

I .... you since the day we met!

f)

Oh no! I .... my pencil!

3 Complete each sentence with a time word or phrase from the box.

| yet | for | ~~since~~ | often | ever | never | already | so far | just | always |

a) Luis has lived in the city centre ....*since*...... 1996.

b) Thanks for the present! I've .... wanted a pet goldfish!

c) Have you .... drunk pineapple juice? It's fantastic!

d) I've .... heard some fantastic news! I've passed my exams!

e) Hurry up! Haven't you finished .... ? You're so slow!

f) Nina has worked in this company .... five years.

g) I've .... been on a big ship before. It's an interesting experience!

h) We're very busy today. .... we've sold over a hundred bikes.

i) I've .... passed this building, but this is the first time I've been inside.

j) Can I have a different book? I've .... read this one.

4 For each question, complete the second sentence so that it means the same as the first, using no more than three words.

a) We started working here three years ago.
We ..*'ve worked here*........... for three years.

b) This is the first time I've been on a plane.
I .... on a plane before.

c) That's strange! My pen isn't here!
That's strange! .... disappeared!

d) Nicky and Jan aren't at this school any more.
Nicky and Jan .... this school.

e) I saw a friend of yours a few moments ago.
I .... a friend of yours.

f) I'm still writing my letters.
I .... writing my letters yet.

g) Is this your first visit to South America?
Have .... to South America before?

h) Oh no! My wallet is still in the car.
Oh no! I .... my wallet in the car.

i) It's a long time since we spoke to your sister.
We .... to your sister for a long time.

j) Is Anna still asleep?
Has .... up yet?

Present perfect 2

Explanations

**Present perfect
continuous: form**

The present perfect continuous is formed with the present perfect of *be*, and the
-ing form of the verb.

> *I've been waiting here all morning.*
> *What have you been doing lately?*
> *I haven't been sleeping well recently.*

**Present perfect
continuous:
meaning**

■ The present perfect continuous, like the present perfect, describes past events
which are connected to the present. But in the continuous form there is a
meaning of an action or situation in progress.

> *What have you been doing lately?*
> *I've been working a lot.*
> *How long have you been living here?*

■ The present perfect continuous can emphasize the length of time of the
action.

> *I've been waiting here all morning.*
> *I've been feeling ill for weeks.*

■ The present perfect continuous can emphasize that the action is temporary.

> *I've been staying in a hotel for the past month.*

■ The present perfect continuous can be used for repeated actions.

> *I've been phoning her for days, but she's never at home.*

■ The action may be finished or continuing, we only know by the situation.

> *Carlos has been studying English for two years and now he's stopped! What a
> shame.*
> *Carlos has been studying English for two years. He's going to do an exam next
> year.*

Time expressions

Typical time expressions that are used with the present perfect continuous
include:

> *all day, all morning, for days, for ages, lately, recently, since, for*

Present perfect or present perfect continuous?

- Often there is very little difference between the two tenses:
  I've worked/been working here for two years.
  I've lived/been living here for two years.

- We often use the present perfect if our attention is on the finished result, but the present perfect continuous if our attention is on the action.
  I've written that email to Jackie. I was meaning to do it for ages.
  I've been writing that email to Jackie and it's taken an hour! I'm exhausted!

- If we give details of how many or how much we do not use a continuous form.
  I've written four emails.
  I've done a lot of cooking and cleaning this afternoon.

Other problems

- Present simple or present perfect?
  We use the present simple to describe habits or states in the present, but we use the present perfect to describe the time until the present.
  I live in Prague.
  (a permanent state – I always live there)
  I've lived in Prague for two years.
  (I arrived two years ago and still live there)

- Past simple or present perfect?
  The past simple describes an event in a completed time period. The present perfect is used for a time period that includes the present.
  I lived in Prague in the nineties.   (now I live somewhere else)
  I've lived in Prague since the nineties.   (I still live there)

  The choice of tense often depends on whether our attention is in the past or the present.
  I had an umbrella, but I left it on the bus.
  (the event is distant in my mind)
  Oh no! I've left my umbrella on the bus.
  (the event is present in my mind)

- *have been* and *have gone*
  If we *have been* to a place, we went there and have now returned. If we *have gone* to a place, we went there but have not returned.
  Melissa has been to China.   (and she has come back)
  Melissa has gone to China.   (and she is still there)

 SEE ALSO

Grammar 4: Past time 1

Practice

1   Underline the correct word or phrase in each sentence.

   a) *I live here/I've lived here* since the end of last year.
   b) I'm afraid the last train *left/has left* an hour ago.
   c) Someone *has just stolen/has just been stealing* my bicycle.
   d) Thank you for your offer, but *I decided/I've decided* not to accept.
   e) Yesterday *I lost/I've lost* my wallet.
   f) Take your umbrella with you. *It started/It's started* raining.
   g) We're enjoying our trip. *We visited/We've visited* two countries so far.
   h) *I'm standing here/I've been standing here* for hours and I feel tired.
   i) This *was/has been* a busy day and it isn't over yet!
   j) I feel really tired. *We went/We've been* to a party last night.

2   Put each verb in brackets into either the present perfect, past simple or present simple.

   a) Last week I (lose) ....*lost*............ my scarf, and now I (just lose) ....*'ve just lost*............ my gloves.
   b) I (work) .... for Blue Bank at the moment but I (decide) .... to change jobs.
   c) We (be) .... here for hours. Are you sure we (come) .... to the right place?
   d) (you see) .... my calculator? I'm sure I (leave) .... it here earlier.
   e) We (have) .... some coffee and then (catch) .... the bus home.
   f) I (never eat) .... octopus, but once on holiday I (eat) .... some squid.
   g) I (hope) .... you aren't a vegetarian. I (cook) .... you some lamb chops.
   h) Recently a lot of young people (take up) .... kite surfing.
   i) When we (reach) .... the cinema, there (not be) .... any tickets left.
   j) Please come quickly! Nick (have) .... an accident, and he (go) .... to hospital.

3   Complete each mini-dialogue by putting the verbs given in brackets into either the present perfect or present perfect continuous.

a) A: Terminator 2 is on at the Rex? (you see) ...*Have you seen*......... it?

   B: No, not yet. Shall we go? I (look forward) ...*'ve been looking forward*...

   to seeing it for ages.

b) A: What's the matter? You look really tired!

   B: I am! I (study) .... all day, and I (not finish)

   .... yet.

   A: Oh well, time for a break.

c) A: I (phone) .... Carol all day, but there's no reply.

   B: I expect she (go) .... swimming with her friends.

d) A: (you hear) .... the news?

   B: What news?

   A: Someone (rob) .... the bank at the end of the road.

e) A: Why is your leg in plaster?

   B: That's a silly question! I (break) .... it, of course.

   A: Someone (write) .... 'Break Time' on the plaster!

4   For each question, complete the second sentence so that it means the same as the first, using no more than three words.

a) I came to live here three months ago.

   I ...*'ve been living*............ here for three months.

b) Sophie is out at the shops at the moment.

   Sophie .... to the shops.

c) I've had French lessons since March.

   I .... French since March.

d) I'm still reading this book.

   I .... reading this book yet.

e) Paul left the room a moment ago.

   Paul has .... the room.

f) It's ages since I last went to the cinema.

   I .... to the cinema for ages.

g) This is the first time I've eaten snails.

   I .... snails before.

h) I don't remember Helen's phone number.

   I've .... Helen's phone number.

5 Complete each sentence with one suitable word.

We've had a very interesting trip (a) ....*so*............. far, and we've had some interesting adventures (b) .... the last time we wrote. We've (c) .... to some beautiful islands, and (d) .... a lot of interesting people. In fact (e) .... we've made friends with some people in a village, and they've been (f) .... us the local language. I haven't managed to learn much (g) .... , but Ann (h) .... picked up quite a lot, and can speak well. She's been (i) .... every day, and she's (j) .... me everything she knows!

6 <u>Underline</u> the errors in these sentences. Rewrite each sentence.

a) My penfriend <u>is</u> writing to me for years.
My penfriend has been writing to me for years.

b) We have started this course three weeks ago.
....

c) 'What have you been doing all day?' 'I've been written letters.'
....

d) When have you arrived in this city?
....

e) You have ever been to India?
....

f) Paula has been stayed in a hotel by the sea.
....

g) I've been feeling ill three weeks ago.
....

h) I live in this city since I was born.
....

i) I wait here for ages. Where have you been?
....

j) Tony has leaved his books on the bus.
....

Explanations

Future time

We can refer to the future in English by using *will, be going to* or by using present tenses. Sometimes we can use different forms and there is little difference between them, other times there is a difference.

will

- Form
  The *will* future is formed with the infinitive without *to*. The negatives of *will* is *won't*. *Will* is usually shortened in speech and informal writing to *'ll*. Some speakers use *shall* to refer to the future in formal situations with *I* and *we*. However this use is becoming very rare. In modern English *shall* is used for suggestions only:
  Shall I open the window?

- Meaning
  We use *will* to talk generally about future beliefs, opinions, hopes and predictions. There is usually a time expression. We can add *perhaps, probably* or *definitely* to show how certain or uncertain we are about our predictions.
  *In the next century, most people **will probably** live in big cities.*
  ***Perhaps it'll** rain tomorrow.*
  *United **will definitely** win tonight.*
  Notice that probably comes after *will* but before *won't*.
  *She'**ll probably** come with us tonight.*
  *She **probably won't** come with us tonight.*

be going to

- Form
  The *be going to* future is formed with the verb *be* + *going* + the infinitive.
  *Jean **is going to learn** to drive.*
  *Tim and Ann **are going to travel** abroad next year.*

- Meaning
  We use *going to* for plans and intentions. The plan may be in the near future, or more distant.
  *I'm **going to do** lots of work this evening.*
  *After I finish University I'm **going to travel** all over Europe by InterRail.*
  We also use *going to* for predictions. We use *going to* when there is some evidence in the present situation, for example we can see something.
  *Look out! Those books **are going to fall**!*

Present continuous

■ Form
See Grammar 2 for the form of the present continuous.
   I'm meeting my mother for lunch at one.

■ Meaning
We use the present continuous to talk about things we have arranged to do, in particular social arrangements and appointments. There is nearly always a time expression.
   A: *Are you doing anything on Friday evening?*
   B: *Not really. Why?*
   A: *I'm having a party. Would you like to come?*

Problems

■ *will* or *going to*?
Will and *going to* are both used for predictions, and on most occasions either is possible.
   *I think **it's going to/it'll probably** rain tomorrow.*
However if there is strong evidence in the present situation, then *going to* is usually used:
   *I think **it's going to** rain this afternoon.*
   (looking up at black clouds in the sky)

■ *going to* or present continuous?
Going to and the present continuous are both used for plans and arrangements, and on most occasions either is possible.
   I'm going to have/I'm having a party on Friday.
However, *going to* can suggest that the details are not yet finalized – it's still just a plan. Whereas the present continuous can suggest that the arrangement is more fixed, with a time and a place.
   *Jean **is going to have** another driving lesson soon.*
   (a plan, with no specific time)
   *Jean **is having** her driving lesson this afternoon.*
   (it's fixed, in her diary)

■ other meanings of *will*
Will has other meanings, for example spontaneous decisions that come into our head at the moment of speaking, promises etc.
   Is that the phone ringing? I'll answer it.   (a spontaneous decision)
   I'll do the best that I can to help you.   (a promise)

■ *be*
With *be* we use *will* or *going to*, not the present continuous.
   *I'll **be** back on Friday.*
   *I'm going to **be** back on Friday.*

→ SEE ALSO

Grammar 2: Present time 1
Grammar 9: Future 2

Practice

1 <u>Underline</u> the correct sentence, 1 or 2, in each mini-dialogue.

a) A: Can you come dancing tomorrow night?
   B: 1 Sorry, I'll play basketball.
      2 <u>Sorry, I'm playing basketball.</u>

b) A: What are your plans for the summer?
   B: 1 I'll spend a month in the mountains.
      2 I'm going to spend a month in the mountains.

c) A: What do you think about the weather?
   B: 1 It'll probably rain tomorrow.
      2 It's raining tomorrow.

d) A: What about tomorrow at about 5.30?
   B: 1 OK, I'll see you then.
      2 OK, I'm seeing you then.

e) A: Mary is buying a dog next week.
   B: 1 Really? What is she calling it?
      2 Really? What is she going to call it?

f) A: It would be nice to see you next week.
   B: 1 Are you doing anything on Wednesday?
      2 Will you do anything on Wednesday?

2 Put each verb in brackets into a form of *will*, *going to* or present continuous. More than one answer may be possible.

a) Have you heard the news? Harry (join) ...*is joining/is going to join*...... the Army!

b) Sorry to keep you waiting. I (not be) .... long.

c) According to the weather forecast, it (snow) .... tomorrow.

d) I'm sorry I can't meet you tonight. I (go out) .... with my parents.

e) Careful! You (knock) .... that jug off the table!

f) In fifty years' time, most people (probably ride) .... bicycles to work.

g) Our teacher (give) .... us a test tomorrow.

h) I (go) .... to Manchester at the end of next week.

i) Look out! You (hit) .... that tree!

j) I think our team (probably win) ....

3 Complete the second sentence so that it has a similar meaning to the first sentence.

a) My party is on Thursday.

I ..*'m having a party*.... on Thursday.

b) Tomorrow's weather forecast is for rain.

It's .... tomorrow.

c) I predict a victory for our team.

I think .... win.

d) Tomorrow I'll be absent, Mrs Jones.

I .... here tomorrow, Mrs Jones.

e) Terry intends to finish painting the kitchen this evening.

Terry .... painting the kitchen this evening.

f) Meet me outside the station at 5.30.

I .... outside the station at 5.30.

g) What's our arrangement for lunch?

Where .... for lunch?

h) Everyone expects lots of tourism in this country next summer.

Everyone thinks a large number of tourists .... this country next summer.

4 <u>Underline</u> the sentences which are incorrect. Rewrite them. If the sentence is correct, put a tick (✓).

a) <u>I go swimming next Saturday. Would you like to come?</u>

..*I'm going swimming next Saturday. Would you like to come?*

b) What are you going to discuss at the next meeting?

....

c) The boat is turning over! I think it will sink!

....

d) Sue is going to lend me her roller-skates.

....

e) The weather forecast says it's definitely sunny tomorrow.

....

f) There is a lot to do. Is anyone going to help you?

....

g) Sorry, I'm not seeing you tomorrow. I have to go to London.

....

h) Bye for now. I see you later this evening.

....

5 **Rewrite each sentence so that it contains *will* or *going to*.**

a) I plan to study engineering in France.
   I'm going to study engineering in France.

b) I've arranged a party for next Friday.

   ....

c) We've got an appointment at the doctor's, so we can't come.

   ....

d) Kelly is likely to get the job.

   ....

e) Martin's wife is pregnant again.

   ....

f) Sarah doesn't plan to get married yet.

   ....

g) There's a possibility of snow tomorrow.

   ....

h) I predict a score of 3–0.

   ....

Future 2

Explanations

Future continuous

■ Form

The future continuous is formed with *will* + *be* + the *-ing* form of the verb.

*This time tomorrow **I'll be eating** lunch on the plane.*

■ Meaning

The future continuous is used when we imagine an activity in progress in the future.

We often use it when we compare what we are doing now with what we will be doing in the future. There is nearly always a time expression.

*Where **will you be living** in five years' time?*

We also use the future continuous to say that something will definitely happen.

***We'll be holding** a meeting soon, so we can decide then.*

Future perfect

■ Form

The future perfect is formed with *will* + *have* + the past participle.

*By the time we get to the cinema, the film **will have begun**.*

■ Meaning

We use the future perfect to look back from one point in the future to an earlier event. We often use *by* or *by the time* with the future perfect.

*By next week **I'll have collected** over 1000 euros for charity.*

The situation has not happened yet, but at a certain time in the future it will happen.

Present simple

■ We often use the present simple to talk about events in the future based on a fixed timetable, programme or calendar.

*Jim's plane **leaves** at 12.00.*

*Our head teacher **retires** next year.*

■ We use the present simple to refer to the future after these words: *when, after, before, unless, in case, as soon as, until, by the time, the next time.*

***When I see** her again, I'll tell her your news.*

*Let's run home **before it rains**.*

*Take an umbrella, **in case it rains**.*

***As soon as we're ready**, we'll phone you.*

*Please wait here **until Mrs Hall comes** back.*

We can also use the present perfect with these words to emphasize that an action is complete.

*Hand in your paper **as soon as you have finished**.*

Functions using *will* **and** *shall*

When we say that a verb form has a 'function', we mean that we use it for a purpose like 'promising' or 'suggesting' rather than to refer to time. Many uses of *will* and *shall* are more easily described in this way.

- Promise

    I'll try *as hard as I can.*

- Threat

    Stop doing that, or *I'll tell* *my dad.*

- Decision made at the moment of speaking.

    A: *'Which one do you want?'*
    B: *'I'll take* *the blue silk one.'*   (in a shop)

- Offer

    I'll give *you a lift in my car.*
    Will you have *some more coffee?*
    Shall I open *the door for you?*

- Request

    Will you carry *this bag for me?*

- Suggestion

    Shall we play *tennis?*

- Parting remark

    I'll see *you tomorrow.*

 SEE ALSO

Grammar 24: Functions

Practice

1 Underline the correct word or phrase in each sentence.

a) This time next week Billy *will lie/will be lying* on the beach.
b) Please stay in your seats until the bell *rings/will ring*.
c) *We'll have moved/We'll be moving* to our new house on Tuesday.
d) What time *does your train leave/will your train leave*?
e) Don't forget to turn off the lights before *you're leaving/you leave*.
f) Where *will you work/will you be working* in ten years' time?
g) Wait for me. *I'll be/I'll have been* ready in a moment.
h) John *won't stop/won't have stopped* talking all the time!

2 Complete each part sentence (a–h) with one of the part sentences (1–8). More than one answer may be possible.

a) As soon as I hear from Sharon, ...*5*...
b) By the time Mary arrives ....
c) Please take a seat ....
d) This time next week ....
e) The next time you see me ....
f) We'll have time to have some lunch ....

1 until the dentist is ready.
2 the match will be over.
3 I'll have had my hair cut and you won't recognize me.
4 before the train leaves.
5 I'll ask her to phone you.
6 we'll be enjoying ourselves on holiday.

3 Underline the inappropriate verb forms and write the correct form in the space. If the sentence is correct, put a tick (✓).

a) By the time the police get here, the burglars will have vanished. ....✓.................
b) When you'll grow older, you'll change your mind about this. ....
c) The bus leaves at 1.00, so we'll leave the house at 11.30. ....
d) I won't leave until you will give me the money. ....
e) As soon as the taxi will arrive, I'll be letting you know. ....
f) Will you have been using the video next lesson? ....
g) By the time we get to Helen's house, she'll leave. ....
h) 'Do you want me to carry this?' 'No that's all right, I'm doing it.' ....

4 Rewrite each sentence so that it contains *will/shall* or *going to*, and the verb underlined.

a) How playing tennis?

Shall we play tennis?

b) I've decided to study Arabic in Cairo.

....

c) I promise to be home by midnight.

....

d) I hope to meet you later.

....

e) I'd like you to go to the shops for me.

....

f) We promise not to make too much noise.

....

g) Would you like me to help you with those bags?

....

h) We could come back later if you like.

....

5 Complete the second sentence so that it has a similar meaning to the first sentence.

a) The work won't take us longer than an hour.

We *'ll have finished* .... the work in an hour.

b) I promise to phone you before our next meeting.

Before we .... you.

c) Would you like me to check the spelling for you?

Shall .... for you?

d) Sheila refuses to let me share her book.

Sheila won't .... book.

e) How about having a game of chess?

Shall .... a game of chess?

f) Please stay here until I come back.

Please don't .... come back.

g) After the lesson we'll meet and play tennis.

When .... we'll meet and play tennis.

h) What job will you have in twenty years' time?

What will .... in twenty years' time?

1 <u>Underline</u> the correct word or phrase in each sentence.

a) When I was a child _I used to ride/I was riding_ a tricycle.

b) That looks very heavy. _Will I/Shall I_ help you?

c) I'm waiting for Sue. _Have you seen her/Did you see her_?

d) How long _are you working/have you been working_ here?

e) I can't come out because _I haven't finished/I didn't finish_ my homework yet.

f) When the phone rang _I washed/I was washing_ my hair in the bathroom.

g) Why _do you stare/are you staring_ at me like that?

h) I've finished my exams so _I'm having/I have_ a party tomorrow.

i) We'd better wait here until the rain _stops/will stop_.

j) When _did you last go/have you last been_ to the cinema?

2 Put each verb in brackets into the present simple or continuous, or the past simple or continuous.

a) 'What (you do) ...._do you do_........ ?' 'I'm an engineer.'

b) The door was open so the dog (run) .... into the living room.

c) When we arrived home Jan (sit) .... outside the door.

d) Can you help me? I (not understand) .... Spanish.

e) At the beginning of the film I (realize) .... I'd seen it before.

f) I'm sorry, I can't talk long. I (study) .... for an examination.

g) At the moment of the earthquake Pat (read) .... in bed.

h) I'll phone you as soon as I (know) .... the results.

i) I (stay) .... at the Hotel Tirol. Why don't you call me?

j) 'What (you do) .... when you saw the snake?' 'I ran!'

3 For each question, complete the second sentence so that it means the same as the first, using no more than three words.

a) Steve left before my arrival.
When I ...._arrived, Steve had_... already left.

b) Do you need any help with your suitcase?
Shall .... you with your suitcase?

c) What's your usual time of arrival at school?
When .... arrive at school?

d) Alice started playing tennis six months ago.
Alice .... tennis for six months.

e) I'll wait here until it stops raining.

When it stops raining .... leave.

f) In the middle of my meal, the phone rang.

While I .... my meal the phone rang.

g) Jack has come to stay for the weekend.

Jack .... with me for the weekend.

h) I last saw David in 1990.

I .... David since 1990.

i) Are you free tomorrow evening?

Are .... anything tomorrow evening?

4 **Decide which answer (A, B, C or D) best fits the space.**

Maria's homecoming

When the bus (1) .....C..... in a small square, Maria (2) .... her magazine and
didn't realize that she (3) .... at her destination. 'This is Santa Teresa,'
Martin said. '(4) .... home! I suppose your cousin (5) .... for us. Come
on. (6) .... the bags.' Maria thought, 'All those years when I (7) .... in
New York, I (8) .... of this moment. And now it's real, I can't believe it! Here
I am, (9) .... in the square'. Santa Teresa was Maria's birthplace, but she
(10) .... the town at the age of six. She had some memories of the town, and
some photos, but (11) .... here still? She (12) .... Nobody (13) ....
in the square. Perhaps her cousin Pablo (14) .... Maria's letter. 'What
(15) .... now?' asked Martin. 'There isn't even a hotel here!'

1) A has stopped	B stops	C stopped	D was stopped
2) A was reading	B read	C had read	D used to read
3) A arrived	B arrives	C has arrived	D had arrived
4) A You arrive	B You're arriving	C You've been arriving	D You've arrived
5) A waits	B will be waiting	C has waited	D is going to wait
6) A I'll carry	B I carry	C I've carried	D I carried
7) A live	B have lived	C was living	D am living
8) A dream	B am dreaming	C used to dream	D will dream
9) A I really stand	B I was really standing	C I had really stood	D I'm really standing
10) A was leaving	B had left	C used to leave	D has left
11) A will she belong	B did she belong	C has she belonged	D does she belong
12) A wasn't knowing	B hasn't known	C hadn't known	D didn't know
13) A was waiting	B is waiting	C waits	D waited
14) A wasn't receiving	B didn't use to receive	C hadn't received	D hasn't received
15) A are we going to do	B have we done	C did we do	D are we doing

5   Put a suitable time word or expression in each space. Each space is for one word.

Just a quick note (a) ..*before*...... I leave for the airport. Sorry I haven't been in touch (b) .... Wednesday, but I've been busy getting ready (c) .... , and I haven't collected my ticket (d) .... from the travel agency. (e) .... I get to Sydney, I'll write you a letter. I've (f) .... been to Australia before but I've been reading a lot about it (g) .... It sounds great! I'll be in Sydney (h) .... the end of next week, and then I'm travelling to Melbourne. I'll be there (i) .... a month. (j) .... I get back all my friends will have forgotten me!

6   Look carefully at each line. Some lines are correct but some have a word which should not be there. Tick (✓) each correct line. If a line has a word which should not be there, write the word in the space.

Dear Emma,

I'm sorry I haven't been written to you lately, but I've	1	*been*
been working hard. When I received your last letter	2	✓
I was acting in a play at school, and when	3	....
I have finished that, I went on holiday with some friends.	4	....
I meant to send you a postcard, but I had forgot to take	5	....
your address with me. How are you getting on at	6	....
college? You didn't say very much about this in	7	....
your letter. I hope you are still like it, and don't	8	....
been work all the time! Do you still want to come	9	....
and will stay for a few days? I'm starting work in	10	....
London after I shall leave school in July, and I want	11	....
to see you before then. I have know you're busy,	12	....
but by the time your term finishes, I'll have	13	....
started my job. I've been done so many things	14	....
lately! I've just learned to drive and my parents	15	....
have sometimes lend me their car, so I often go out	16	....
with friends. Maybe I'll be drive to Nottingham and	17	....
see you one day.		

Best wishes, Luisa

7 <u>Underline</u> the errors in these sentences. Correct the error.

a) By the time I got to the phone it <u>stopped</u> ringing.
   it had stopped ringing.
   ....

b) I'm not very good at this game. You see, I didn't play it before.
   ....

c) When has Pete written to you last?
   ....

d) What do you do at weekends? Are you ever going to the cinema?
   ....

e) When I was on holiday last summer I was going to the beach every day.
   ....

f) Julie can't meet you tomorrow. She will play basketball.
   ....

g) You're always late! I'm waiting here for ages!
   ....

8 In everyday spoken English, we often leave out the subject pronoun and auxiliary. Instead of saying, *'Do you like it?'* we say, *'Like it?'*. Rewrite each sentence so that the verb <u>underlined</u> has a subject pronoun.

a) <u>Finished</u> yet? We're all waiting!
   Have you finished yet?..

b) Bye for now! <u>See</u> you tomorrow!
   ....

c) Good holiday? <u>Had</u> a nice time?
   ....

d) Paul's a bit difficult. <u>Know</u> what I mean?
   ....

e) Hi, Tim. <u>Coming</u> out for a drink later?
   ....

f) <u>Been</u> waiting long? Sorry for the delay.
   ....

Problem check

1 Check the difference between the present simple and present continuous in Grammar 3. How can you show this difference in your language?

2 Does your language have a tense with the same form as the present perfect? Is it used in the same way? Can you show the difference in your language between the present perfect and past simple?

3 Do you have a future tense in your language? Does it express all the meanings of *will*, *going to* and the present continuous?

Reported speech 1

Explanations

Reported speech

We often tell people what other people have said. This is called reported or indirect speech. We rarely report the exact words, usually we just give a general summary.

Sandra speaking to Petra: *'Bye, Petra, it's been great seeing you again. I'll call **you** sometime next week when I get a chance.'*

Petra reporting the conversation to Roberta: *'I saw Sandra yesterday. She said she'd call **me** next week.*

We usually change tenses (*will → would* in the example above) and also other references like people, places and times (*you → me* in the example above).

Tense changes

Statements are usually reported with a past tense verb (like *said*) and an optional *that*. The form of the verb that follows then 'moves back' in time. This is sometimes called backshift.

Present simple to past simple	*'I **need** some help.'* *She said (that) she **needed** some help.*
Present continuous to past continuous	*'We **are having** our lunch.'* *She said that they **were having** their lunch.*
Present perfect to past perfect	*'I've **lost** my keys.'* *He said (that) he **had lost** his keys.*
Past simple to past perfect (or stays the same)	*'I **wrote** two letters to her.'* *He said (that) he **had written** two letters to her.* *He said (that) he **wrote** two letters to her.*
be going to to *was going to*	*'They **are going to** come back.'* *She said (that) they **were going to** come back.*
will to *would* *can* to *could*	*'I **will be** home at 6.00.'* *She said (that) she **would be** home at 6.00.*

- There is no change for *must, might, could, should, would.*
    *'I **must leave** straightaway for Brussels.'*
    *He said he **must leave** straightaway for Brussels.*
  But in the case of *must* we can also use *had to.*
    *He said he **had to leave** straightaway for Brussels.*

- Note that if the actual words were in the past simple, the report can change or stay the same.

- Note that if we write down the actual words that someone says we use speech marks (inverted commas). But if we write down a report of the words there are no speech marks.

No tense changes

- If the report is about something which is always true, it is not necessary to change tenses.

  *'I **like** apples more than I **like** oranges.'*

  *She said that she **likes** apples more than she **likes** oranges.*

But in cases like this it is still possible to change tenses if you want to.

- If the report is about something that has immediate relevance, we usually do not change tenses.

  Jack speaking to Ted: *'**I'm going** to the cinema tonight. Do you want to come?'*

  Ted reporting the conversation to Peter: *'Jack is on the phone. He **says he's going** to the cinema tonight.'*

Speakers in reported speech

When we write down the actual words, the speaker can be mentioned at the beginning or end of the sentence. Notice the position of the comma and the final full stop in relation to the speech marks.

  Jack said, 'We're going to miss the train.'

  'We're going to miss the train,' said Jack.

But in reported speech the speaker is only mentioned at the beginning of the sentence.

  Jack said (that) they were going to miss the train.

People, places, times

In reported speech references to people, places and times often change, because the point of view changes.

  *'I'll see **you here tomorrow**,' said Sue.*

  *Sue said (that) **she** would see **me there the next day**.*

  *'I bought **this** book **yesterday**,' said Martin.*

  *Martin said (that) **he** had bought **the** book **the day before**.*

Summarizing

We usually just summarize what people say when we make reports.

  *'Look, actually, tell him **I'll** give him a call or email him next week, OK?'*

  Reported as: *She said (that) **she'd** get in touch next week.*

If we report the exact words it is called verbatim reporting.

say, tell, speak

We *say* something and we *tell* somebody. *Say* and *tell* can be followed by the optional *that*.

  'It's warm today,' she said.

  *She **said** (that) it was warm.*

  *She **told me** (that) it was warm.*

We can use *to* after say, but we never use *to* after tell.

  'I come from Slovenia'

  *She **said to me** (that) she comes from Slovenia.*

  *She **told me** (that) she comes from Slovenia.*

Speak describes the act of talking.

  *Simon **spoke** to me in the supermarket yesterday.*

Practice

1   <u>Underline</u> the errors in these sentences. Rewrite each sentence.

a) Sally <u>told</u> that she'd lost her keys.
   Sally said that she'd lost her keys.

b) Chris said me that he must leave early.

....

c) Maria and Tony said they shall see us tomorrow.

....

d) Tom said, I'm coming to your party.

....

e) Sue said that she had wrote a letter to Lisa.

....

f) Steve said us that he was arriving at 8.00.

....

g) 'I had bought a new bike Pam told us.'

....

h) 'What's the matter? Ellen told.

....

2   Rewrite each sentence in direct speech, ending as shown.

a) Anna told us that she'd finished.
   ' *I've finished* .... ,' Anna told us.

b) Simon said that he would be back at 6.00.
   '... ,' Simon said.

c) Beth said she was going to go shopping.
   '... ,' said Beth.

d) Paul said that he wanted to make a phone call.
   '... ,' said Paul.

e) Tina told the teacher she'd forgotten her homework.
   '... ,' Tina told the teacher.

f) David said he had to be back by 3.30.
   '... ,' David said.

g) Jan told me she would let me know.
   '... ,' Jan told me.

h) Bill said he was going to be late.
   '... ,' Bill said.

3 Match each sentence in direct speech (a–e) with its summarized version in reported speech (1–5).

a) 'Look, sorry about this, but I'm afraid I'm going to be a bit late.' ....*3*....

b) 'Actually I've no idea at all where I am!' ....

c) 'The thing is, I know it's silly but I've missed the bus.' ....

d) 'Anyway, I'll be back in next to no time.' ....

e) 'I did ring, you know, earlier in the evening.' ....

1 She said she would be back soon.

2 She said she had missed the bus.

3 She said she was going to be late.

4 She said she had already rung.

5 She said she didn't know where she was.

4 Complete each sentence, using *say, tell* or *speak* in an appropriate form.

a) Daniel ...*told*..... me that he was playing in the school basketball team.

b) I .... to Helen, and she .... she would phone you.

c) 'You're lucky,' .... Steve. 'I .... you that you would win!'

d) A translator .... the President what everyone was ....

e) 'Look,' I .... her, 'why don't you .... me what you mean?'

f) I .... my teacher that I .... Chinese, but she didn't believe me.

5 Rewrite each sentence in reported speech, beginning as shown.

a) 'I won't be there because I'm having a party,' said Lucy.

Lucy told us that she ..*wouldn't be there because she was having* .... ..*a party.*..

b) 'I've lost the map and I don't know the way,' said Jack.

Jack told me that he ....
....

c) 'When I finish the book, I'm going to watch television,' said Jessica.

Jessica said that when ....
....

d) 'I'm doing some homework but I won't be long,' said Mike.

Mike said that he ....
....

e) 'I got up late and I missed the bus,' said Richard.

Richard said that he ....
....

Reported speech 2

Explanations

Reporting questions

■ We can report questions with verbs like *ask*, *wonder* and *want to know*. Tense change rules are the same as in Grammar 11.

> *'**Where do** you **live**?'* he asked.
> He **asked** me where I **lived**.   (NOT ~~where I did live~~)
> *'**Do** you **live** in Athens?'* he asked.
> He **wanted to know** if I **lived** in Athens.   (NOT ~~If I did live~~)

■ Look at more examples of 'Wh- questions' (using *when, what, why, how* etc). Study the tense changes and word order carefully. Notice that the word order in a reported question is like a normal statement, with the subject before the verb.

> *'Where **is the bus station?**'* she asked.
> She asked where **the bus station was**.   (NOT ~~where was the bus station~~)
> *'What **are you doing?**'* he asked.
> He wanted to know what **I was doing**.
> *'Why **did you go** there?'* she asked.
> She wondered why **I had gone** there.
> *'Where **have you come** from?'* he asked.
> He asked me where **I had come** from.

■ Look at more examples of *Yes/No* questions (*Do you, Did you, Are you* etc.). When we report *Yes/No* questions we use *if* or *whether*.

> *'**Does** the London train **stop** here?'* she asked.
> She asked me **if** the London train **stopped** here.
> *'**Did you speak** to Rachel?'* he asked.
> He wanted to know **whether I had spoken** to Rachel.
> *'**Are you** a student?'* she asked.
> She asked me **if I was** a student.

Reporting commands and requests

■ Commands are reported with *tell* and the infinitive.

> *'Wait! Wait!'*
> I **told** him to wait.

■ Requests are reported with *ask* and the infinitive.

> *'Please wait!'*
> I **asked** her to wait.

Other reporting verbs

■ Grammar 11 used *say* as the reporting verb, but there are many others. Here are some of the most common:

advise	*'I wouldn't buy that car, Janos, if I were you.'*
	I **advised** *Janos not to buy the car.*
agree	*'OK, I'll give you a lift,' said Jenny.*
	Jenny **agreed** *to give her a lift.*
	'Yes, Jill, I think you're right,' said Mike.
	Mike **agreed** *with Jill.*
apologize for	*'I'm really sorry for being so late,' said Maria.*
	Maria **apologized for** *being late.*
ask	*'Do you think you could help me, Sue?'*
	I **asked** *Sue to help me.*
congratulate on	*'Well done, Tina, you've passed the exam!'*
	I **congratulated** *Tina* **on** *passing her exam.*
decide	*'I'll have the fish soup, please,' said Bill.*
	Bill **decided** *to have the fish soup.*
deny	*'No, I didn't take it! I wasn't even there!' said Alice.*
	Alice **denied** *taking it.*
invite	*'Would you like to come to the cinema on Saturday, Pam?'*
	I **invited** *Pam to the cinema on Saturday.*
offer	*'Shall I carry your case, Dawn?' said Peter.*
	Peter **offered** *to carry Dawn's case.*
promise	*'I'll definitely be home by eight,' said Ann.*
	Ann **promised** *to be home by eight.*
refuse	*'No, I won't open the door!' said Carol.*
	Carol **refused** *to open the door.*
remind	*'Don't forget to send your mother a birthday card, Joe.'*
	I **reminded** *Joe to send his mother a birthday card.*
suggest	*'How about spending the day at the beach?' said Carlos.*
	Carlos **suggested** *spending the day at the beach.*

■ Reporting verbs can have one or more different patterns. A good dictionary shows this information. Study the example sentences in the previous section in relation to the patterns below.

Verb + *to* infinitive:	*agree, decide, offer, promise, refuse*
Verb + object + *to* infinitive:	*advise, ask, invite, remind*
Verb + *-ing* form:	*deny, suggest*
Verb + preposition + *-ing* form:	*apologize for, congratulate on*

→ SEE ALSO

Grammar 11: Reported speech 1

47

Practice

1 **Put one suitable word in each space.**

a) Fiona asked me ...*whether*... I ....*was*.......... going to school or not.

b) David asked his mother .... she .... be coming home.

c) Peter asked us .... we .... ever been to Hungary.

d) Costas asked me .... I .... many photographs.

e) Maria asked a policeman .... the museum was.

f) Dora asked her sister .... she .... fed their dog.

2 **Complete each question in direct speech, ending as shown.**

a) Jack asked me whether I was having lunch or going out.
   '..*Are you having lunch or going out*................ ?' Jack asked me.

b) Carol asked Ann what she had done the day before.
   '.. , Ann?' asked Carol.

c) John asked us if we often went sailing.
   '.. ?' John asked us.

d) Christine asked me how many German books I had read.
   '.. ?' Christine asked me.

e) Kevin asked Sue if she was going to change schools.
   '.. , Sue?' asked Kevin.

f) Alice asked me who I sat next to in class.
   '.. ?' Alice asked me.

3 **Rewrite each sentence in reported speech, beginning as shown. Do not change the meaning.**

a) 'Are you staying here all summer?' the little girl asked me.
   The little girl asked me *if/whether I was staying there all summer...*

b) 'What does 'procrastinate' mean?' I asked my teacher.
   I asked my teacher ....

c) 'Have you done your homework, or not?' my mother asked me.
   My mother asked me ....

d) 'When is your birthday?' I asked Sue.
   I asked Sue ....

e) 'Did you remember to lock the door,' my father asked me.
   My father asked me ....

f) 'Why have you turned off the television?' Ellen asked me.
   Ellen asked me ....

4 Use a verb from the box to rewrite each sentence in reported speech, beginning as shown. Do not change the meaning.

advised	apologized	congratulated	invited	offered
~~promised~~	refused	suggested		

a) 'I'll definitely be at your house before 8.00, Sue,' said Mike.

Mike ..*promised*.. Sue ..*he would be at her house before 8.00*......

b) 'Would you like to come to the cinema, Jean?' asked Chris.

Chris ....

c) 'I wouldn't eat too much if I were you, Dave,' said Patsy.

Patsy ....

d) 'How about going for a walk?' said Nick.

Nick ....

e) 'I'm terribly sorry for breaking the window,' said Carol.

Carol ....

f) 'Shall I do the washing-up?' said Bill.

Bill ....

g) 'Well done, you've passed your driving test,' said Tina's mother.

Tina's mother .... her ....

h) 'No, I won't open my mouth!' said Pat.

Pat ....

Explanations

Conditions and results

■ Sentences with *If* are called conditionals. The *If* ... clause is the condition and the other part of the sentence is the result. Here are four examples of conditionals, used for talking about checking in at the airport for a flight:

1 *If you **arrive** early, you **get** a better seat.*
2 *If you **arrive** early, you'**ll get** a better seat.*
3 *If you **arrived** early, you'**d get** a better seat.*
4 *If you **had arrived** early, you'**d have got** a better seat.*

■ Sentence 1 is talking generally about something that is always true. It is sometimes called a zero conditional.
Sentence 2 is talking about something that is likely to happen in the future. It is sometimes called the first conditional.
Sentence 3 is talking about something that is unlikely to happen in the future, or an imaginary situation. It is sometimes called the second conditional.
Sentence 4 is talking about something that is imaginary in the past. It is sometimes called the third conditional.

■ Zero, first and second conditionals are covered in this unit. The third conditional is covered in Grammar 14.

Zero conditional: *If* + present simple, ... present simple

■ This type of sentence describes things that are always or generally true. We can use *when* or *if* to introduce the sentence.
*It's a tropical country, and so **if it rains** hard, everyone **stays** indoors.*
***When it rains** hard, everyone **stays** indoors.*

■ There can be an imperative structure in the result clause: just the bare infinitive with no subject. An imperative is when we tell people what to do.
*If you **feel dizzy, stop** taking the tablets.*
*If you **change** your mind, **give** me a ring.*

First conditional: *If* + present simple, ... will/won't

■ This type of sentence describes future events that will happen, or are likely to happen. It is a real possibility in the speaker's mind, not imaginary (for imaginary situations see the second conditional).
*If we **walk** so slowly, we'**ll be** late.*
*If we **run**, we **won't be** late.*
*If we **don't run**, we **will be** late.*

■ Example: You are at the supermarket with a friend. Your friend has put some eggs in a bag, and is picking up lots of other bags at the same time. You say:

*If you **carry** too many bags, you**'ll drop** the eggs.*
*If you **drop** the eggs, they**'ll break**.*
*If the eggs **break**, there **will be** an awful mess on the floor!*
*If you **are** careful, you **won't break** them.*

■ In the condition clause it is possible to use other present tenses, not just the present simple.

*If you**'re driving**, I'll come with you.* (present continuous)
*If I**'ve seen** the film before, I'll let you know!* (present perfect)

Second conditional: *If +* **past simple, ...** *would/wouldn't*

■ This type of sentence describes future events that are imaginary, unlikely or impossible.

*If I **had** a helicopter, I**'d fly** to school.*
*If I **flew** to school, I **wouldn't be** late.*

■ Example: You start talking to a friend about aliens. You say:

*If some **aliens landed** on earth, I**'d make friends** with them.*
*If they **didn't speak** English, I**'d use** sign language.*
*If they **took** me back to their planet, I**'d learn** their language.*
*If anyone **believed** my story, I**'d become** famous!*

■ Note that *would* is usually contracted in speech.

*I**'d become** famous.* (= I **would** become famous.)

■ Note that the past simple is used in the condition clause, but the time reference is the future.

■ The regular past simple of *to be* is *I was* and *He/She was*. We can use these forms in second conditionals, or alternatively we can use *If I were* and *If he/she were*. The *were* form is more formal.

*If I **was/were** an astronaut, I'd enjoy being weightless!*

unless

Unless means *If not*. Compare these sentences which have the same meaning.

*We'll go out for a walk **if it doesn't rain**.*
*We'll go out for a walk **unless it rains**.*

Other uses of *would*

We use *would* in other situations which do not involve conditional sentences.

Reporting what someone said:	*He said he **would call back** later.*
Polite offer:	***Would you like** some more tea?*
Polite request:	***Would you open** the window, please?*
Someone refused to do something:	*The minister **wouldn't answer** the question.*

 SEE ALSO

Grammar 14: Conditionals 2

Practice

1   <u>Underline</u> the correct word or phrase in each sentence.

   a) If *we'd be*/<u>*we're*</u> late for class, our teacher <u>*will be*</u>/*was* angry.
   b) If we *would live/lived* on another planet, *we'll see/we'd see* the Earth in the sky.
   c) If we *take/will take* a taxi, *we arrived/we'll arrive* sooner.
   d) If we *won't hurry/don't hurry*, *we'll be/we'd be* late.
   e) If we *were/are* birds, we *would be able to/are able to* fly.
   f) If you *don't wear/wouldn't wear* your pullover, *you'll feel/you felt* cold.
   g) If I *studied/will study* harder, I *get/would get* better marks.
   h) If I *have/had* a motorbike, *I rode/I'd ride* it to school.
   i) If you *will lend/lend* me your bike, *I'll let/I let* you borrow my skateboard.
   j) If I *had/have* lots of money, *I gave/I'd give* some to all my friends.

2   Complete the sentence for each situation using the verbs given.

   a) You're standing very close to the edge of a swimming-pool. You're wearing
       all your clothes, not a swimming costume. A friend says:
       If you (fall in) ...*fall in*..... , your clothes (get) ....*will get*... wet!
   b) You're sitting in the classroom on a hot day. You're day-dreaming about
       going to the beach. You think:
       If today (be) .... a holiday, I (go) .... to the beach.
   c) You can't answer a question in your English book. You ask a friend to help,
       but she doesn't know the answer. She says:
       If I (know) .... the answer, I (tell) .... you.
   d) You're walking towards the bus stop with a friend. Suddenly the bus arrives.
       The bus stop is far away, but you think there is a chance of catching the bus.
       You say:
       If we (run) .... , we (catch) .... it!
   e) You're planning to go to the beach tomorrow with some friends. You are not
       sure about the weather, because it sometimes rains at this time of the year.
       You arrange to meet tomorrow afternoon and say:
       If it (rain) .... , we (go) .... to the cinema instead.
   f) You're very busy, because you have lots of school work, and you also play in
       two teams. A friend asks you to join a computer club. You say:
       If I (have) .... more free time, I (join) .... the club.
       But it's impossible at the moment because I'm too busy!

3   Complete each sentence using *if, unless* or *would*.

a) If he asked me to help him, I ...*would*........ .

b) We'll have lunch outside in the garden, ... it's too cold.

c) John .... win more races if he trained harder.

d) Come on! .... we hurry, we'll miss the plane!

e) .... you like to see my stamp collection?

f) The manager won't be long. .... you take a seat, please.

g) I'm sure that Connie .... go to the cinema with you, if you asked her.

h) .... you feel like a chat, phone me tonight.

i) What .... you do if you saw a snake?

j) I don't feel happy .... I swim every day.

4   Complete each sentence (a–j) with an ending (1–10).

a) If you play the music too loud, ...*8*.....

b) If the North Pole melted, ...

c) If we don't have enough ice-cream, ...

d) If I found someone's wallet, ...

e) If a burglar broke into this house, ...

f) If my train isn't late, ...

g) If you were famous, ...

h) If my father lends me the money, ...

i) If you took more exercise, ...

j) If you tell me what you want, ...

1 the alarm would go off.

2 I'll buy a new bike.

3 I'll be in Paris at 6.00.

4 you wouldn't see me any more!

5 you would feel better.

6 the water would flood many cities.

7 I'll buy it for you.

8 you'll wake up the neighbours.

9 we'll get some more.

10 I'd take it to the police station.

5 Complete each sentence as either a first conditional or a second conditional sentence using the verb in brackets.

a) If I (have) .....*had*..... arms five metres long, I (be able) .....*'d be able*..... to reach the top of that shelf!

b) Don't worry, you've just got a cold. If you (take) .... an aspirin, you (feel) .... better.

c) Vegetarians believe that if nobody (eat) .... meat, everyone (live) .... longer.

d) If I (become) .... a famous rock star, I (buy) .... my parents an enormous house.

e) It says 'No Parking'. If you (leave) .... the car here, the police (give) .... you a parking fine.

f) It's not far. If you (follow) .... this path, you (come) .... to the station.

g) If people (use) .... bikes instead of cars, there (not be) .... so much pollution.

h) Actually, Brutus is a very friendly dog. If you (touch) .... him, he (not bite) .... you.

i) If you (leave) .... your books on the desk, I (give) .... them back to you at the end of the lesson.

j) If you (own) .... a pet tiger, your friends (not visit) .... you!

14 | Conditionals 2

Explanations

Third conditional:
If + past perfect, ...
would/wouldn't +
have + past
participle

- This type of sentence describes a past event that is different to what really happened.

    *If you **had arrived** earlier, we **wouldn't have missed** the train.*
    *If you **hadn't warned** me about the sun, I **would have got** sunburnt.*

- Example: You went for a long walk, but you did not take your umbrella. It rained, and you got wet.

    *If I **had taken** my umbrella, I **wouldn't have got** wet.*
    *If I'**d heard** the weather forecast, I **wouldn't have gone** out.*
    *If I **hadn't gone** out, I **would have finished** my homework.*

Modal verbs in
conditional
sentences

- The examples in Grammar 13 and this unit have all used *will/won't* or *would/wouldn't* in the result clause. But we can use any other modal verb, like *can, could, may, might, must* and *should*.

    *If you ever **come** to Istanbul, I **can** show you around the city.*
    *If you ever **come** to Istanbul, you **must** phone me.*

- We often use *might* and *could* in conditional sentences when we want to say that we are not certain about the results. Compare:

    *If you **carry** too many bags, you **will drop** the eggs.*   (certain result)
    *If you **carry** too many bags, you **might drop** the eggs.*   (uncertain result)
    *If anyone **believed** my story, I **would become** famous!*   (certain result)
    *If anyone **believed** my story, I **could become** famous!*   (uncertain result)

    In third conditional sentences we use *could have (done)* or *might have (done)* .
    *If I **had brought** some more money with me, I **could have taken** a taxi.*

Conditionals
without *if*

In everyday speech we can use *imagine* or *supposing* in place of *if*.
    ***Imagine you saw** a snake, what would you do?*
    ***Supposing you owned** a helicopter, what would you use it for?*

If I were you, ...

We can give advice by using a second conditional sentence beginning *If I were you.*
    ***If I were you**, I'd spend more time on your written work.*
    ***If I were you**, I wouldn't eat so much chocolate!*
It is also possible to put the *if*-clause at the end.
    *I'd be more careful, **if I were you**.*

 SEE ALSO

Grammar 13: Conditionals 1
Grammar 18: Modals 1
Grammar 19: Modals 2

Practice

1 Rewrite each comment, beginning as shown. Do not change the meaning.

a) Supposing you had wings, what would you do?
   What *would you do if you had wings* ?

b) Why don't you leave now? That's what I'd do.
   If ....

c) Imagine you lived on Mars. How would you feel?
   How .... ?

d) I think you should buy a bike. That's what I'd do.
   If ....

e) Imagine you were rich. What would you do?
   What .... ?

f) Supposing Jim came with us, what would you say?
   What .... ?

g) Why don't you take the bus. That's what I'd do.
   If ....

h) Imagine you owned a robot. What would you do?
   What .... ?

2 <u>Underline</u> the correct word or phrase in each sentence.

a) If you *phoned/<u>had phoned</u>* me yesterday, I *had given/<u>would have given</u>* you the news.

b) If you *took/would have taken* more exercise, you *might feel/had felt* better.

c) If Tim *drove/had driven* more carefully, he *wouldn't have crashed/didn't crash*.

d) If you *had come/came* to see the film, you *had enjoyed/would have enjoyed* it.

e) If *I'd known/I would know* it was your birthday, I *would send/would have sent* you a card.

f) If people *had helped/helped* one another more often, the world *might be/was* a better place.

g) If our team *had scored/scored* more goals, we *had won/could have won*.

h) If you *would have worn/wore* a coat, you *wouldn't get/didn't get* wet.

3 Complete the sentence for each situation.

a) Charlotte didn't leave early, and so she missed the bus.
   If Charlotte .... *had left early* .... , she
   .... *wouldn't have missed* .... the bus.

b) I didn't buy more milk, so I didn't have enough for breakfast.
   If I .... , I
   .... enough for breakfast.

c) We forgot to take a map, so we got lost in the mountains.
   If we .... , we
   .... in the mountains.

d) I didn't go to bed early, so I didn't wake up at 7.00.
   If I .... early, I
   .... at 7.00.

e) Mike didn't make a shopping list, and he forgot to buy some coffee.
   If Mike .... , he
   .... some coffee.

f) I didn't realize you were tired when I asked you to go for a walk.
   If I .... , I
   .... for a walk.

g) The Romans didn't sail across the Atlantic, so they didn't reach America.
   If the Romans .... , they
   .... America.

h) I didn't turn left at the station, and I lost my way.
   If I .... , I
   .... my way.

Explanations

Wishes about the present

- For wishes about the present we use *I wish* + the past simple. Note the relationship with the second conditional.

  *I wish I **owned** a helicopter. If I owned a helicopter, I would be happy.*
  *I wish I **didn't have to go** to school! If I didn't go to school, I would be happy.*

- *could*

  We use *I wish I could* to refer to something that is difficult or impossible. This can refer to the present or future.

  *I wish I **could** fly!*
  *I wish I **could** stay at home tomorrow.*

- As in the second conditional, the past simple form does not refer to past time.

Wishes about the past

For wishes about the past we use *I wish* + the past perfect. Note the relationship with the third conditional.

*I wish I **had lived** in the eighteenth century! If I had lived in the eighteenth century, I would have been happy.*
*I wish I **hadn't eaten** so much! I feel awful! If I hadn't eaten so much, it would have been better for me!*

hope

If the wish is a good one, we use *I hope*. This is not followed by a conditional form – it is simply followed by the present simple or *will*.

*I hope you **have** a good time at the party.*
*I hope the weather **will be** fine tomorrow.*

If only

We can replace *I wish* with *If only* for emphasis. We stress *only* in speech.

*If only I **owned** a helicopter.*
*If only I **hadn't eaten** so much!*

 SEE ALSO

Grammar 13: Conditionals 1
Grammar 14: Conditionals 2

Practice

1 <u>Underline</u> the correct word or phrase in each sentence.

a) I'm sunburnt. I wish I <u>*hadn't sunbathed*</u>/*didn't sunbathe* for so long.

b) I don't feel well. I wish I *could stay/stayed* at home tomorrow.

c) I'm not a good swimmer, but I wish I *could swim/would swim* well.

d) I wish I *had/have* a puppy or a kitten!

e) I wish I *could see/saw* you tomorrow, but it's impossible.

f) I wish Jim *didn't sit/doesn't sit* next to me. He's so annoying!

g) If only we *had/would have* some money we could take the bus.

h) I hope you *enjoyed/enjoy* yourselves at the dance tomorrow.

i) I wish I *can/could* speak English better!

j) I hope *I'll/I'd* win the lottery!

2 <u>Underline</u> the correct continuation for each sentence.

a) I've got lots of work to do, and I'm tired, but I can't stop.

    1 I wish I had taken a rest.   2 <u>I wish I could take a rest.</u>

b) I wasn't paying attention in class, and now I can't do my homework.

    1 I wish I listened to my teacher.   2 I wish I'd listened to my teacher.

c) Sarah painted her room green, but she doesn't like it.

    1 She wishes she'd painted it blue.   2 She wishes she painted it blue.

d) This is a very puzzling problem!

    1 I wish I'd known the answer.   2 I wish I knew the answer.

e) It's really cold and miserable here in the winter.

    1 I wish we lived in a warm place.   2 I hope we live in a warm place.

f) I can't repair my bike because I haven't got any tools.

    1 If only I would have a screwdriver.   2 If only I had a screwdriver.

g) I'm worried about my basketball team. Perhaps they won't win!

    1 I wish they play well.   2 I hope they play well.

h) You promised not to tell anyone my secrets but you did!

    1 I wish I hadn't told you.   2 I wish I didn't tell you.

i) I've been feeling ill all week.

    1 I hope I feel better soon.   2 I hope I'd feel better soon.

j) I want to see my sister. I haven't seen her for ages.

    1 I wish I could speak to her.   2 I wish I spoke to her.

3 **Complete each sentence with a suitable form of the verb in brackets.**

a) I'm soaked to the skin! If only I (bring) ...*had brought*....... an umbrella!

b) This pullover was cheap. I wish I (buy) .... two of them!

c) I like your school. I wish I (go) .... there too.

d) I must get in touch with Sue. If only I (know) .... her phone number!

e) This bus is really slow! I wish we (take) .... the train.

f) I'm disappointed in this camera. I wish I (not buy) .... it.

g) I answered three questions well. If only I (finish) .... the whole test!

h) I can't understand Marie! I wish I (speak) .... French.

4 **Complete each sentence in a suitable way.**

a) I'm hungry. If only ....*I had a sandwich*... with me.

b) Enjoy your holiday. I hope .... time.

c) This is a lovely place. I wish we .... before.

d) It's a pity you live so far away. If only you .... nearer.

e) Ellen is a fantastic dancer. I wish I .... as well as her!

5 **Rita isn't very happy at the moment. Complete her words.**

a) Rita wasted a lot of money on DVDs.
   'I wish I ...*hadn't wasted*........... so much money on expensive DVDs!'

b) Rita thinks new jobs are difficult to find.
   'I wish new jobs .... so difficult to find.'

c) Rita thinks new jobs are difficult to find.
   'I wish new jobs .... easier to find.'

d) Rita can't go on holiday this summer.
   'I wish I .... on holiday.'

e) Rita doesn't have very good qualifications.
   'I wish I .... better qualifications.'

f) Rita has to do the washing up. She hates doing it.
   'I wish I .... do the washing up.'

g) Rita is sorry her family moved to the suburbs.
   'I wish we .... to the suburbs.'

h) Rita thinks she is very untidy.
   'I wish I .... so untidy.'

Explanations

Passive: form

- To make the passive we use *be* and a past participle. Compare the active and passive forms in these examples:

- Present simple   *The Government **builds** hundreds of houses every year.*
  *Hundreds of houses **are built** every year.*

- Present continuous   *The authorities **are questioning** two men.*
  *Two men **are being questioned** by the authorities.*

- Present perfect   *We **have chosen** Helen as the new president.*
  *Helen **has been chosen** as the new president.*

- Past simple   *The police **arrested** one protester.*
  *One protester **was arrested**.*

- *will*   *They **will play** the match on Wednesday evening.*
  *The match **will be played** on Wednesday evening.*

- Notice how the object in the active form (*hundreds of houses, two men, Helen*) moves to the front in the passive sentence and becomes the subject.

Passive: use

- Focus on important information
  Compare:
  (active)   ***The Government** built hundreds of houses last year.*
  (passive)   ***Hundreds of houses** were built by the Government last year.*

  In the active sentence more emphasis is given to who did the action – the Government.
  In the passive sentence more emphasis is given to the thing affected by the action – the number of houses.
  Emphasized information usually comes at the beginning of the sentence.

- Spoken and written
  The passive is used more in writing and formal speech.

Using *by* and *with*

- The person or organization that does the action is called 'the agent'. If we want to say who does the action then we use *by*.
  Hundreds of houses were built last year.
  *Hundreds of houses were built **by the Government** last year.*
  A lot of stones were thrown.
  *A lot of stones were thrown **by angry football fans**.*

- The thing that is used to perform an action is called 'the instrument'. If we want to include this we use *with*.
  *The windows were broken **with a baseball bat**.*

Sentences without an agent

It is not always necessary to mention the agent. There are several reasons for this:

- Agent not known: *Brenda's motorbike **was stolen** last night.*
  If we knew who had stolen it, we would mention the name of the person. But we don't know and the agent is not mentioned.

- Agent obvious: *One protester **was arrested**.*
  It is not necessary to add the words 'by the police', because we know that it is always the police who do this. However, it is possible to add these words if we want to.

- Agent unimportant: *A lot of English grammar books **are sold** every year.*
  Exactly who sells the books is not important. If it was important we could use *by* and the names of the people or shops who sell the books.

Transitive and intransitive verbs

- Verbs which have objects are called transitive verbs (example: *help*). In this sentence, 'the old lady' is the object.
  *A young man **helped the old lady** across the road.*

- Verbs which do not have objects are called intransitive verbs (example: walk).
  *Diane **walks** to college.*

- Dictionaries show this information with T or I. Only transitive verbs can be made passive.
  The old lady was helped across the road by a young man.

Practice

1 <u>Underline</u> phrases which are not necessary in these sentences. Sometimes every phrase is necessary.

a) My wallet has been stolen <u>by someone</u>.

b) We were taught by a different teacher yesterday.

c) Nick was operated on at the hospital by a doctor.

d) The meal was served by a waiter in a red coat.

e) We were shown round the museum by a guide.

f) Two letters were delivered this morning by the postman.

g) Three men have been arrested by the police.

h) Yesterday a window was broken by someone.

2 Complete each sentence with a passive verb.

a) The police questioned George.

George ....*was questioned*........ by the police.

b) Millions of people watch this programme.

This programme .... by millions of people.

c) They will finish our new house at the end of the month.

Our new house .... at the end of the month.

d) They've elected a new president.

A new president ....

e) They're rebuilding the damaged stadium.

The damaged stadium ....

f) They've closed the mountain road.

The mountain road ....

g) Students write most of this magazine.

Most of this magazine .... by students.

h) A burglar stole my laptop.

My laptop .... by a burglar.

i) Somebody will meet you at the bus station.

You .... at the bus station

j) United won the cup last year.

Last year the cup .... by United.

3 <u>Underline</u> the errors in these sentences. Rewrite each sentence.

a) Many pet dogs <u>are losing</u> every year.
   Many pet dogs are lost every year.

b) The injured man was been taken to hospital.
   ....

c) A new bridge is be built across the river.
   ....

d) All the food at the party was ate.
   ....

e) Nothing will being decided before next Saturday.
   ....

f) The match is playing on Friday evening.
   ....

g) The robber unlocked the door by a false key.
   ....

h) This book was writing by Sam's father.
   ....

4 For every question, complete the second sentence so that it means the same as the first, using no more than three words.

a) Archaeologists have discovered a new tomb in Egypt.
   A new tomb *has been discovered* by archaeologists in Egypt.

b) The President will open the new sports stadium on Saturday.
   The new sports stadium .... by the President on Saturday.

c) Picasso painted this portrait.
   This portrait .... Picasso.

d) They will announce the results of the competition tomorrow.
   The results of the competition .... tomorrow.

e) They're redecorating our school during the summer holidays.
   Our school .... during the summer holidays.

f) The police in New York have arrested three terrorists.
   Three terrorists .... in New York.

g) Our company sells more than 1,000 cars every week.
   More than 1,000 cars .... our company every week.

h) They're building a new museum in the city centre.
   A new museum .... in the city centre.

5 Rewrite each sentence with a passive verb, and so that the names of people are not mentioned.

a) The authorities have closed the casino.

...*The casino has been closed.*...

b) The clubs have postponed the match.

....

c) People all over the world speak English.

....

d) The authorities have opened the new swimming pool.

....

e) Someone left this purse in the classroom yesterday.

....

f) The city council has banned traffic from the city centre.

....

g) People have elected a new government.

....

h) Someone broke into the flat last week.

....

Explanations

Verbs with two objects

■ Some verbs can have two objects. We can:
  give, lend, offer, promise, sell, send, take **something** to **somebody**
  buy, keep, make, prepare, save **something** for **somebody**.

■ In active sentences we can use these verbs in two ways:
  *Peter gave **Karen a present**.*
  *Peter gave **a present to Karen**.*
  Each way can be made passive:
  ***Karen** was given **a present** by Peter.*
  ***A present** was given **to Karen** by Peter.*

■ The form without *to/for* is more usual, in both active and passive sentences.

to be born

To be born is a passive form but does not have an obvious passive meaning.
  ***I was born** in Uruguay.*

have something done

■ When a professional person, e.g. a mechanic, a plumber etc. does some work for us, we can use *have something done*. *Have* can be used in any tense.
  *We **had our house painted** last year.*
  *I'm **having my car serviced** tomorrow.*
  *I've **had my room decorated**.*

■ We also use this for unpleasant happenings.
  *She **had her house broken into**.*
  *Tim **had his arm broken** playing rugby.*

Passive + infinitive

■ The verbs *believe, expect, know, report, say, think, suppose, understand* are often used in the present simple passive followed by an infinitive (*to do/to be doing*). This use is common in news reports.
  *The economy **is expected to grow** by 2% this year.*
  *Beckham **is said to be considering** a transfer from Manchester United.*
  *The new shopping centre **is supposed to open** next spring.*

Practice

1 <u>Underline</u> the correct word or phrase in each sentence.

a) I'm having my hair *cutting/<u>cut</u>/to have cut* tomorrow.

b) The children were *took/taken/taking* to the seaside for the day.

c) I was *sending/sent/send* here by the manager.

d) Kate is having her car *services/servicing/serviced* tomorrow.

e) Sue had her windows *breaking/broken/broke* by vandals.

f) David has been *offer/offering/offered* a new job in Brazil.

g) Where exactly *were you born/did you born/did you bear*?

h) I've just had my bike *repaired/repair/repairing*.

i) I *was given/gave/did give* this book by Emily.

j) This cake *makes/made/was made* for her birthday.

2 Rewrite each sentence beginning and ending as shown. Do not change the meaning.

a) Someone stole Bob's bike.

Bob ..... *had his* ..... bike stolen.

b) John lent me this book.

This book .... John.

c) The dentist took out one of my teeth yesterday.

Yesterday I .... out.

d) Cairo is my place of birth.

I .... in Cairo.

e) A rock concert ticket was sold to me by a friend.

I was .... by a friend.

f) Someone broke into Tom's house last week.

Tom had .... last week.

g) When is your date of birth?

When exactly .... born?

h) My parents gave me this ring.

I .... parents.

i) I'm keeping this bottle of wine for a special occasion.

This bottle of wine .... for a special occasion.

j) We will send you a letter with your exam results.

A letter .... to you with your exam results.

3 Rewrite each sentence so that it has a similar meaning and contains the word in **bold**.

a) They're servicing my car tomorrow.

having

I'm having my car serviced tomorrow.

b) Yesterday they stole my bike.

had

....

c) Last year they painted our house.

had

....

d) They're taking out my tooth tomorrow!

having

....

e) They've just cut my hair.

had

....

f) They're fitting our new carpet tomorrow.

having

....

g) They've just painted Ann's portrait.

had

....

4 Rewrite the first sentence as a news report using present simple passive + infinitive.

a) Lots of people believe the criminal is living abroad.

The criminal ...*is believed to be living*... abroad.

b) Economists suppose that inflation will fall next year.

Inflation .... next year.

c) Everyone expects that Arsenal will win the League.

Arsenal .... the League.

d) People think the Government is planning a new airport.

The Government .... a new airport.

e) They say he is making a new movie about the Civil War.

He .... a new movie about the Civil War.

f) Journalists report that the Finance Minister disagrees with the President.

The Finance Minister .... with the President.

GRAMMAR 18

Modals 1: present and future

Explanations

Modal verbs: form and meaning

- Modal verbs are auxiliary verbs – they are used with other main verbs. Modal verbs are *can, could, will, would, may, might, shall, should* and *must*.

- Note these important rules:
  - two modal verbs cannot be put together
    (NOT ~~He can will meet you tomorrow.~~)
  - modal verbs are followed by the infinitive without *to*.
    (NOT ~~He must to meet you tomorrow.~~)
  - modal verbs do not have third person *s*
    (NOT ~~He cans meet you tomorrow.~~)
  - modal verbs do not form tenses with *-ing, -ed* etc.
    (NOT ~~I'm sorry I canned not meet you yesterday.~~)
  - modal verbs use inversion in questions (like the verb *be*), not *do/does*
    (NOT ~~Do can you meet me tomorrow?~~)

- Questions are made by putting the modal in front of the subject. Negatives are made by putting *not* immediately after the modal (often shortened to *-n't* in spoken and informal written English).

Can I ...?	*I cannot (can't)*
Could I ...?	*I could not (couldn't)*
Will I ...?	*I will not (won't)*
Would I ...?	*I would not (wouldn't)*
May I ...?	*I may not*
Might I ...?	*I might not*
Shall I ...?	*I shall not (shan't)*
Should I ...?	*I should not (shouldn't)*
Must I ...?	*I must not (mustn't)*

- Modal verbs show the speaker's attitude or feelings about a situation. For example how probable or necessary something is, or that the speaker is offering or requesting something. The same modal verb can be used in different ways with different meanings – you only know from the situation.

Ability

- To talk about ability we use *can* and *can't* (or *cannot* in formal writing)
  I can swim.   Can you swim?

- Pronunciation: *can* is normally unstressed /kən/, but is stressed for emphasis /kæn/.
  A: *Can you speak Chinese?*
  B: *No, but I can speak Japanese.*

69

■ We sometimes use *be able to* instead of *can*. *Be able to* forms tenses.
   Will you be able to *help me move my furniture tomorrow?*

■ *Can* and *can't* are also used for permission: to describe what is allowed or not allowed.
   Can I leave *early, please?*
   I **can't come** *skating tomorrow.*

Certainty and uncertainty

■ Study this table of probability and the notes below:

100%	certainty	*will*
95%–100%	deduction	*must, can't*
80%	expectation	*should*
30%–70%	uncertainty	*may, might, could*
0%	certainty	*won't*

■ We use *will* and *won't* when we are certain about something in the future.

■ We use *must* and *can't* for another type of certainty called 'deduction'. This is when we know something is certain because it is logical, or when we make an assumption because of the facts of the situation.
   He **must be stuck** *in the traffic.*
   (I'm sure he is – it's the only possibility)
   She **can't be in Italy**! *I saw her today!*
   (I'm sure she isn't – it's impossible)

■ We use *should* when we expect that something will happen.
   They **should arrive** *here at about 6.30.*

■ We use *may, might* and *could* for uncertainty.
   I **may not have** *time to finish tonight.*   (I don't know)
   President Jones **might win** *the next election.*   (It's possible)
   I **may /might have** *some news for you next week.*   (perhaps I will)
   He **could be** *stuck in the traffic.*   (perhaps he is)

Obligation

■ We use *must* or *have to* to explain that something is necessary.
   I **must finish** *my homework before 8.00.*
   I **have to phone** *Jan at 9.00.*

■ In writing there is no real difference between *must* and *have to*. In speech there is a small difference:

We use *have to* when the situation makes something necessary, for example because of official rules.
   At our school, we **have to wear** *a uniform.*
   Every player in a football team **has to have** *a number.*
   When the traffic lights are red, you **have to stop**.
In everyday speech, we can use *have got to* instead of *have to*.

We use *must* when the speaker personally feels that something is important.

*You really **must** stop working so hard and try to relax.*

*You **must** be here by 8.00, or the bus will leave without you.*

Note that we do not use *to* after *must*.

■ In their negative forms *mustn't* and *don't have to* have different meanings.

Mustn't describes an action which is prohibited/forbidden.

*You **mustn't cross** the road when the red light is showing.*

Don't have to describes an action which is not necessary – you have a choice.

*You **don't have to turn on** the central heating. It's automatic.*

Opinions and advice

■ We use *should* and *shouldn't* to give an opinion about what is the best thing to do. When we speak to another person our opinion becomes advice.

I think the police should arrest hooligans. (opinion)

I think you should talk to your teacher about it. (advice)

Note the other use of *should* for expectation, mentioned earlier in this unit.

■ We can use *ought to* and *ought not to* in the same way as *should* and *shouldn't*. *Ought to* is not as common as *should* and is a little more formal.

I think you ought to talk to your teacher about it.

■ Note that with *think* in the negative, we use *I don't think + should* rather than the negative forms of *should* and *ought to*.

*I don't think you **should/ought to** go.*

■ *Had better* is used for strong opinions. *Had* is usually contracted.

*I think **you'd better talk** to your teacher about it.*

***We'd better not forget** to turn off the computer!*

 SEE ALSO

Grammar 24: Functions

Practice

1   Underline the correct word or phrase in each sentence.

a) Look at those clouds. I think it *can/might/must* rain.

b) This is impossible! It *can't be/mustn't be/may not be* the answer.

c) Well done! You *may be/must be/might be* very pleased!

d) I've no idea where Jane is. She *could be/must be* anywhere!

e) I suppose it's possible. I *might/can/must* come to your party.

f) I'm not sure. I *must not/may not* be able to get there in time.

g) That *can't be/mustn't be/may not be* David. He hasn't got a bike.

h) Lisa isn't here yet. She *can be/must be* on her way.

i) There's someone at the door. It *can be/could be* the postman.

j) Sorry, I *can't come/may not come* out tonight. I have to do my homework.

2   Rewrite each sentence, using *can, can't, might* or *must,* and beginning and ending as shown.

a) Sarah is really good at swimming.

Sarah ....*can swim really*............... well.

b) It's possible that our team will win.

Our team .... win.

c) I'm sure this isn't the right road.

This .... the right road.

d) I'm sure you work very hard!

You .... very hard.

e) Caroline isn't allowed to come to our party.

Caroline .... to our party.

f) It's possible that I'll see you tomorrow, but I'm not sure.

I .... , but I'm not sure.

g) I'm afraid that your teacher is unable to come today.

I'm afraid that .... today.

h) I'm sure it's very hot here in summer.

It .... here in summer.

i) Excuse me, is it all right if I open the window?

Excuse me, ... the window?

j) I suppose you're Mrs Perry. How do you do?

You .... Mrs Perry. How do you do?

3 Decide whether each pair of sentences have a similar meaning, or whether they are different. Write *S* for *same* or *D* for *different*.

a) You'd better go.   You should go. ...*S*...

b) You don't have to press this button.   You mustn't press this button. ....

c) You should have a rest.   You ought to have a rest. ....

d) You must be crazy!   You should be crazy! ....

e) You must be here before 8.30.   You have to be here before 8.30. ....

f) You mustn't do that!   You don't have to do that! ....

g) You shouldn't eat so much.   You ought not to eat so much. ....

h) We have to work harder.   We must work harder. ....

i) I'd better write my letters.   I must write my letters. ....

j) I ought to leave now.   I have to leave now. ....

4 Rewrite each sentence so that it has a similar meaning and contains the word in **bold**.

a) It would be a good idea for you to see a dentist.
   ought
   ...*You ought to see a dentist.*...

b) It's not necessary for us to go to school tomorrow.
   have
   ....

c) I'm sure that isn't John, because he's in Paris.
   be
   ....

d) Perhaps Ann is at home.
   be
   ....

e) You ought to wear a warm coat today.
   had
   ....

f) It's possible that I'll be late.
   may
   ....

g) I wouldn't go skiing if I were you.
   think
   ....

h) It is forbidden to leave your bike here.
   can't
   ....

5 **Complete each sentence with one suitable modal auxiliary.**

a) Soldiers ......*have*........ to obey orders.

b) I think you .... take your umbrella.

c) Sorry, I .... go now. I don't want to be late.

d) I'm not sure, but I .... be able to help you.

e) Francesca isn't at home, so she .... be on her way here.

f) We .... better not leave any windows open.

g) It .... be a star, it's too bright. Perhaps it's an alien spaceship!

h) I don't .... to go to work today. It's a holiday.

i) Sorry, but I wasn't .... to finish all the work you gave me.

j) I think you .... to ask your teacher for some advice.

6 **Rewrite each sentence so that it does not contain the phrase in *italics*.**

a) *If I were you* I'd take more exercise.
    I think you'd better/you should take more exercise.

b) *I expect* the plane will land soon.

    ....

c) You *are not allowed to* use a dictionary.

    ....

d) *It's impossible for that* to be Sue. She's abroad.

    ....

e) *It's possible that* I'll come to your party.

    ....

f) *It's against the law to* drop litter in the street.

    ....

g) *It's not necessary for you* to wait.

    ....

h) *You'd better* stay in bed today.

    ....

Modals 2: past

Explanations

Ability

■ To talk about general past ability we use *could, couldn't* and *was able to.*
   *Jane **could swim/was able to swim** when she was ten.*
   To talk about one specific past action we only use *was able to.*
   *When David fell in the river, Jane **was able to** rescue him.*

Certainty and uncertainty

The form is: modal + *have* + past participle. Compare with Grammar 18:
   *You **must have left** your passport on the plane.*
   (deduction: I'm sure you did)
   *Lina **can't have written** this.*
   (deduction: I'm sure she didn't)
   *Maria **might/may/could have taken** the bus.*
   (uncertainty: perhaps she did)

Obligation

■ To talk about obligation in the past we use *had to, didn't have to, didn't need to, needn't have done.* There is no past form of *must.*
   *When I was at school, we **had to/didn't have to wear** a uniform.*

■ In strict grammar there is a difference between *didn't need to* and *needn't have done.*

*I **didn't need to do** any homework yesterday.*	(I had a choice)
*I **needn't have done** any homework yesterday.*	(I did it, but it wasn't necessary)

   But in everyday speech we use *didn't need to* for both cases.

Opinions and advice

■ The form is: modal + *have* + past participle. Compare with Grammar 18:
   *I think you **should have worked** harder.*
   *You **shouldn't have eaten** so much!*
   We can use *ought to have done* and *ought not to have done* in the same way.

■ These forms mean that we are making a criticism. So in the examples above we are saying 'I think you were wrong'.

→ **SEE ALSO**

Grammar 18: Modals 1

Practice

1 **For each question, complete the second sentence so that it means the same as the first, using no more than three words. Contractions count as one word.**

a) I'm sure you dropped your wallet at the bus stop.

You ...*must have dropped*.. your wallet at the bus stop.

b) Maybe Joanna missed the last bus.

Joanna .... the last bus.

c) Peter knew how to skate when he was twelve.

Peter .... skate when he was twelve.

d) Emma was wrong not to tell you the answer.

Emma .... you the answer.

e) It wasn't necessary for us to pay to get in.

We .... pay to get in.

f) I'm sure that Diana didn't take your books.

Diana .... your books.

g) Perhaps David didn't notice you.

David .... noticed you.

h) Terry arrived early, but it wasn't necessary.

Terry .... arrived early.

i) It wasn't necessary for me to buy any food yesterday.

I didn't .... any food yesterday.

j) It was a bad idea for us to be rude to the policeman!

We .... been rude to the policeman!

2 **Rewrite each sentence beginning as shown. Do not change the meaning.**

a) You were wrong to study so late!

You shouldn't ...*have studied so late*... .

b) Did you manage to stop him?

Were .... ?

c) It wasn't necessary to work hard.

I didn't ....

d) Perhaps Tim has lost his way.

Tim might ....

e) It was possible for you to hurt yourself.

You could ....

f) It would have been a good idea to tell me.

You should ....

g) I'm sure the class enjoyed it.

The class must ....

h) I helped her but it wasn't necessary.

I needn't ....

i) It was a mistake to leave.

You ought ....

j) I'm sure the butler didn't do it.

The butler can't ....

3   Complete each sentence so that it contains the words in **bold**.

a) I'm completely soaked! We *should have taken an umbrella.* ....

should/umbrella

b) I've lost my bag. I think I ....

must/bus

c) I tried to phone Sam, but I ....

couldn't/get through

d) I forgot Kate's birthday. I ....

should/present

e) The cat doesn't like fruit! It ....

can't/orange

f) Jo isn't here yet. I suppose she ....

might/address

g) I did badly in the test. I ....

ought/harder

h) It's a shame we didn't go on holiday. We ....

could/fun

1 <u>Underline</u> the correct word or phrase in each sentence.

a) Jim *asked*/*told* the teacher if the book was his.

b) I *have had/had* two teeth taken out last week.

c) I can't do these sums. I wish I *have/had* a calculator with me.

d) Ann *refused/said she didn't want me to* borrow her bike.

e) Helen *can't have stolen/must have stolen* the money from the office. She didn't come in to the office on the day it was stolen.

f) If I *have/had* more money, I'd pay for you too.

g) It's getting very late, so I think *you'd better/you could* leave.

h) Tracey phoned earlier and said that she *had been/would be* late.

i) The next two lessons *were been/have been* cancelled.

j) If *we'd remembered/we remembered* to bring the map, we wouldn't have got lost.

2 Look carefully at each line. Some lines are correct but some have a word which should not be there. Tick (✓) each correct line. If a line has a word which should not be there, write the word in the space.

Do-It-Yourself

Last week my brother and I decided to paint our	1 ....✓.........
bedrooms if while our parents were out for the	2 ....*if*............
day. Our parents usually they have the painting done	3 ....
by a local firm, but we thought we could to save some	4 ....
money if we did paint it ourselves. We had watched the	5 ....
painters the last time the house had to been painted,	6 ....
so we thought we would be able to do the job.	7 ....
'First all the surfaces must have to be washed,' my	8 ....
brother said. 'That can't have be very difficult,' I	9 ....
replied. 'We'd better if put some newspapers on	10 ....
the carpet. If we can make a mess, we'll get into	11 ....
trouble.' After that had been have done, we looked	12 ....
for some paint in the garden shed. 'We could use	13 ....
this red paint,' I was suggested. My brother said that	14 ....
he preferred green paint. Just as if we were going to	15 ....
start, our parents arrived home. 'You should have been	16 ....
asked us first,' my mother said us. 'You can paint the	17 ....
rest of the house too!'	18 ....

3   **Decide which answer (A, B, C or D) best fits the space.**

Making arrangements with Paul

A few days ago Paul phoned me and (1) ....*C*.... whether I (2) .... looking after his dog when he (3) .... away. I (4) .... that I didn't really like dogs, but he said that he (5) .... all his other friends, and that I (6) .... his only hope. He invited me round to his house (7) .... to meet the dog, and he told me that he (8) .... dinner for me. An hour later he phoned again and said that he (9) .... after all, so I (10) .... meeting the following day for lunch. The next morning he cancelled this appointment and, after he (11) .... , said that he (12) .... the dog to my house at 6.00. 'I don't know exactly (13) .... ,' he said. 'Could you tell me how (14) .... there?' I quickly said I (15) .... out and put the phone down. Luckily I haven't heard from him since.

1) A told	B said me	C asked me	D spoke
2) A would mind	B want	C like	D will help
3) A has gone	B went	C would go	D will go
4) A told him	B said him	C asked him	D replied him
5) A asks	B would ask	C will ask	D had already asked
6) A am	B will be	C had been	D was
7) A this evening	B that evening	C the evening	D in evening
8) A is cooking	B will cook	C would cook	D had cooked
9) A had to go out	B went out	C goes out	D has to go out
10) A had suggested	B would suggest	C suggested	D suggest
11) A has done	B told me sorry	C asked	D had apologized
12) A would bring	B had brought	C brought	D brings
13) A where is it	B if it is	C where it is	D how was it
14) A do I get	B I get	C I will get	D I'm getting
15) A went	B go	C will go	D was going

4   **Complete each sentence with one of the words or phrases from the box.**

could	~~don't have to~~	might have	must	mustn't	should	
had to	have to					

a) We ..*don't have to*.... wear a uniform at my school.

b) You .... play with matches! It's very dangerous!

c) I'm not sure, but I think I .... left my wallet in the bank.

d) I'm getting up early, because I .... go running before school.

e) Sorry I can't stay any longer, but I really .... go home.

f) If you want to, we .... go swimming this afternoon.

g) Sorry I'm late, but I .... take my dog to the vet's.

h) I think you .... go to bed earlier, and stop drinking coffee.

5 Complete the second sentence so that it has a similar meaning to the first sentence.

a) I don't know the answer, so I can't help you.

If I *knew the answer, I would help you* ....

b) Don't run fast, or you'll feel tired.

If ....

c) An off-duty policewoman arrested the robber.

The robber ....

d) We didn't leave early, so we missed the train.

If we ....

e) I ate all the ice-cream, and now I regret it.

I wish ....

f) Where is the bus station?

Could you .... ?

g) The local council is building a new sports centre.

A new sports centre ....

h) I think you should go to the doctor's.

If I ....

i) Someone used a hammer to break the window.

The window ....

j) 'Don't forget to buy some milk, Amy,' I said.

I reminded ....

6 For each question, complete the second sentence so that it means the same as the first, using no more than three words.

a) It wasn't necessary for me to go to work yesterday.

I didn't *have to go* .... to work yesterday.

b) I'd like to be rich!

I wish .... rich!

c) I'm going to the hairdresser's tomorrow.

I'm having .... tomorrow.

d) Perhaps Mark missed the bus.

Mark might .... the bus.

e) Marconi was the inventor of radio.

Radio .... by Marconi.

f) I think you were wrong to forget the keys!

You shouldn't .... the keys!

g) It would be a good idea for us to take an umbrella.

We .... better take an umbrella.

h) I'm sure that Maria worked very hard.

Maria .... very hard.

i) Helen gave a camera to Richard.

Richard .... a camera by Helen.

j) It was unnecessary for us to buy so much food.

We .... bought so much food.

7 For each question, complete the second sentence so that it means the same as the first, using no more than three words.

a) The painters are coming to our house tomorrow.

We are ...*having our house*..... painted tomorrow.

b) Someone stole Peter's car last week.

Peter .... stolen last week.

c) 'I've lost my ticket, Kate,' said Danny.

Danny told Kate that .... lost his ticket.

d) Carl advised Diane not to take the job.

'I .... the job if I were you, Diane,' said Carl.

e) When does the play start?

Could you .... the play starts?

f) Let's go for a picnic if the weather's good.

Let's go for a picnic .... the weather's bad.

g) I stayed up late because I didn't feel tired.

If I had felt tired I .... stayed up late.

h) Jim lived in Spain then, so it was impossible that you met him here.

You .... met Jim here, because he lived in Spain then.

i) 'Do you have to leave early tomorrow, Ann?' asked Mary.

Mary asked Ann if she .... leave early the next day.

j) 'Do you think you could pass me the salt, Peter?' I said.

I .... Peter to pass the salt.

8   <u>Underline</u> the errors in these sentences. Correct the error.

a) War and Peace was <u>writing</u> by Leo Tolstoy.
.. *written* ....

b) That mustn't be David! He's on holiday in Bermuda.
....

c) Andrea asked a passer-by where was the train station.
....

d) If I had lived in Ancient Greece, I might be a slave!
....

e) In the army, you'd better wear a uniform.
....

f) Kate told me that she must to finish her homework.
....

g) I think someone must open your bag. That's the only explanation.
....

h) I wish I am taller!
....

i) I repair my car by a qualified mechanic.
....

j) If I saw a snake, I'll scream and run away!
....

Problem check

1   **Do you change tenses when you use reported speech in your language?**
If you need to check the punctuation of direct speech you can look at Grammar 48.

2   **Check the difference between the second and third conditionals. Remember that the past tense verb in a second conditional does not refer to past time.**

3   **When do we use the passive? Does your language use passives like English does?**

4   **How do we use *must, have to* and *should*? When might you say:**
a) Jim has to get up early every day.
b) Jim must get up early every day.
c) Jim should get up early every day.

5   **Explain the difference between each pair of sentences.**
a) I'm cutting my hair.
I'm having my hair cut.
b) I must have lost my keys.
I can't have lost my keys.
c) I didn't need to buy any food yesterday.
I needn't have bought any food yesterday.
d) If you came by bus, you'd get here faster.
If you had come by bus, you would have got here faster.

Explanations

Purpose: *to* and *for*

■ We use the *to* infinitive to describe purpose, to say why we do things. This is called 'the infinitive of purpose'.

*Alistair went to the station **to meet** his parents.* (NOT ~~for to meet~~)

■ In formal speech and writing we can use *in order to*. This is not as common as the infinitive of purpose.

*The President made a speech **in order to explain** the policy.*

■ We can use *for* followed by a noun to say why we do something. This is especially common following verbs of motion.

*I **went** to the shops **for some milk**.*

Purpose: *so that*

■ We can use *so (that)* to express purpose. After *so (that)* we use subject + verb.

■ For a habitual purpose we use *can* or the present simple.

*I leave the window open **so (that)** the cat **can get** in and out.*
*Bill wears thick socks in bed **so (that)** his feet **don't get** cold.*

■ For a future purpose we use *can, will* or the present simple.

*Dora is going to leave class early **so (that)** she **can go** to the dentist.*
*We'll take an umbrella **so (that)** we **don't get** wet.*

■ For a past purpose we use *could, would* or the past simple.

*Dora left class early **so (that)** she **could go** to the dentist.*
*We took an umbrella **so (that)** we **wouldn't get** wet.*
*We took an umbrella **so (that)** we **didn't get** wet.*

■ If the subject of the first part of the sentence and the subject of the purpose clause are different, we can't use the infinitive of purpose *to*. We have to use *so (that)*.

*Helen played the piano **to entertain** her friends.*
***Helen** played the piano **so (that) everyone else** could dance.*

Practice

1 Put one suitable word in each space. Contractions count as one word.

a) I wrote the date in my diary ...*so*............. ...*that*.......... I wouldn't forget it.

b) Most tourists come here .... visit the ancient temples.

c) Mary called a meeting .... announce the team.

d) The thief .... in black so that nobody .... see him.

e) Jack came to me .... advice.

f) Our teacher made us sit far apart so that we .... cheat!

g) I'll leave the box open so that you .... help yourself.

h) Lisa got up early so that she .... finish her homework.

2 Rewrite each sentence so that it contains to word in **bold**.

a) I went to the shops to get some eggs.

for

...*I went to the shops for some eggs.*......................................

b) Nicola came here for a meeting with the director.

to

....

c) We went on holiday to have a rest.

for

....

d) Mike plays chess for relaxation.

to

....

e) I opened the window to let in some air.

for

....

f) Cristina went shopping to buy some new clothes.

for

....

g) I went to a private school for English lessons.

to

....

h) Sam went to a specialist to get treatment.

for

....

3 Complete the second sentence so that it has a similar meaning to the first sentence.

a) Paul had to go to the doctor's, and left work early.

Paul ....*left work early*.......... so that ......*he could go*........ to the doctor's.

b) The school was rebuilt because it wasn't large enough.

The school .... in order to ....

larger.

c) Sophia wanted Jack to call her, and gave him her phone number.

Sophia .... so that .... her.

d) I might get sunburnt, so I'll put on some suntan oil.

I'll .... so that .... sunburnt.

e) Cathy hid the presents and nobody saw them.

Cathy .... so that .... them.

f) We wanted people to dance, so we had the party in a large hall.

We .... so that .... dance.

g) Dick wanted to get a good seat, so he arrived early.

Dick .... so that .... a good seat.

h) I couldn't see well in the cinema, and changed seats.

I .... so that .... better.

i) We didn't want to feel hungry, so we took some sandwiches.

We took .... so that we ....

j) Harry wanted his friends to notice him so he wore a funny hat.

Harry .... so that .... him.

Explanations

Reason and result

- We use *because, as* and *since* when we want to explain the reason for something. *As* and *since* are more common in formal speech and writing.

  *Tim didn't feel well, **because** he had eaten fifteen ice-creams.*
  ***As/since** Tim had eaten fifteen ice-creams, he didn't feel very well.*
  *Tim didn't feel well, **as/since** he had eaten fifteen ice-creams.*

- *As* and *since* can come at the beginning of the sentence. Normally we do not begin sentences with *because*, but this is possible in informal speech.

  ***Because** Tim had eaten fifteen ice-creams, he didn't feel very well.*

- We use *so* to express a result. Note the relation between *because* and so.

  *Tim had eaten fifteen ice-creams, **so** he didn't feel very well.*

so and *such* for emphasis

- We use *so many/much (that)* and *so few/little (that)* with nouns, for emphasis. *That* is usually left out in informal speech and writing. Note the rules:

  Countable nouns
  *I bought **so many books (that)** I couldn't carry them all.*
  *There were **so few people in the theatre (that)** the actors didn't perform well.*
  Uncountable nouns
  *There is **so much rain** at the moment **(that)** we hardly ever go out.*
  *We have **so little free time (that)** we don't watch television.*

- We use *so* + adjective + *that* with adjectives by themselves.

  *Last night was **so hot (that)** I couldn't sleep.*
  *The trainers were **so cheap (that)** I bought two pairs.*

- If we have an adjective followed by a noun, we use *such a*.

  *It was **such a lovely day (that)** we went for a walk in the country.*
  *It was **such a good film (that)** I saw it twice.*

too and *not enough* for a difficulty

- *Too* + adjective means 'more than is necessary or good'. It suggests a difficulty, and that something cannot be done.

  *It was **too far**.*   (so I didn't go)
  *It was **too difficult**.*   (so I didn't do it)

- If we say what the action is we use *to* + infinitive.

  *It was **too far to walk** so we took a taxi.*
  *The mountain was **too difficult** (for us) **to climb**.*

- *Not* + adjective + *enough* means 'less than is necessary or good'. Compare the use of *too* and *not enough*.

    *Little Gerry is **too young to walk** to school.*
    *Little Gerry is **not old enough to walk** to school.*

- With nouns we can use *too many/much, too few/little* and *not enough*.
    Countable nouns

    *There are **too many** people in the class.*
    *There are **too few** books.*
    *We **haven't** got **enough** books.*

    Uncountable nouns

    *There are **too many** things to do.*
    *There's **too little** time.*
    *We **haven't got enough** time.*

- Notice from the above examples that *enough* comes after adjectives ('old') but before nouns ('books'/'time').

so and too

- It is a common mistake to confuse *so* and *too*.
    So is like *very*, and is used for emphasis. The speaker's opinion can be positive or negative.
    Too means 'more than enough'. It suggests a difficulty, that something cannot be done or will not happen.

    *It's **very** expensive.*   (a fact)
    *It's **so** expensive.*   (I'm surprised, but I still might buy it)
    *It's **too** expensive.*   (so I won't buy it)

- Look back at the examples in the previous two sections to see these uses of *so* and *too*.

Result phrases: *as a result, in the end, eventually*

We can also express result with a linking phrase like *as a result*, or a time expression like *in the end* or *eventually*. These are more common in formal speech and writing.

    *Two metres of snow fell during the night. **As a result**, several main roads were blocked.*   (in speech we would just use *so* here)
    *It started raining while we were having our picnic, and **eventually** we decided to go home.*
    *Kate and Tim waited for the bus for a long time, and **in the end** they took a taxi.*

Linking words

- Words like *because* and *so* are called 'linking words'.

→ SEE ALSO

Grammar 47: Linking words

Practice

1   Underline the correct word or phrase in each sentence.

a) It was _such_/so a delicious drink, that I had to have another glass.

b) Andrew ate _so much/so many_ cakes that he could hardly walk!

c) Kate's offer sounded _so/too_ good to be true!

d) There are _so few/so little_ good programmes on TV that I rarely watch it.

e) I felt _so/too_ weak that I couldn't stand up.

f) We had _so much/so many_ free time, that we got bored.

g) I waited for Elaine for ages, and _as a result/in the end_ I gave up.

h) There was _so much/so many_ rain last night, that the roads were flooded.

i) David was _too tall/tall enough/enough tall/very tall_ to reach the shelf.

j) I had _so few/so little_ knowledge of the subject that I got zero in the test.

2   Complete the sentences with one of these words: _too, enough, so, such, much, many, little, few._

a) It's ....._so_............. late and there are still lots of people in the club.

b) It's .... late to catch a bus. I'll have to get a taxi home.

c) I have so .... work to do!

d) I have so .... jobs to do!

e) I don't have .... money to go on holiday this year.

f) I have too .... money to go on holiday this year.

g) I have too .... euros in my bank account to go on holiday this year.

h) It was .... an exciting film.

i) The film was .... exciting.

j) It's .... hot on the beach. I don't like it. I'm going back to the hotel.

k) It's .... hot on the beach! I love it. I'm really relaxed.

3   Put one suitable word in each space.

a) My tea is ....._too_........... hot to drink at the moment.

b) I had to stand at the back, ... there weren't any seats left.

c) Thomas had .... homework, that he had to stay up late.

d) There were .... people in front of us that we couldn't see.

e) Helen missed the bus, ... she took a taxi.

f) There were .... customers that the shop closed down.

g) The room wasn't large .... for so many guests.

h) Hannah was .... tired that she fell asleep on the train.

i) We had .... money that we couldn't even buy a drink.

j) .... it was raining, the school picnic was postponed.

4 Rewrite each sentence so that it has a similar meaning and contains the word in **bold**.

a) I felt really tired, so I stayed at home and had a rest.

because

I stayed at home and had a rest because I felt really tired.

b) I didn't use that piece of string, because it was too short.

enough

....

c) The question was so difficult that I had to ask for help.

such

....

d) There weren't enough seats for all the guests.

few

....

e) There weren't enough seats for all the guests.

many

....

f) We can't put that box in the car as there isn't much space.

little

....

g) I haven't got enough time to do all my work.

too

....

h) I've got such a lot of work that I can't go out.

so

....

i) She had lots of children and didn't know what to do.

many

....

j) It was such a good play that the audience cheered.

so

....

5 <u>Underline</u> the errors in these sentences. Rewrite each sentence.

a) Sorry, but I haven't got <u>little</u> time.

...*Sorry, but I haven't got enough time.*...

b) Erica is not enough old to drive a car.

....

c) Paul has so much friends that he's always busy.

....

d) We had too few time to go sight-seeing.

....

e) It's too hot that I can't think!

....

f) There was too much snow that we couldn't travel.

....

g) It was so a long way that we decided to drive there.

....

h) So that I had run a long way, I felt exhausted.

....

6 Complete the second sentence so that it has a similar meaning to the first sentence.

a) I'm afraid you're not fast enough to be in the running team.

I'm afraid you're too ...*slow to be in the running team.*.....................

b) It's not very far to the house, so we can walk.

We can walk ....

c) The film was so long that we missed our last bus.

It was ....

d) Tina felt unhappy and she cried.

Tina felt so ....

e) Tom has lots of money, and doesn't know what to do with it.

Tom has so ....

f) Jim is too young to get married.

Jim isn't ....

g) I can't afford to buy this bike.

I haven't got ....

h) There are too few plates I'm afraid.

There aren't ....

Explanations

but, yet and
although

■ We can use *but* and *although* to make a contrast. *Although* is more typical of careful or formal speech or writing.

*Maria felt ill, **but** she went to school.*

*Maria went to school **although** she was ill.*

The clause with *although* can come at the beginning.

***Although** she was ill, Maria went to school.*

■ We can emphasize *but* and *although* with *still* and *anyway*.

*Maria felt ill, **but** she went to school **anyway**.*

*Maria felt ill, **but** she **still** went to school.*

***Although** she was ill, Maria went to school **anyway**.*

■ We can use *yet* instead of *but* in writing.

*Maria felt ill, **yet** she went to school.*

even though and
though

■ We can use *even though* like *although* to give a stronger contrast.

***Even though** she felt very ill, Maria went to school.*

■ We can use *though* like *although* in informal speech and writing. We often make two separate sentences and put *though* at the end.

*Maria went to school. She was ill, **though**.*

while and *whereas*

■ *While* and *whereas* can be used in formal speech and writing to compare two facts and emphasize the difference between them.

***While/Whereas** some experts expect the Government to win the election, most believe that the opposition will win.*

despite and
in spite of

■ *Despite* and *in spite of* are also used to make a contrast. But they are followed by a noun or noun phrase (not subject + verb like *although*). The *-ing* form of the verb acts like a noun here.

***Despite her illness**, Maria went to school.*

(NOT ~~Despite she felt ill, Maria~~ ...)

***Despite being ill**, Maria went to school.*

***In spite of her illness**, Maria went to school.*

***In spite of being ill**, Maria went to school.*

however and *on the other hand*

■ *However* introduces or completes a contrasting sentence. *However* always has punctuation before and after.

> *Maria was ill.* **However***, she went to school.*
> *Maria went to school. She was ill,* **however***.*

However is more common in formal speech and writing.

■ Note that we cannot say:

> ~~However she was ill, Maria went to school.~~

■ *On the other hand* introduces a contrasting opinion. It is more common in formal speech and writing.

> *Television has many advantages. It keeps us informed about the latest news, and also provides entertainment in the home.* **On the other hand***, television has been blamed for the violent behaviour of some young people, and for encouraging children to sit indoors, instead of taking exercise.*

Linking words

■ Words like *but, although* and *however* are called 'linking words'.

→ SEE ALSO

Grammar 47: Linking words

Practice

1 <u>Underline</u> the correct word or phrase in each sentence.

a) I read the book you suggested. I didn't enjoy it, *although/<u>however</u>*.

b) *In spite of/Although* we warned him, Harry still got lost.

c) *Although/However* I like it here, I won't stay here long.

d) Cars are convenient. *On the other hand/Whereas*, they cause pollution.

e) I didn't have much time, *but/however* I managed to visit lots of places.

f) Catherine won the race, *although/despite* falling over.

g) *Although/In spite of* the delay, the train arrived on time.

h) I didn't manage to jump over the wall, *although/yet* I tried twice.

2 Complete each sentence with one suitable word.

a) ...*Although*. Tim felt tired, he stayed up to finish his homework.

b) Sam didn't like skating, ... he went with his friends all the same.

c) I found French hard at first. .... , I soon started to enjoy it.

d) Jane kept running, ... though she knew she couldn't win.

e) Mike was lost, but he .... refused to look at the map.

f) Carol went to see the film, ... she had seen it before.

g) .... the rain, the school sports were a great success.

h) Helen won the swimming competition, in .... of her cold.

3 Rewrite each sentence beginning as shown. Do not change the meaning.

a) Although it was snowing, we went out for a walk.
   Despite ...*the snow, we went out for a walk*...............................

b) Some experts think prices will fall, but others disagree.
   While ....

c) Even though they were losing at half-time, City won in the end.
   Despite ....

d) Despite the heat, Diana wore her winter clothes.
   Although ....

e) Whereas last summer was good, this summer it's rained all the time.
   Last summer was good ....

f) James had a headache, but he still read until late.
   In spite of ....

g) Although Jon hadn't studied, he did well in the test.
   Jon hadn't studied ....

Functions

Explanations

What is a function?

- A function is a way of describing language according to its purpose (how it is used). Functions can be short phrases as well as single words. Typical functions are: offering something, asking for permission, making a suggestion etc.

- The same function can be expressed in different ways. Our choice of words depends on:
  - The situation we are in: is it public or private? who else is present?
  - The person we are talking to: someone of our own age? how well do we know them?
  - What we are talking about: is the topic sensitive? or is it light and unimportant?

- The functions below are classified as formal (= polite), neutral or informal, but remember that the choice of words depends on many things. You might be talking to a friend and you want to borrow a pen, so you are informal. But if you are talking to the same friend and you want to borrow a large amount of money you will use more formal language.

Asking for information

- To ask for information we can use an indirect question:

  Can you tell me what time the bus from Glasgow arrives? (neutral)
  Could you tell me what time the bus from Glasgow arrives?
  → *Of course. It arrives at 9.30.* (neutral)
  Would you mind telling me what time the bus from Glasgow arrives?
  → *Of course not. It arrives at 9.30.* (formal)

- Note the indirect question form (NOT ~~what time does~~ ...).

Offers

Offering help:
  Shall I carry this suitcase for you? (neutral)
  Let me carry your suitcase. (neutral)
  → *Thank you very much. / Thanks, but I can manage.*
Offering things:
  Would you like a soft drink? (neutral)
  → *Yes, please, I'll have an orange juice. / No thanks, it's OK.*
  Would you like tea or coffee? (neutral)
  → *I'd rather have coffee, please. / I'd prefer tea, please. / I don't mind.*

Permission	*Is it all right* if I leave early?	(informal)
	Can I leave early, please?	(neutral)
	→ *Yes, of course.*	
	→ *Sorry, but you can't. You have to stay to the end.*	
	Could I possibly leave a bit early, please?	(formal)
	→ *Yes, you can.*	
	May I leave early, please?	(formal)
	→ *Yes, you may.*	

When we reply we often repeat the modal verb, but notice that when we reply to *Could I* we say *can* not *could*.

Promising	*I'll be back at 11.30.*	(neutral)
	I won't do anything silly!	(neutral)

The word *will* is used in many functions.

Requests	*Can you open the window, please?*	(neutral)
	Can you help me?	(neutral)
	Could you open the window please?	(formal)
	Will/Would you wait here, please?	(formal)

We can reply to a request by agreeing or refusing:
→ *Sure. / No problem. / Of course.*
→ *Actually, it's a bit inconvenient. / I'm sorry but that's not possible.*

Requests with mind

- Requests with *mind* are confusing for learners because *Would you mind ...* means 'Is it a problem for you?'. So we say 'no' if we want to be helpful.
  Would you mind helping me?
  → *No, of course not.*
  → *Actually, I'm quite busy at the moment. Perhaps later.*

- Note that we use an *-ing* form after *Would you mind*.

Suggesting and advising	*Let's go to the cinema.*	(neutral)
	Why don't we go to the cinema?	(neutral)
	How about going to the cinema?	(neutral)
	We could go to the cinema.	(neutral)

If we make a suggestion to another person it is advice:
I think you should stay at home. (formal)
If I were you, I'd stay at home. (formal)

 SEE ALSO

Grammar 9: Future 2
Grammar 28: Questions 2

Practice

1 **Match what people say (a–j) with the functions (1–10).**

a) Would you like a cup of tea? .....4.....

b) Excuse me, do you know what time the museum opens? ....

c) Actually, I think I'd rather have a Chinese meal. ....

d) I know, we could walk along the river. How about that? ....

e) Sorry, but I won't do it. ....

f) That looks difficult. Shall I help you? ....

g) Excuse me, but do you think you could turn your music down a bit? ....

h) Well, to be honest, I think you should go to the police. ....

i) Is it all right if I go out to the shops for a moment? ....

j) I'll definitely be there at 6.00. I won't be late! ....

  1 Giving advice
  2 Asking for information
  3 Offering help
  4 Offering something
  5 Asking permission
  6 Refusing to do something
  7 Expressing a preference
  8 Making a promise
  9 Making a request
10 Making a suggestion

2 <u>Underline</u> **the correct word or phrase in each sentence.**

a) I'm very busy. *Let's/<u>Would you mind</u>* giving me a hand?

b) *If I were you, I'd write/How about you write* the letter again.

c) Why don't we *go/going* to the theatre tomorrow?

d) *Would you mind/Could you* close the door please?

e) *Do you like/Would you like* some more water?

f) I promise *I won't do it/I don't do it* again.

g) I'm quite good at cooking too. *Shall I help/Would I help* you?

h) I've a suggestion. *Why don't you go/Could you go* to the beach?

i) *Would I borrow/Could I borrow* your ruler?

j) Are you tired? I think you *can go/should go* to bed early.

3 Replace the parts in *italics* with a more appropriate or accurate expression.

a) Look, don't worry about me, there's a bus at 12.30. So *I'm back* by 2.00, I promise!

.........*I'll be back*...

b) A: Would you like an ice-cream? Or some cake perhaps?

   B: *I choose ice-cream*, please.

   ....

c) A: I'm having problems at school. What do you think I should do?

   B: *I talk it over with your parents.*

   ....

d) A: This suitcase is really heavy, and my back is killing me!

   B: *Do I carry it?*

   ....

e) A: I'm not sure what to do this evening. Any ideas?

   B: *You will go to the cinema, perhaps?*

   ....

f) A: I've got an appointment at the dentist's. *Shall I leave school early?*

   B: Have you brought a note from your parents?

   ....

g) Excuse me, I want to catch a bus from here to London. *Tell me how much does it cost.*

   ....

h) A: I feel really hungry. Have you got anything to eat?

   B: *Do you like some lemonade?*

   ....

i) A: It's very hot in here. *Are you opening the window?*

   B: Of course.

   ....

j) A: Come on, hurry up! Tidy your room and make your bed!

   B: *No, I don't!* It's not fair!

   ....

4 **For each question, complete the second sentence so that it means the same as the first, using no more than three words.**

a) Please take a seat.

Would ...*you mind taking*........................... a seat?

b) Fruit juice would be better for me.

I .... fruit juice.

c) I'd like you to wait for me.

.... for me, please?

d) Will you allow me to leave the room?

.... the room?

e) I'd like you to turn off the television.

Could .... the television?

f) Let's go for a walk.

.... for a walk?

g) I promise not to talk to Richard again.

I .... to Richard again.

h) Would you like me to help you?

.... you?

i) When does the plane arrive?

Would you .... when the plane arrives?

j) My advice is to see a doctor.

If I .... I'd see a doctor.

5 **Complete each sentence with one suitable word. More than one answer may be possible.**

a) I think you ...*should*..... spend more time on your homework.

b) .... you help me carry these bags?

c) Excuse me. .... you tell me what street this is?

d) What a terrible noise! .... you please be quiet!

e) .... go skating tomorrow.

f) Would you .... telling me what time it is?

g) Thanks for the offer, but I'd .... stay at home.

h) .... you sign your name here, please, sir?

i) .... you like another slice of pizza?

j) Please .... I leave the table?

Relative clauses 1

Explanations

Relative clauses

Relative clauses are short phrases beginning with words like *who, that* and *which* (called 'relative pronouns') that define or describe people and things. There are two types:

- Defining relative clauses: we use these to identify exactly which person or thing we mean. The information is necessary for the sentence to make sense.
  *The doctor **who treated me** told me not to worry.*
  In this example there is more than one doctor and we only know which one by the relative clause.

- Non-defining relative clauses: we use these to give extra information. The information is not necessary for the sentence to make sense. To show this in writing we use commas.
  *Pablo Picasso, **who died in 1973**, was a painter and sculptor.*

Relative pronouns

- *which, that*
  Which refers to things and *that* refers to people and things. *That* is more common, especially in speech.
  *The bus **which** goes to Cairo leaves from here.*
  *The woman **that** we spoke to gave us directions.*
  *The road **that** we took led to an ancient temple.*

- *who* and *whom*
  Who and *whom* refer to people.
  In formal speech and writing we can use *whom* instead of *who* where *who* is the object of the sentence (see below). We can also use *whom* after a preposition. However, this is becoming less common and in modern English speakers rarely use *whom* – instead they use *who* or *that*.
  *The people **who** live next door make a lot of noise.*
  *The people **that** live next door make a lot of noise.*
  *It was the same boy **whom** I met yesterday.*
  ('I' is the subject, 'whom' is the object)
  *No one knows **by whom** the victim was shot.*
  (after the preposition 'by', but very rare in modern English.)
  *No one knows **who** the victim was shot **by**.*
  (normal usage in speech and writing)

- *whose*
  Whose shows that something belongs to someone.
  *The girl **whose** case had been stolen went to the police station.*

Leaving out the relative pronoun

■ To understand whether you can leave out the relative pronoun you first need to look at whether the relative clause refers to the subject or object of the sentence.

A relative clause that refers to the subject of the sentence:
The doctor who treated me told me not to worry.
<u>The doctor</u> (subject) *treated <u>me</u>* (object).

A relative clause that refers to the object of the sentence:
The doctor that/who/whom I spoke to told me not to worry.
<u>I</u> (subject) *spoke to <u>the doctor</u>* (object).

■ We can leave out the relative pronoun in a defining relative clause that refers to the object.
The doctor I spoke to told me not to worry.

■ We cannot leave out the relative pronoun in a defining relative clause that refers to the subject.
The doctor who treated me told me not to worry.

■ In a non-defining relative clause we must keep the relative pronoun.
Pablo Picasso, who died in 1973, was a painter and sculptor.

■ We can also leave out the relative pronoun after a superlative.
That was the best meal (that) I've ever eaten!

Practice

1 <u>Underline</u> the correct word in each sentence.

a) An old man, <u>who</u>/which was carrying a suitcase, knocked at the door.
b) The winner, *which/whose* bike was an unusual design, won a medal.
c) The girl *who/which* spoke to me turned out to be in my class.
d) The museum, *which/whose* was in a beautiful building, was closed.
e) A policewoman *that/which* we asked told us how to get there.
f) The boy *whose/whom* house I was staying at was an old friend.
g) The last person *which/whose* pen I borrowed didn't get it back.

2 Complete each sentence with *who, whose* or *that*.

a) The friend ...*whose*....... house I stayed in is coming to stay with us.
b) The guidebook .... we bought explained everything.
c) The couple .... house I bought both worked in my office.
d) I'd like you to tell me .... you were talking to.
e) The girl .... ruler I had borrowed wanted it back.
f) I can't remember .... I lent my bike to.
g) Do you know .... Catherine works for?

3 Decide whether the clause in *italics* is Defining or Non-defining. Write D or N next to each sentence.

a) The girl *who was waiting* was becoming impatient. ....*D*..........
b) The room, *which was enormous*, was filled with lines of chairs. ....
c) The students, *who were late*, waited in the playground. ....
d) The food *which was left* was eaten the following day. ....
e) A tall girl, *who was wearing a hat*, came into the room. ....
f) The dog, *which was lying on the sofa*, had long pointed ears. ....
g) The train *which leaves at 8.00* doesn't stop at Bath. ....

4 <u>Underline</u> relative pronouns which can be left out in these sentences.

a) The book <u>that</u> John was reading was a bit frightening.
b) The travel agency which sold me the ticket was near my office.
c) In the end, our holiday was the best that we had ever had.
d) The dentist who I go to isn't very expensive.
e) The film which we saw last week was much better than this one.
f) The people who were leaving couldn't find their coats.
g) The garden, which wasn't very large, was full of flowers.

5 Rewrite each formal sentence as an informal one, ending with the word given.

a) These are the boys with whom I went on holiday.
   ...*These are the boys I went on holiday*............................ with.

b) This is the letter for which I've been waiting.
   .... for.

c) That is the shop from which Sue bought her bike.
   .... from.

d) That is the hotel at which I stayed.
   .... at.

e) Tim is someone to whom I hardly ever write.
   .... to.

f) Do you know by whom this book was written?
   .... by?

g) Ravenna was the most interesting town in which we stayed.
   .... in.

h) United were the best team against which we played.
   .... against.

6 Add a relative pronoun to each sentence.

a) Friday was the last time I saw Jim.
   ...*Friday was the last time that I saw Jim.*...............................

b) The island we visited was extremely beautiful.
   ....

c) The girl I met was a friend of Philip's.
   ....

d) The meal we ate wasn't very tasty.
   ....

e) Gina was the first person I asked.
   ....

f) The book I read didn't explain the problem.
   ....

g) The teacher we usually have was away ill.
   ....

h) The friends I met last night send you their love.
   ....

Explanations

Combining sentences

- Look at these short sentences.

  A bus goes to Cairo. It leaves from here.
  A woman teaches us music. She also plays in an orchestra.
  We took a road. It led to an ancient temple.
  We spoke to a woman. She gave us directions.

  We can combine the sentences using relative clauses.

  *The bus **that** goes to Cairo leaves from here.*
  *The woman **who** teaches us music also plays in an orchestra.*
  *The road **(that)** we took led to an ancient temple.*
  *The woman **(that)** we spoke to gave us directions.*

- Note that articles often change (e.g. from *a/an* to *the*) when sentences are combined.

  A girl's case was stolen. She went to the police station.
  The girl whose case was stolen went to the police station.

  A doctor treated me. She told me not to worry.
  The doctor who treated me told me not to worry.

  *I spoke to **a** doctor. She told me not to worry.*
  The doctor I spoke to told me not to worry.

- Note this common error: ~~The bus that goes to Cairo it leaves from here.~~
  When we combine sentences we do not repeat the subject by adding another pronoun (*The bus ... it*).

Relative clauses with an *-ing* form

The relative clause often has a continuous verb form:

  *Can all the students **who are leaving** tomorrow give back their books?*
  *I sent a card to the girl **who was living** across the street.*

In this case we can leave out both the relative pronoun and the verb *be*.

  *Can all the students **leaving** tomorrow give back their books?*
  *I sent a card to the girl **living** across the street.*

***What* as a relative pronoun**

We can use the relative pronoun *what* to mean *the thing(s) that*.

  *We didn't understand **what** she said.*   (= the things that she said)
  ***What** I want now is a cup of tea.*   (= the thing that I want)

Practice

1 <u>Underline</u> the correct word in each sentence.

a) The train <u>*which*</u>/*who* goes to Brighton leaves from here.

b) *That/What* I like best is an afternoon at the beach.

c) I didn't know *who/which* to ask about my timetable.

d) The people *which/whose* luggage was lost had to wait a long time.

e) Where's the ruler *whose/that* I left on this desk?

f) The shop *what/that* I went to didn't have any milk.

g) Do you know *whom/whose* bag this is?

h) Everyone *who/which* was there will remember the day forever.

i) The second bus, *which/whose* was full, didn't stop either.

j) Jim was helped by someone *who/whom* told him the answer.

2 Some sentences have a word which should not be there. Write the word in the space. If the sentence is correct, put a tick (✓).

a) The man whose his car had been damaged was very angry. .....*his*.....

b) That was the longest film I've ever seen. ....

c) The train which it goes to London leaves from here. ....

d) The policewoman who she stopped me asked me my name. ....

e) The Eiffel Tower, which it was finished in 1889, is made of iron. ....

f) Everyone that Elena spoke to advised her to try again. ....

g) The children that they live next door are my friends. ....

3 Rewrite each pair of sentences as one sentence, and include the word in bold. Begin as shown, and make any necessary changes.

a) We want to visit a museum. It opens at 12.00.

that

The .....*museum that we want to visit opens at 12.00.*.....

b) A boy's bike was taken. He visited the police station.

whose

The ....

c) A friend met me at the airport. He carried my suitcase.

who

The ....

d) Tom cooked a meal. It was delicious.

that

The ....

e) A friend is staying with me. She comes from Paris.

who

The ....

f) I found a man's wallet. He gave me a reward.

whose

The ....

g) I go to a shop in the centre. It is cheaper.

that

The ....

h) I went to a girl's party. She phoned me.

whose

The ....

i) I know someone. This person likes you.

who

I ....

4 **Put one word in each space, or tick (✓) the space if the sentence is correct.**

a) We sent a present to the children ....✓.......... living next door.

b) Mike doesn't really know .... he wants.

c) I started talking to some boys .... sitting by the side of the road.

d) I asked Mary .... she was thinking, but she wouldn't tell me.

e) There were lots of people at the party .... we went to.

f) I don't really know .... you're talking about.

g) .... we need now is a map and a compass.

h) We saw two rabbits .... playing in the garden.

Questions 1

Explanations

Questions with the answer *yes* or *no* are formed with an auxiliary verb + subject + main verb. The auxiliary can be *do, be, have* or a modal verb like *can, will* etc.

Present simple	*Do you live in Prague?*
Present continuous	*Are you sitting comfortably?*
Present perfect	*Have you ever eaten octopus?*
Past simple	*Did you phone Sue?*
Past continuous	*Were you having a bath?*
Past perfect	*Had you already left?*
can/could	*Can you swim? Could you see?*
must/have to	*Must you go? Do you have to go?*

We can also make a question with a question word: *what, why, when, who, whose, which* and *how*. After the question word we use the same structure as a *Yes/No* question: auxiliary verb + subject + main verb.

Present simple	*When do you usually leave?*
Present continuous	*What are you doing?*
Present perfect	*Why have you stopped?*
Past simple	*How did you feel?*
Past continuous	*Where were you living?*
Past perfect	*Who had you told?*
can/could	*What can I do? Where could he go?*
must/have to	*What must I do? What do I have to do?*

Sometimes the question word is the subject of the sentence. In this case we do not use *do/does/did*.

Who did you meet in England?	('you' is the subject)
Who met you at the airport?	('who' is the subject, 'you' is the object)
What do cats eat?	('cats' is the subject)
Who eats seafood?	('who' is the subject, 'seafood' is the object)

Negative questions

A positive question could have a *yes* or *no* answer.

> *Do you like dogs?*
>
> → *Yes, I do. / No, I don't.*

We use negative questions when we expect the answer will be *no*. In social situations this makes it easier for the other person to reply politely. Compare:

> *Do you like Mexican food?*
>
> → **No**, *not really*   (the answer seems very strong)
>
> **Don't you like** *Mexican food?*
>
> → **No**, *not really.*   (the same answer seems more polite)

Short answers

To make a short answer we repeat the auxiliary verb.

*Do **you speak French?*	*Yes, I **do**.*
***Have** you seen this film?*	*No, I **haven't**.*
***Did** you stay long?*	*No, I **didn't**.*
***Will** you be late?*	*No, I **won't**.*
***Have** you got a pen?*	*Yes, I **have**.*
***Can** you drive?*	*No, I **can't**.*

Practice

1 Write a question for each answer.

a) *What time do you usually get up?*   Get up? At about 7.30 usually.

b) .... I was reading *War and Peace*.

c) .... I went there to buy some food.

d) .... So far I've only eaten breakfast.

e) .... Now you have to put it in the oven!

f) .... Yesterday? I felt absolutely awful.

g) .... I'm washing my hair. I can't talk, sorry.

h) .... Because I haven't paid the electricity bill!

i) .... My bike? I left it at school.

j) .... My party? All my friends are coming.

2 Write a *who* or *what* question for each answer.

a) *Who lives next door?* .... A family of three lives next door.

b) .... I play with my little brother.

c) .... Mrs Dawson teaches me maths.

d) .... I usually eat a sandwich for lunch.

e) .... Horror films frighten me.

f) .... I talk most to my friend Dina.

g) .... I sit next to Maria in English.

h) .... Music helps me study.

3 Write a short answer for each question, beginning as shown.

a) Have you been ill long?   No, *I haven't* ....

b) Are you waiting for me?   Yes, ...

c) Did you go to the cinema?   Yes, ...

d) Will you be here tomorrow?   Yes, ...

e) Did you have to pay a lot?   No, ...

f) Can you help me with this problem?   No, ...

g) Do you know where the theatre is?   Yes, ...

h) Is George going to be there?   No, ...

Questions 2

Explanations

Tag questions: form

■ A tag question is a short phrase at the end of a statement that turns it into a question. Tag questions are formed using auxiliaries (*do, be, have* or a modal). A positive statement has a negative tag, and vice-versa.

> *You **speak** French, **don't you**?* (negative tag)
> *You **don't speak** French, **do you**?* (positive tag)

■ Here are some examples of tag questions showing different verb forms and a mixture of positive and negative tags.

Present simple	*You don't know the answer, **do you**?*
Present continuous	*We're enjoying ourselves, **aren't we**?*
Present perfect	*He's moved house, **hasn't he**?*
Past simple	*You didn't tell her, **did you**?*
Past continuous	*I wasn't driving fast, **was I**?*
Past perfect	*She hadn't met him then, **had she**?*
can	*They can't be here yet, **can they**?*
could	*You couldn't give me a hand, **could you**?*
should	*You shouldn't do that, **should you**?*

Tag questions: use

■ Negative tags: if we use a negative tag we expect the answer will be *yes*.
> A: *You **speak** French, **don't you**?*
> B: *Yes, that's right, I do.*

The intonation on the tag can either rise or fall:
– if it rises then it is a real question – the speaker is not sure and needs information. The other person will continue speaking afterwards.
> A: *You speak French, don't you?*
> B: *Yes, that's right, I do. I learned while I lived in France when I was a student.*
– if it falls then it is just a question for confirmation – the first speaker wants to check information and will continue speaking afterwards.
> A: *You speak French, don't you?*
> B: *Yes, that's right, I do.*
> A: *Good, because we need someone to translate this email which we've just received.*

■ Positive tags: if we use a positive tag we expect the answer will be *no*.
> A: *You **don't speak** French, **do you**?*
> B: *No, sorry, I don't.*
The intonation can rise or fall just like with a negative tag.

Problems with tags

- The tag for *I am* is *aren't*. The tag for *let's* is *shall*.
    *I'm a fool, **aren't I?***
    *Let's go to the cinema, **shall we?***

- After an imperative we use *will you?* or *won't you?*
    *Sit down, **will you?***   *Sit down, **won't you?***
    The imperative with *be* also uses *will* or *won't*.
    *Be quiet, **will you?***   *Be quiet, **won't you?** This is an order!*
    The imperative with *have* also uses *will* or *won't*.
    *Have a seat, **won't you?***

Reply questions

We can use a short question to reply to what someone says. We do this to show interest, surprise or uncertainty. The meaning is like *Really?* or *Is that true?*
     I've never eaten spaghetti.
     → ***Haven't you?***   (surprise)
     We're leaving at 6.00.
     → ***Are we?***   (not sure)
The reply question uses an auxiliary verb like a tag question, but there is no change of positive to negative.

Indirect questions

- We can be more polite by beginning a question with a short phrase like:
    Could you tell me ... ?   *Do you know ... ?*

- The word order of an indirect question is like a statement, not like a direct question.
    direct: *Where **is the post office?***
    indirect: *Could you tell me where **the post office is?*** (NOT ~~where is the post office~~)
    direct: *When **does the film start?***
    indirect   *Do you know when **the film starts?*** (NOT ~~when does the film start~~)

- *Yes/No* **questions use** *if*
    direct: ***Is this** the right street?*
    indirect: *Do you know **if this is** the right street?*

Practice

This unit also includes further practice for Grammar 27.

1 **Add a short answer to each sentence.**

a) Have you ever been to Brazil?   No, ...*I haven't*........... .

b) Do you like sausages?   Yes, ...

c) Are you coming to the match tomorrow?   Yes, ...

d) Did Helen phone you today?   No, ...

e) Has Jack done his homework?   Yes, ...

f) Can Robert and Sue skate?   Yes, ...

g) Will you be late?   No, ...

h) Has Julie got a brother?   No, ...

i) Is that your house?   Yes, ...

j) Did Jane give you that book?   No, ...

2 **Add a reply question to each sentence.**

a) We've got a test tomorrow.   ...*Have we*.................... ?

b) I don't understand this sentence.   .... ?

c) Fiona phoned me last night.   .... ?

d) I don't like ice-cream.   .... ?

e) Tom is leaving tomorrow.   .... ?

f) There's a policeman at the door.   .... ?

g) Lisa has just had a baby.   .... ?

h) I haven't eaten Chinese food.   .... ?

i) There isn't any milk in the fridge.   .... ?

j) I met David in France.   .... ?

3 **Add a tag question to each sentence.**

a) We're nearly there, ...*aren't we*.... ?

b) You haven't got a spare pen, ... ?

c) You're coming to my party, ... ?

d) You won't be late, ... ?

e) Harry's fifteen, ... ?

f) Kate and Pat live in Leeds, ... ?

g) You don't feel well, ... ?

h) You like fish, ... ?

i) Richard's bought a new bike, ... ?

j) I shouldn't tell you this, ... ?

4 **Make a new sentence with a tag question which has the same meaning as the first sentence, beginning as shown. Make any necessary changes.**

a) I'm sure that Paul doesn't like football.

Paul ...*doesn't like football*................................. , ...*does he?*..............

b) I'm checking that you've got a sister.

You .... , ...

c) I don't think that you've done your homework!

You .... , ...

d) I'm angry that you sat next to Ellen!

You .... , ...

e) I'm surprised that the guests have arrived.

The guests .... , ...

f) I'm checking that your name is John.

Your name .... , ...

g) I'm surprised to meet you and think that your name might be John.

Your name .... , ...

h) You're certain that you didn't leave your wallet on the desk.

I .... , ...

i) You're surprised that William has got married.

William .... , ...

j) You're checking that this book is by Martin Aimless.

This book .... , ...

5 <u>Underline</u> **the best sentence in each context.**

a) Why did you forget your keys! You are silly!

   1 I didn't tell you to forget them, did I?

   2 <u>I told you not to forget them, didn't I?</u>

b) Ugh! I can't believe it! I'm sure they must taste horrible!

   1 You like eating snails, don't you?

   2 You don't like eating snails, do you?

c) If we go to Brazil, we might have problems with the language.

   1 You speak Portuguese, don't you?

   2 You don't speak Portuguese, do you?

d) I told you to keep the party a secret. It's supposed to be a surprise for Stella. So, I just want to make sure.

   1 You didn't tell her, did you?

   2 You told her, didn't you?

e) Well, Mr Robinson, I think it's time you told the police the truth. You see, we've found your fingerprints on the murder weapon.
   1 You didn't murder Lord Chumley, did you?
   2 You murdered Lord Chumley, didn't you?

f) Only two minutes to the end of the match and United are still 5–1 in the lead. It looks certain now.
   1 United aren't going to win, are they?
   2 United are going to win, aren't they?

g) I haven't see Ann for ages. She's working abroad I think.
   1 She's got a job in France, hasn't she?
   2 She hasn't got a job in France, has she?

h) I just can't answer this question. It would be nice to have some help.
   1 You could help me, couldn't you?
   2 You couldn't help me, could you?

6 **Rewrite each question, beginning as shown. Do not change the meaning.**

a) What's the time?
Could you tell me ...*what the time is?*...

b) What does this mean?
Do you know ....

c) How much does this cost?
Could you tell me ....

d) What time does the museum open?
Do you know ....

e) Am I in the right seat?
Could you tell me ....

f) Where's Asham Street?
Do you know ....

g) Is this Trafalgar Square?
Could you tell me ....

h) When does this bus leave?
Do you know ....

it and *there*

Explanations

Introducing new information

■ We often use *there* to introduce new information. Typical structures are:

something exists:	**There are** *many possibilities.*
something happens:	**There's** *a football match every Saturday.*
number or amount:	**There are** *twelve students in this class.*
modals:	**There could/may/shouldn't** *be a problem.*
There seems/appears to be:	**There seems/appears to be** *a mistake.*

■ We can also use *it* to introduce new information. Typical structures are:

times, days, dates:	**It's** *one o'clock.* **It's** *Tuesday.*
the weather:	**It's** *raining.* **It** *rained all night.*
opinions:	**It** *was a difficult choice.*
adjectives:	**It's strange** *that we've never spoken before.*
It looks like:	**It looks like** *the sun is going to come out this afternoon.*
It seems/appears:	**It seems/appears (that)** *our new teacher is Jane.*

■ Note these structures with *look, seem* and *appear*. *Look* is usually followed by *as if* + subject + verb, or by *like* + noun phrase.

It looks as if *Carol has won.* **She looks like** *a real champion.*

Seem and *appear* are followed by (*that*) + subject + verb.

It seems (that) *the Brazilians are going to win.*

It appears (that) *one of the customers called the police.*

Referring back

It refers back to something already mentioned.

There is a shop at the end of the street. **It** *is open every day.*

Notice in this example how the new information is introduced with *there*.

Referring to a place

There can refer to a place.

A famous writer used to live **there**.

Who is that over **there**?

it's and *its*

It's is a contraction of *it is* or *it has. Its* is the possessive form of *it*.

I like this hotel. **It's** (= it is) *comfortable and* **its** *restaurant is good.*

It's (= it has) *got a lovely swimming-pool, too.*

they're and *their*

They're is a contraction of *they are. Their* is the possessive form of *they*.

Nancy and Dominique have arrived. **They're** *both wearing the same dress!*

Ask them to leave **their** *coats in the hall.*

→ SEE ALSO

Grammar 46: Possession

Practice

1 <u>Underline</u> **the correct word in each sentence.**

a) Are *their/<u>there</u>* any eggs in the fridge?

b) *It's/Its* really cold this morning.

c) Peter says *they're/there* arriving at about 5.00.

d) I like this bike but *its/it's* wheels are too small.

e) Is *there/they're* anybody *their/there*?

f) *It's/Its* a pity we missed the opening of the film.

g) Patrick and Bridget have sold *their/they're* house.

h) What a lovely dog. What's *it's/its* name?

2 **Put *it* or *there* in each space.**

a) ....*There*.... is a tree in the garden. ....*It*........ is an apple tree.

b) .... looks as if .... is going to rain.

c) .... is strange that .... are no restaurants in this town.

d) 'Who's that at the door?' '............... is only me!'

e) 'Which house is yours?' '............... is the one at the end of the street.'

f) .... seems to be something under the cupboard, but what is .... ?

g) .... appears that .... was nobody .... when I phoned.

3 **Rewrite each sentence, ending as shown, so that it has a similar meaning to the first sentence, and so that it contains *it* or *there*.**

a) Near the hotel is a small restaurant.
...*There is a small restaurant*............................ near the hotel.

b) You went to Thailand for your holiday too, which is strange.
.... to Thailand
for your holiday too.

c) My road has a big tree at the end of it.
.... road.

d) Brian seems to have left.
.... has left.

e) Today is really cold!
.... today.

f) Budapest is a long way from here.
.... to Budapest.

g) Your torch hasn't got any batteries in it.
.... torch.

h) We appear to be lost again!
.... lost again!

30 Place and position

Explanations

in, inside, out, outside

- *In* describes something contained by something else.
    > *There are some cups **in** that cupboard.*
    Inside has the same meaning but is used for emphasis.
    > *Luckily there was nobody **inside** the burning house.*

- *Out* means 'away from the inside' and also 'not in the place where you usually are'.
    > *Close the door on your way **out**.*
    > *I'm sorry, Kate's not here right now. She's **out**.*   (= she's not at home)
    Outside means 'out of a particular room or building, but still near it'.
    > *Kate's **outside** in the garden. I'll just call her.*

Expressions with in

There are many expressions with *in*. This is a selection. Note that sometimes the definite article *the* is not used.

countries	*My parents are **in Canada** at the moment.*	(no article)
cities	*My sister lives **in Madrid**.*	(no article)
streets	*Jack lives **in Garden Avenue**.*	(no article)
roads	*She was walking **in the road**, not on the pavement.*	
'the mirror'	*Tony could see his face **in the mirror**.*	
'hole/crack in'	*There was a **hole in** my shoe.*	
'hand'	*Ellen had a bunch of flowers **in one hand**.*	
'armchair'	*She sat **in an armchair**.*	
'the country'	*Paul and Mary live **in the country**, not in the city.*	
hospital	*Sally is ill and is **in hospital**.*	(no article)
prison	*Keith stole some money and ended up **in prison**.*	(no article)

on

On describes a thing touching the surface of another thing.
> *Don't leave your bag **on** the floor.*
> *There's a photograph of London **on** the wall.*

Expressions with on

There are many expressions with *on*. This is a selection.

transport	*There were few passengers **on the plane/bus/train**.*
'chair'	*She sat **on a chair**.*
'television'	*What's **on television/the radio** this evening?*
'wall'	*Let's hang this picture **on that wall**.*
injuries	*Tim cut his foot **on a piece of glass**.*
'left'/'right'	*There's a cinema **on the left**.*
'side'	*There are small houses **on this side** of the street.*
'pavement'	*She was walking in the road, not **on the pavement**.*

at, in or *to?*	■ *At* and *in* are both used to describe a person's position. *At* shows a general location at a point or place. *In* is used with the name of a container, place or area to show that someone or something is inside it. Study these examples.

*We met **at the airport**.*	(the place in general)
*We met **in the airport building**.*	(inside the building)
*I'll see you **at the cinema**.*	(the place in general)
*I'll see you **in the cinema**.*	(inside the building)
*We arrived **at Prague Airport**.*	(the place)
*We arrived **in Prague**.*	(the city)

■ *To* is used with verbs of motion.
*Last night we **went to** the cinema.*
*Could you **take** this letter **to** the post office?*
*I **sent** a parcel **to** my sister.*

Expressions with *at*	There are many expressions with *at*. This is a selection, and note that sometimes the definite article *the* is not used.

'the beginning'/'the end'	*There's a café **at the end** of the street.*	
'the front'/'the back'	*Do you sit **at the front** or **at the back** of the class?*	
'school'	*John isn't **at school**.*	(no article)
'home'	*He's **at home**.*	(no article)
'work'	*Mr King wasn't **at work** yesterday.*	(no article)

above/below, over/under	■ *Above/below* mean 'higher/lower than'. They can be used without an object. *You can see the top of the tower **above the trees**.* *From the mountain, I could see the lake **below**.*

Over/under mean 'directly above/below'. They both need an object.
*The alien spaceship hovered **over the building**.*
*I keep my suitcase **under my bed**.*

■ *Over* can also be used like 'across' or 'covering'.

*There is a footbridge **over the motorway**.*	(= across)
*There was a plastic sheet **over the hole** in the roof.*	(= covering)

next to/beside, near/by	■ *Next to* and *beside* mean 'exactly at the side of'. *Beside* can be more formal. *Maria sits **next to** Paula.* *Come and sit **beside me** on the sofa.*

■ *Near* means 'close to'. *By* mean 'at the side of' and is often used in descriptions of rooms.
*Tom's house is **near** the sports centre.*
*There was a table **by** the window. He was standing **by** the door.*
*We had a holiday **near** the sea.* (close to the sea – a few kilometres away)

opposite	■ *Opposite* means 'exactly on the other side of' a space. *There is a baker's **opposite** our house.*

Practice

1 Underline the correct word in each sentence.

a) There's a small shop <u>at</u>/by the end of the road.

b) Paula was standing *on/with* one foot.

c) Laura has moved *at/to* Barcelona.

d) Don't walk *at/in* the road! It's dangerous!

e) From the plane we could see the mountains *below/under*.

f) Brian spent his holiday *at/in* Hungary.

g) When the horse came to a small stream it jumped *above/over* it.

h) Julia's house is *at/on* the other side of the street.

i) Lisa cut her foot *at/on* some broken glass.

j) Tim was sitting *in/on* an armchair.

2 If the word <u>underlined</u> is not appropriate, write a new word in the space. Tick (✓) the space if the word is correct.

a) Jane's sister has a job <u>at</u> Manchester Airport. ....✓..........

b) I met David yesterday <u>by</u> the city centre. ....

c) Ellen had a large hole <u>at</u> her left boot. ....

d) Jack sits <u>in</u> the back of the class. ....

e) There was a small table <u>at</u> the bed. ....

f) The robber was holding a gun <u>in</u> one hand. ....

g) There was a beautiful portrait hanging <u>at</u> the wall. ....

h) William didn't feel well and his doctor sent him <u>to</u> hospital. ....

i) The children usually sit <u>at</u> the back seat of the car. ....

j) To reach our village we take a road <u>above</u> the mountains. ....

3 Complete each sentence with one suitable preposition.

a) Maria lives ....*in*............ Bellingham Road.

b) Can you put the plates back .... the shelf please?

c) Please don't stand .... your desks!

d) I'd really like to live .... the country.

e) Go down this street, and you'll see the cinema .... the right.

f) The police searched the building but there was no one ....

g) I met Anna .... the bus yesterday.

h) Sorry, George isn't here at the moment. He's ....

i) Alice wants to know what's .... television this evening.

j) Just as Tom arrived .... the bus stop, the bus left.

4 **Complete each sentence with one suitable preposition.**

a) The statue was holding a sword ....*in*............ one hand.

b) What's on .... the cinema this week?

c) When I look .... the mirror, I don't recognize myself!

d) What have you got .... your bag?

e) Pete found someone's wallet .... the pavement.

f) My family moved from the country .... the city.

g) You've got a small hole .... your pullover.

h) The burglar climbed .... the fence and into the garden.

5 <u>Underline</u> **the correct word or phrase in each sentence.**

a) Karen is living *at/<u>in</u>* London Street.

b) Maggie sits *by/next to* Sally in the physics class.

c) I want to send this letter *at/to* Brazil.

d) When I opened the box, there was nothing *in/inside*.

e) Exactly *by/opposite* the cinema, there's a really good restaurant.

f) We had a holiday in a small village *by/near* Monte Carlo.

g) Paula lay down *at/on* the floor to do her exercises.

h) We had a lovely meal *in/on* the plane.

6 **Complete each sentence with one suitable preposition.**

a) Bye for now. I'll see you ...*at*............ school tomorrow.

b) We put a blanket .... the injured man to keep him warm.

c) It's not far. We're getting ....

d) We found our cat hiding .... a car.

e) Daniel hung his coat .... the back of a chair.

f) I decided to go to the shops .... my bike.

g) What time is the news .... the radio?

h) I decided to visit my grandmother .... hospital.

1 <u>Underline</u> the correct word or phrase in each sentence.

a) We arrived early, *so that we/in order to* get tickets.

b) It was *too/enough* long to wait, so we went home.

c) Tim and Helen have arrived, and *they're/there* waiting outside.

d) The boy *which/whose* bike I borrowed had forgotten about it.

e) We went to the beach *for/so that* a swim.

f) Ann felt lonely *because/so* no one had invited her to the party.

g) *Despite/Although* I felt tired, I worked until late.

h) We spent a lovely holiday *in/into* the country.

i) Yesterday was *so/such* cold that I stayed at home.

j) *However/In spite of* the rain, we went for a walk.

2 For each question, complete the second sentence so that it means the same as the first, using no more than three words.

a) Although it was late, we decided to go for a walk.

It was late ...*but we decided*... to go for a walk.

b) John is someone with whom I used to work.

John is someone I .... with.

c) The exam was so difficult that I couldn't finish it.

It was .... difficult exam that I couldn't finish it.

d) Although it was raining, we worked in the garden.

Despite .... , we worked in the garden.

e) Let's spend the afternoon at the beach.

How .... the afternoon at the beach?

f) Ann's house has got four large bedrooms.

.... four large bedrooms in Ann's house.

g) We might feel hungry, so we'll take some sandwiches.

We'll take some sandwiches so that we .... hungry.

h) The cat hasn't come home, which is strange.

.... that the cat hasn't come home.

i) Harry can't afford to go on holiday.

Harry hasn't got .... to go on holiday.

j) Where's the National Museum?

Would .... telling me where the National Museum is?

3 Decide which answer (A, B, C or D) best fits each space.

A case of mistaken identity
When Diana got off the train, (1) ....*B*.... was a woman waiting for her
(2) .... the platform. '(3) .... ?' she asked. '(4) .... a car waiting for
you (5) ....' Diana was not very surprised, (6) .... she thought that her
aunt must have been (7) .... busy to meet her (8) .... the station.
(9) .... she did not recognize the woman, (10) .... was dressed very
formally, and had a small briefcase (11) .... her arm, she was (12) ....
tired after the journey that she was happy to get (13) .... the car. The
woman, (14) .... , just said a few words to the driver, and then walked away.
Diana wondered (15) .... she was. 'It's strange that she didn't even introduce
herself,' she thought.

1) A who | B there | C whose | D it
2) A below | B to | C on | D in
3) A You Diana, are you | B You're Diana, isn't it | C Are you Diana | D You aren't Diana
4) A There's | B Theirs | C Its | D It's
5) A out | B in | C inside | D outside
6) A so | B despite | C too | D as
7) A so | B too | C enough | D very
8) A at | B to | C in | D for
9) A However | B Since | C In spite of | D Although
10) A she | B who | C and | D whose
11) A at | B in | C under | D by
12) A enough | B so | C too | D very
13) A with | B by | C at | D into
14) A however | B despite | C although | D in spite of
15) A whether | B there | C who | D however

4 Complete each sentence with one suitable preposition.

There was another woman (a) ....*on*.... the bus, and Kate sat
(b) .... her and started chatting. She said she was going
(c) .... Forbes Road too. 'I've got an interview (d) .... a place
called Murcott House,' said Kate. 'Is it (e) .... the bus stop?' 'It's not
far. It's (f) .... the right (g) .... the end of the street,' the
woman replied. 'In fact, I live (h) .... When I look out of my
window, I can see people working (i) ....' When they arrived
(j) .... the stop, they got off and walked up the street together.

5 **What would you say in these situations?**

a) You want to know if Andrew has ever been to America. Ask him.
   Have you ever been to America?

b) You want to know if Andrew has ever been to America. Ask Amanda.
   Has Andrew ever been to America?

c) You want to know if Rita likes rap music. Ask Isabel.
   ....

d) You want to know if Rita likes rap music. Ask her.
   ....

e) You want to know if Nigel enjoyed the film. Ask him.
   ....

f) You want to know if Nigel enjoyed the film. Ask Petra.
   ....

g) You want to know if Maria is going to London next summer. Ask her.
   ....

h) You want to know if Maria is going to London next summer. Ask Patricia.
   ....

i) You want to ask Patricia if you can borrow her mobile phone. Ask her.
   ....

j) You want to ask Patricia if she could lend you her mobile phone. Ask her.
   ....

6 **Complete each sentence, using the verb given where necessary.**

a) '(have got) ...*You've got*................ a book, haven't you?' 'Yes, thanks.'

b) 'They'll be back by 6.00, ... ?' 'I expect so.'

c) '(go) .... for a walk, shall we? 'Good idea!'

d) 'You (leave) .... now, are you? Stay a bit longer.'
   'Sorry, I can't. I have to catch the bus.'

e) 'Jim and Sara have seen the film, ... ?' 'Yes, I think so.'

f) 'You can meet Helen at the station, ... ?' 'Yes, of
   course I can.'

g) '(be) .... here yesterday, were you?' 'No, I wasn't.'

h) 'You don't happen to know the time, ... ?' 'Sorry, I
   don't.'

i) 'Both drivers were driving too fast, ... ?' 'Yes, that's
   right.'

j) 'You (forget) .... the milk, did you?' 'No. Here it is.'

7 **Rewrite each pair of sentences as one sentence. Do not change the meaning.**

a) Sue read a book. She really enjoyed it.

which

Sue ...*read a book which she really*... enjoyed.

b) Some friends visited me. They brought me a present.

who

The friends .... present.

c) I stayed in a hotel. It was cheaper than this one.

that

The hotel .... this one.

d) I borrowed a friend's bike. He wanted it back.

whose

The .... back.

e) I saw the vase in the shop. I wanted to buy it.

that

I wanted .... shop.

f) A girl sings in the group. She's got green hair.

who

The girl .... green hair.

g) I met a girl. Her brother is in my class.

whose

.... class.

h) We're taking the train. It leaves at 4.30.

that

The train .... at 4.30.

i) A man knocked at the door. He was selling brushes.

who

The man .... brushes.

j) I saw a film with Luke. It was interesting.

which

The film .... interesting.

8 Look carefully at each line. Some lines are correct but some have a word which should not be there. Tick (✓) each correct line. If a line has a word which should not be there, write the word in the space.

A case of mistaken identity

After a few minutes, the car stopped in front of	1 ....✓.........
a large hotel. The driver who opened the door, and	2 ...*who*...........
said, 'Please follow me.' They went up in to a lift.	3 ....
Then there was a long corridor with two or three	4 ....
doors. Although it seemed strange so that the car hadn't	5 ....
taken her to her aunt's house, Diana who wasn't surprised.	6 ....
Her aunt, who she was very rich, owned several large	7 ....
hotels, which she often stayed in them. I suppose she felt	8 ....
so much bored at home that she decided to stay here.	9 ....
'Please you wait here, will you?' said the driver, and	10 ....
disappeared into a room at the end of the corridor.	11 ....
There seemed to be a lot of people that in one of the	12 ....
rooms. Then the driver, who he hadn't been gone long,	13 ....
came back at and asked Diana to follow him. They went	14 ....
into a large room full of people, who all started clapping.	15 ....
There was a poster that it said, 'Diana Harris, Supermodel.'	16 ....
'Oh dear,' said Diana, 'I think so there's been a mistake!'	17 ....

Problem check

1 Check the different uses of *so, too* and *enough* in Grammar 22. When do we use *so* and *such*?

2 Check the differences between *although, however* and *despite/in spite of* in Grammar 23.

3 Can you add any more expressions to the list of functions in Gramar 24? How important is the intonation of your voice in sounding polite? What do you say in similar situations in your language?

4 Check in Grammar 25 for when you can leave out relative pronouns.

5 Check in Grammar 29 for the meaning of *they're, their* and *there*.

6 Check in Grammar 30 for the differences between *at, in* and *to*.

32 Time expressions

Explanations

in, on and at

■ *in*

Years	*in* *1999*
Months	*in* *January*
Seasons	*in the summer*
Parts of the day	*in the morning/afternoon/evening*

■ *on*

Days of the week	*on Wednesday*, *on Friday morning*
Special days	*on my birthday*, *on Christmas Day*

■ *at*

Times of the day	*at 4.00*, *at midday*, *at midnight*
'the weekend'	*at the weekend*
Holiday periods	*at Christmas/Easter*
Meals	*at breakfast/lunch/dinner*
Parts of the day: 'night'	*at night*

Relation to today

5 September	*the day before yesterday*
6 September	*yesterday*
7 September	*today*
8 September	*tomorrow*
9 September	*the day after tomorrow*

Parts of yesterday, today and tomorrow

yesterday morning	*yesterday afternoon*	*last night*
this morning	*this afternoon*	*tonight*
tomorrow morning	*tomorrow afternoon*	*tomorrow night*

Calendar references

■ In the UK people say *the seventh of September* or *September the seventh*.
People write *7 September* or *7th September* or *September 7th*.
Full dates are written Day/Month/Year: *7/9/03*.

■ In the US people say *September seven* and write *September 7*.
Full dates are written Month/Day/Year: *9/7/03*.

for, since and ago

We use *for* and *since* with the present perfect to talk about time. *For* refers to a period of time and *since* refers to when it started.

I've lived here ***for six years****. I studied French* ***for two years****.*
I've lived here ***since 2001****. I've been waiting* ***since 3.30****.*

Ago means 'before the present'

We arrived ***five hours ago****. I knew that* ***ages ago****!*

during or *for*?	*During* and *for* are both used to talk about periods of time. *During* answers the question 'When?'. *For* answers the question 'How long?'.
	    *I didn't feel nervous **during** the performance.*
	    *The performance lasted **for** forty-five minutes.*

by or *until*?	*By* means 'on or before'. *Until* means 'up to'.	
	*We'll be there **by 6.00**.*	(perhaps earlier)
	*I waited for Alex **until 6.00**, and then I left.*	(all the time up to 6.00)
	*Please give me your homework **by Friday**.*	(Thursday would be fine)
	*I'll be away **until Friday**.*	(all the time up to Friday)

on time or *in time*?	*On time* means 'at the right time'. *In time* means 'with enough time to do something'.
	    *The plane took off exactly **on time**.*
	    *We arrived **in time** to have a meal before the plane left.*

once and *one day*	*Once* means 'at one time in my life' and only refers to the past. *One day* can refer to the past or the future.
	    ***Once I owned** a motorbike.*
	    ***One day I was walking** through the town centre when I met Jill.*
	    ***One day I'll be** famous!*

now and *nowadays*	*Now* means 'at the present time' or 'immediately'. *Nowadays* also means 'at the present time' and is used to make a strong contrast with the past.
	    *Peter used to live in Rome, but **now he's living** in Florence.*
	    *You have to finish ... **Now!***
	    ***Nowadays** people are not as polite as they used to be.*

Note that the word 'actually' in English does not mean 'at the present time'. It means 'in fact' or 'really'. This is a common mistake.

then, afterwards, after and *later*	■ *Then* and *afterwards* are similar. *Then* is used like 'next' in a sequence, *afterwards* is used like 'at a later time'. *Afterwards* can come at the end of the sentence.
	    *We went to the cinema, and **then** we had a pizza.*
	    *We went to the cinema, and **afterwards** we had a pizza.*
	    *We went to the cinema, and had a pizza **afterwards**.*

	■ *After* is usually followed by an object. ***After the film** we had a pizza. **After that** we went home.*
	■ *Later* means 'after some time'. *Mrs James isn't here at the moment. Can you come back **later**?*

at the end, in the end and *at last*	■ *At the end* refers to a point in time. ***At the end** of the film we all cried.*
	■ *In the end* means 'after a lot of time' or eventually'. *We waited for Tim for ages, and **in the end** we left.*
	■ *At last* makes a comment that we are pleased a long wait has ended. ***At last** we can be together!*

Practice

1 <u>Underline</u> the correct word or phrase in each sentence.

a) I met Tina *a day/<u>one day</u>* last week.

b) *In these days/Nowadays* everyone seems to watch too much television.

c) *This morning/The morning* I was busy in the garden.

d) We have to finish this project *by/until* the end of the week.

e) Bye. I'll see you *the day after tomorrow/the next day*.

f) *During/While* the film I remembered where I'd left my keys.

g) John played tennis, and *after/afterwards* had a shower.

h) Helen's birthday is *in/on* January 10th.

2 Complete the second sentence so that it has a similar meaning to the first sentence.

a) We had lunch, and afterwards we went for a coffee.

After *we had/had had lunch, we went for a coffee* .

b) Jill is never late for lessons.

Jill is always ....

c) I won't leave before 8.00.

I'll be here ....

d) I've been living here for three months.

I started living here ....

e) When we met for lunch it was 12.00.

We met for lunch ....

f) What do you do in your country on January 1st?

What do you do in your country on the .... ?

g) I'll see you not tomorrow but the next day.

I'll see you the ....

h) It's 10.00 and I've been waiting here since 7.00.

I've been waiting here .... hours.

3 Complete each sentence with one suitable word.

a) Would you like to go out .....*on*............ my birthday?

b) Rita moved to this town four years ....

c) I won't phone Jason now. I'll phone him ....

d) I woke up twice .... the night.

e) .... midnight the frog turned into a prince.

f) People in cities used to take the bus, but .... most use their cars.

g) Luckily Rachel arrived just .... time to catch the train.

h) We felt fine in the restaurant, but we both felt ill ....

4 Rewrite each sentence so that it has a similar meaning and contains the word in **bold**.

a) I spend the summer at the seaside.

in

.... *I go to the seaside in the summer.* ....

b) I started at this school in 1997.

since

....

c) George had a bath and after that washed his hair.

then

....

d) Dina left my house at 10.00.

until

....

e) The train arrived exactly when it was supposed to.

on time

....

f) I won't arrive later than 2.00.

by

....

g) Paul tried hard but finally gave up.

end

....

h) I was too late to say goodbye to Lisa.

time

....

5 Complete each sentence with one suitable word.

a) Did you sleep well ... *last* .... night?

b) .... the hot weather, we have our meals in the garden.

c) .... the lesson, Mike and Carmen decided to play basketball.

d) John hasn't seen Cristina .... three weeks.

e) I know that .... day you will be a star!

f) It's very important to arrive .... time for the examination.

g) The robber ran out of the bank and was arrested shortly ....

h) There is a lot of noise in our street .... night.

Countable and uncountable nouns

Explanations

Countable and uncountable

- A countable noun has a singular and a plural form. The plural may be irregular. We can use numbers with it.

  one book, three books   one possibility, two possibilities,   one piece, four pieces
  one person, three people   one child, two children   one woman, four women

- An uncountable noun has only one form. We cannot use numbers with it.

  work   love   progress   water   information   English (language)

- Typical uncountables are:

Materials and substances:	*plastic, iron, wood, paper, water, air, coffee*
Abstract ideas:	*life, fun, freedom, progress, health, time*
Activities:	*work, travel, sleep, football, help, research*
Human feelings:	*happiness, anger, honesty, hope, respect, courage*

- Note the words below which are uncountable in English but countable in many other languages:

  accommodation, advice, behaviour, business, cash, equipment, furniture, health, homework, information, knowledge, luggage, money, permission, rubbish, scenery, traffic, travel, weather, work

Countable and uncountable: grammar

- Countable nouns can be singular or plural.
  *The book **is** over there.*
  *The book**s are** over there.*
  Uncountable nouns are always singular.
  *French **is** difficult.*
  *His advice **was** very useful.*

- With countable nouns we can use *a/an* and *some*.
  *Sue has got **a book/some books** about Ancient Egypt.*
  With uncountable nouns we cannot use *a/an*.
  *Sue has got **some money** to go on holiday this year.*
  *Could I have **some information**?*

some **or** *any*?

- *Some* is common in positive sentences. *Any* is common in questions and negatives.
  *We've got **some juice**, but we haven't got **any glasses**.*
  *Have you got **any cups**?*

- But we can use *some* in a question if it is an offer or request.
  ***Could I have some** more tea, please?*
  And we can use *any* in positive sentences if we mean 'it doesn't matter which'.
  *I'm free **any day** next week.*

■ *Any* always has the meaning of 'no limit'. Compare:

*Is there **something** I can do to help?* (I know what to do)

*Is there **anything** I can do to help?* (I'll do whatever I can)

*Have you got **some letters** for me?*

(There are particular letters I am expecting)

*Have you got **any letters** for me?*

(I have no idea if you have letters for me or not)

many and *much*

Many is used for countable nouns and *much* is used for uncountable nouns. They are used mainly in questions and negatives.

How many *chairs are there?*   *There aren't **many cushions**.*

How much *money have we got?*   *There isn't **much water** here.*

Change of meaning

■ Some words can be countable or uncountable with a change in meaning. The countable meaning is specific and the uncountable meaning is general.

a fish (the animal)	*some fish* (a portion of food)
a business (a company)	*business* (in general)
a noise (a specific noise)	*noise* (in general)
a hair (a single piece)	*hair* (all together)
a painting (one object)	*painting* (the activity/hobby)
a work (a work of art)	*work* (in general)
a loaf (a loaf of bread)	*some bread* (in general)
a coffee (a cup of coffee)	*some coffee* (the material)
a paper (a newspaper)	*some paper* (the material)
a wood (a small forest)	*some wood* (the material)
an iron (for pressing clothes)	*some iron* (the material)
a glass (for drinking)	*some glass* (the material)

■ Look at these examples:

*I heard **a strange noise**.*   *I can't stand **noise**.*

*I bought **a painting** last week.*   *Do you like **painting**?*

*Diana had **a very good education**.*   ***Education** is very important.*

***A knowledge** of boats is useful.*   ***Knowledge** is the key to success.*

*Can you buy **a loaf** from the shop?*   *Can you buy **some bread** from the shop?*

Other problems

■ One group of nouns only has a plural form and takes a plural verb: *clothes, contents, feelings, glasses* (for your eyes), *jeans, stairs, trousers*

*My trousers **are** too tight.*   *The stairs **are** very steep.*

■ One group of nouns can be followed by either a singular or plural verb: *army, audience, class, company, crowd, family, government, group, public, team*

*The Government **has/have** decided to resign.*

■ The word 'news' is followed by a singular verb.

*The **news is** on.*

■ The word 'police' is followed by a plural verb

***The police** are coming.*

Practice

1   Underline the correct word or phrase in each sentence.

a)   *How much/How many* pasta have we got?

b)   Where *is/are* my new trousers?

c)   I put *some/any* chocolate somewhere, but where is it?

d)   Peter went to buy *a/some* glass so he could fix the broken windows.

e)   I'm afraid we haven't got *much/many* time.

f)   *How much/How many* furniture shops are there?

g)   I've found the milk but I can't find *a/some* glass.

h)   Mary's advice *was/were* not very useful.

2   Put one word in each space. Put a dash (–) if the space should be blank.

a)   My trousers need ironing. Have you got ...*an*............. iron?

b)   Could you go to the baker's and buy .... loaf, please?

c)   I'd like .... information about trains to Paris.

d)   Louise has .... very good health.

e)   The war ended .... years ago.

f)   Vanessa bought .... paper and read it on the bus.

g)   Could you give me .... advice, please?

h)   Do you know .... people in this village?

3   Complete the second sentence so that it has a similar meaning to the first sentence and contains the word in **bold**.

a)   Let me tell you what I think you should do.
     advice
     Let me .*give you some advice.*...

b)   I need a clean pair of trousers.
     any
     I haven't got ....

c)   There isn't a lot of water in the pool.
     much
     .... water in the pool.

d)   I have to wash my hair.
     washing
     My hair ....

e)   The book didn't contain any information.
     in
     The information ....

4   **Choose the best alternative, 1 or 2, to complete each sentence.**

a)   The fire is going to go out. Can you go and get ....*some wood*.................... .
1 a wood   2 some wood

b)   .... money all over the floor!
1 There was   2 There were

c)   Lemonade? Sorry, no, we haven't got ....
1 some   2 any

d)   Peter keeps .... at the bottom of his garden.
1 a chicken   2 some chicken

e)   The information we were given ....
1 were very useful   2 was very useful

f)   .... people were there on the bus?
1 How many   2 How much

g)   Look at Rita's hair. .... !
1 It's green   2 They're green

h)   I've called the police and ....
1 they're on their way   2 it's on its way

i)   The assembly hall was full of ....
1 a noise   2 noise

5   **Complete each sentence with one suitable word.**

a)   I wanted to have a bath but there wasn't any hot ....*water*....... .

b)   When is the .... on? I haven't heard any today.

c)   Tim's eyesight was bad and he had to have new ....

d)   Laura had to pay extra at the airport because she had too much ....

e)   If you want to make an omelette there are some .... in the fridge.

f)   You can't cut that with a knife. You need some ....

g)   We need some bread. Could you go and buy a large ....

h)   When the burglar ran out of the house he was arrested by a ....

Explanations

Indefinite article:
a/an

■ We use *a/an* when the listener does not know which person or thing we are talking about. Compare:

> *Tim works in **a factory**.*   (we don't know which factory)
> *Tim works in **the factory** down the road.*   (we know which factory)

■ If we refer to something for the first time it will be new information for the listener and so we use *a/an*. Other references to the same thing use *the* because now the listener knows what we are talking about.

> *I've bought **a** new mobile **phone**. It's great. **The phone** connects to the Internet.*

■ We use *a/an* to describe something.

> *It's **a lovely day**.*   *Kazakstan is **an enormous country**.*

Note these two ways of saying the same thing:

> *An ocelot is **a wild animal**, similar to **a leopard**.*
> *Ocelots are **wild animals**, similar to **leopards**.*

■ We use *a/an* to describe the job or the character of a person.

> *Mary is **an engineer**.*   *Peter is **a fool!***

■ *A/an* mean 'one', so we cannot use *a/an* with uncountable nouns.

> *I've **got a brother and a sister**.*   (not two)
> *Can you give me **some information**?*   (not ~~an information~~)

■ Note that *a/an* are unstressed, and are pronounced /ə/ and /ən/.

Zero article
(no article)

■ We use zero article with plurals and uncountable nouns when we are talking generally. Compare:

> ***Dogs** are not allowed in this shop*   (dogs in general)
> ***The dogs next door** bark all night.*   (some particular dogs)
> ***Milk** is good for you.*   (milk in general)
> ***The milk** on the top shelf is fat-free.*   (we know which milk)

Here are some examples showing the use of zero article to talk generally:

Materials:	*This chair is made of **plastic** and **leather**.*
Food and drink	*I love **chocolate**. I don't like **orange juice**.*
Abstract ideas:	***War** is a terrible thing.*
Languages:	***Spanish** is spoken by about 300 million people.*
Activities:	***Speaking** is not permitted during the examination.*

■ Zero article is used with most countries, states and cities.

> *Marie comes **from France**.*
> ***Los Angeles** is in **California**.*

But countries which are a group or plural have a definite article.

> *We left **the United Kingdom** and crossed to **the Netherlands**.*

Note also that *Great Britain* has zero article.

■ Zero article is used with geographical areas, lakes, mountains and islands.
   *We visited **Lake Victoria**. It's in **East Africa**.*
   *They climbed **Mt. Everest** in record time.*
   *Helen spent her holidays on **Crete**.*

■ Zero article is used with most streets.
   *I bought this dress from a shop **in Bond Street**.*
   But we use *the* for the phrase ***the High Street*** (this means the main shopping street in a town).

■ Zero article is used with names of buildings with a place name before.
   *We visited **Blenheim Palace** and **Coventry Cathedral**.*
   But we use *the* when there is a phrase with *of* after the noun.
   *We visited **the Houses of Parliament**.*

■ Zero article is used with names, but *the* is used with titles.
   ***Carol Parker** is **the Minister of Communications**.*

■ Zero article is used with meals when we refer to them in general.
   ***Dinner** is at 7.30.*
   But compare with these examples where we are not talking generally:
   *At the end of the conference there was **a dinner**.*   (mentioned for first time)
   ***The dinner** they serve here is really fantastic.*   (we know which dinner)

■ Zero article is used with general historical references
   ***Prehistoric Europe/Ancient Rome** is a fascinating period of history.*

■ Zero article is used with *by* for general forms of transport.
   *We went there **by car**.*
   But compare with these examples where we are not talking generally:
   *We went there in **a really old car**.*   (mentioned for first time)
   *We went there in **the car** my sister uses.*   (we know which car)
   Note also that we say *on foot*.

■ Zero article is used with certain buildings, where the purpose of the building is more important than the place itself. Compare:
   *Jim is **in prison**.*   (which prison is not important)
   *My company is rebuilding **the prison**.*   (one particular building)
   Words of this type are:
   be in or *go to*   *hospital, prison, bed, class, court*
   be at or *go to*   *work, school, university, sea*
   with 'home'   *be at home, go home*

→ SEE ALSO

Grammar 33: Countable and uncountable nouns

Practice

See Grammar 35 for activities including *the*.

1 **Underline** the errors in these sentences. Rewrite each sentence.

a) Have you ever visited <u>United Kingdom</u>?
   ...Have you ever visited the United Kingdom?..................

b) On our trip, we visited the Canterbury Cathedral.
   ....

c) Love is wonderful thing.
   ....

d) The pets are not permitted in this hotel.
   ....

e) Rabbit is small wild furry animal with long ears.
   ....

f) The New York is in United States of the America.
   ....

2 Put *a/an* or leave the space blank.

a) ...—.... love makes the world go round.
b) Sheila has got .... German car.
c) Rita works in .... office in .... West Street.
d) I've got .... friend who is .... electrician.
e) Paul goes to .... special school for .... musicians.
f) Jack is in .... hospital and can't go to .... school.
g) Valerie wants to go to .... university and study to be .... doctor.

3 For each question, complete the second sentence so that it means the same as the first, using no more than three words.

a) Mary teaches English.
   Mary ...*is an*........................... English teacher.
b) Charles has a factory job.
   Charles works .... factory.
c) You are not allowed to park here.
   .... not allowed here.
d) Fabio is on a ship at the moment.
   At the moment .... sea.
e) We walked to the station.
   We went to .... foot.

135

Explanations

Definite article: *the*

- We use *the* when it is clear which thing or person we are talking about. The points below explain this in more detail. Compare:

  The war between the two countries *lasted for six weeks.*

  (we know which war)

  War *is a terrible thing.*

  (war in general, so zero article)

- We often use *the* when we refer to something that we mentioned before, using *a/an*.

  *We saw **a** good **film** last night. It was **the new film** by Berghini.*

  But we can use *the* for the first time that we refer to something if it is clear from the context which one we mean.

  *Where's **the newspaper**?*

- We often use *the* with phrases including *of*. Compare:

  *The film was about **the love of a girl** for her cat.*

  Love is a wonderful thing!   (love in general, so zero article)

- We use *the* when there is only one of something. It is clear which one we mean.

  *How many astronauts have landed on **the moon**?*

- We use *the* for nationalities and other groups.

  *I really admire **the Italians**.*

  ***The old**, **the sick** and **the unemployed** need our special care.*

- Note these other uses of *the*:

Playing musical instruments:	*Do you play **the guitar**?*
Time:	*In **the past**/in **the future***
	But: *at present*
Superlatives	*This is **the biggest** one. / You are **the first**.*
Fixed phrases	***The** sooner **the** better.*
Names of ships	*We sailed on **the Neptune**.*
Oceans	***The Pacific, the Atlantic***
Rivers	***The Amazon, the Danube***

- *The* is usually pronounced /ðə/ before consonants and /ðiː/ before vowels.

  The beginning.   The end.

> → SEE ALSO
>
> **Grammar 38:** Making comparisons

Practice

1 <u>Underline</u> the correct word in each sentence.

a) Where's *an/the* electric heater? I can't find it.

b) What happened at *an/the* end of *a/the* film?

c) David has *an/the* appointment at *a/the* optician's.

d) *An/The* old person sometimes feels lonely.

e) Peter owns *a/the* largest model plane in *a/the* world.

f) Luckily *a/the* fire brigade soon came and put out *a/the* fire.

g) Harry's mother bought him *a/the* guitar for his birthday present.

h) I'm thinking of buying *a/the* new pair of trousers.

i) In the end there was *a/the* war between the two countries.

j) I didn't know *an/the* answer to *a/the* question, so I left it out.

2 Complete the second sentence so that it has a similar meaning to the first sentence.

a) Frances is a very good pianist.
Frances ...*plays the piano*.......................... very well.

b) Poor people need help from the Government.
The Government should .... poor.

c) Tracey's bike is faster than everyone else's.
Tracey's .... fastest.

d) Tom has a doctor's appointment.
Tom .... doctor's.

e) The film was about an artist's life.
The film .... of an artist.

f) The only goal of the match was scored by Italy.
The only goal of the match .... Italians.

3 Put *a/an* or *the* in each space or leave the space blank.

a) ....The. President is ...*the*. largest cruise ship in ...*the*. world.

b) Everyone in .... class agreed that .... happiness was important.

c) There's .... strange person at .... door.

d) Someone who saw .... robbery called .... police.

e) At .... beginning of .... film, ... tall man sat in front of me.

f) When I arrived at .... station, I ate .... sandwich and waited for .... train.

g) .... person with .... good education usually gets .... good job.

h) Have you seen .... new film at .... Embassy cinema?

Practice

Includes practice of Grammar 34 and 35.

1 **Put *a/an/the* in each space, or leave the space blank.**

a) ..*The*.... Chinese eat ..*a*....... lot of ...*–*...... rice.

b) .... most people thought that .... Beatles were .... very good group.

c) I usually drink .... glass of .... milk in .... morning.

d) What's .... difference between .... rabbit and .... hare?

e) .... first person who crosses .... finishing line is .... winner.

f) .... playing .... guitar is .... interesting .... hobby.

g) .... Rebecca got on .... bus and bought .... ticket.

h) There's .... newspaper shop at .... end of .... street.

i) In .... past, most of .... population lived in .... country.

j) I needed .... new pair of trousers so my mother gave me .... money.

2 **Correct the errors in these sentences by adding or removing *a/an/the*.**

a) Could you get loaf of bread from baker's?

   ..*Could you get a loaf of bread from the baker's?*..........................

b) The milk is good for the children.

   ....

c) The John is at a work at moment.

   ....

d) We travelled to the Hungary by a car.

   ....

e) Have you got a brother or the sister?

   ....

f) War between two countries was longest in the history.

   ....

g) Who was first astronaut who walked on moon?

   ....

h) Nile is longest river in world.

   ....

3 Rewrite each sentence so that it has a similar meaning and contains the word in **bold**.

a) We travelled there by train.

on

..... *We travelled there on the train.* ....

b) There isn't a larger size than this one.

largest

....

c) Clara sings for her living.

singer

....

d) People who are unemployed often feel depressed.

the

....

e) Anna is learning to be a guitarist.

play

....

f) Mike is an office-worker.

works

....

g) Marie is a Frenchwoman.

France

....

h) David is still working.

at

....

4 Put *a/an/the* in each space, or leave the space blank.

(a) ...A.... friend of mine, Sally Milton, wanted to become (b) .... dancer when she was (c) .... girl. (d) .... every morning before (e) .... school she used to practise in (f) .... living room at (g) .... home. (h) .... dancers need (i) .... lot of (j) .... exercise, so Sally used to go to (k) .... gym two or three times (l) .... week. In (m) .... end she got (n) .... job in (o) .... theatre company and became (p) .... actress. In (q) .... fact, (r) .... last week I saw her in (s) .... programme on (t) .... television!

5 Complete the second sentence so that it has a similar meaning to the first sentence.

a) I didn't expect to see Darrel.

....*Darrel was the*........................ last person I expected to see.

b) Do you have a dog in your house?

Do .... home?

c) Nick teaches chemistry.

Nick is .... teacher.

d) My friends gave me a wonderful present.

.... gave me was wonderful.

e) The Australian capital is Canberra.

Canberra .... Australia.

f) The French lesson is the first tomorrow.

.... French.

g) Someone is phoning you.

There's someone on ....

h) We saw a very entertaining film last night.

.... was very entertaining.

6 In each pair of sentences, fill in one space with *the* and the other space with a dash (–) to show no article.

a) 1 For me, ...–..... football is my life.

2 ..*The*.. football in the second division is a much lower standard.

b) 1 They say that .... love makes the world go round.

2 They say that .... love of a mother for her child is the strongest kind.

c) 1 .... information in this article will be very useful for my project.

2 .... information about the Government's defence plans is hard to find.

d) 1 .... students in my new class all seem very friendly.

2 .... students should be in their classes by 9.00.

e) 1 I need .... help!

2 Thanks very much for .... help you gave me yesterday.

f) 1 .... computers in the January sale are not too expensive.

2 These days everybody needs to know how to use .... computers.

g) 1 .... English are famous for their strange sense of humour.

2 .... English programmes are quite easy to find on satellite TV.

h) 1 Many of my friends are studying .... business at university.

2 My father is involved in .... business of buying and selling houses.

36 | Determiners and pronouns

Explanations

all, some

■ *all*

All is usually followed by a plural noun and verb.

> **All students are expected** to arrive on time.

In the expressions *all day, all night, all the time*, the noun is singular.

We can also say *All (of) the ...* , and in this expression we can replace *the* by a possessive adjective (*my* etc.).

> **All (of) the tickets** for the match had been sold.

> **All (of) my friends** have bikes.

Not is also used with *all*.

> **Not all students** have bikes.

> **Not all (of) my friends** have bikes.

All is also used as a pronoun at the beginning of a sentence.

> **All I want** is some peace and quiet!

> **All I need** is £400! **All I have** is £50!

All is not normally used as a single-word object. Instead we use *everything*.

> Tell me **everything** that happened on your holiday.

> (NOT *Tell me all that happened* ...)

■ *some*

Some is used in the same way. *Some* is not used with *not*.

> **Some students** are expected to help.

no, none

■ *no*

We can use *no* with a singular noun or a plural noun.

> **No students** arrived on time for the last lesson!

> **No student** arrived on time for the last lesson!

We do not use *no* if there is another negative word. In this case we use *any*.

> I did**n't** see **any** students arriving on time for the last lesson.

■ *none*

We do not use *No of ...* or *No the ...* . Instead, we use *none of the* or *none* on its own.

> **None of the guests** are here yet.

> 'Were there any letters for me?' Sorry, **none** for you. '

Note that in the first example there is a plural verb 'are'. This is more common, although a singular verb is possible.

To emphasize the idea of *none* we can use *none at all*, or *not one*, or *not a ...* .
> *'How many people were surfing?'* → *'**None** at all! '*
> *'How many people were surfing?'* → *'**Not one**! '*
> *'How many people were surfing?'* → *'**Not a** single one!'*

Other examples:
> ***Not one person** has done any homework!*
> *I **haven't** had **a** single phone-call today.*

each, every

The meaning of *each* and *every* is similar and often either word is possible. They are both followed by a singular noun.
> ***Each person** in the room was wearing a hat.*
> ***Every person** in the room was wearing a hat.*

- *each*

  We use *each* when we think of the members of a group separately, one by one.
  > *She spent some time talking to **each** person in the room.*

  Each is often used with *one*.
  > *There were ten people in the room. **Each one** was wearing a hat.*

  Each of ... can be used.
  > ***Each of you** can carry one parcel.*

  Each can be used after the subject, or at the end of a sentence.
  > *My sisters **each have** their own room.*
  > *My uncle gave my brother and I $50 **each**. (= gave $50 to each of us.)*

- *every*

  We use *every* when we think of all the members of a group together.
  > ***Every box** was wrapped in coloured paper.*

  We cannot say *every of*.

  We cannot use *every* after the subject, or at the end of a sentence.

both, either, neither

- *both*

  Both refers to two things and means 'the one and the other'. It is used with a plural noun and verb. Note the structures and positions.
  > ***Both people/Both the people/Both of the people** in the room were wearing hats.*
  > *The people in the room were **both wearing hats**.*
  > *There were two people in the room. **Both** (of them) were wearing hats.*
  > ***Both of you** can help me.*
  > ***You can both** help me.*

- *either*

  Either means 'this one or the other one'. It is followed by a singular noun and verb.

  > *We can paint it green or blue. **Either colour** matches the walls.*

  But note that when we use *either* with the words 'end' or 'side' then the meaning changes to *both*.

  > *There are trees on **either side** of the street.*

  We can use *either of*.

  > ***Either of the books** will be very useful.*

- *neither*

  Neither means 'not this one or the other one'.

  > *We can't paint it green or blue. **Neither colour** matches the walls.*
  >
  > *There are trees on **neither side** of the street.*
  >
  > ***Neither of these books** will be very useful.*

→ SEE ALSO

Grammar 45: Pronouns

Practice

1 <u>Underline</u> the correct word or phrase in each sentence.

a) There were *none/<u>no</u>* people at the bus stop.
b) My two brothers *each/every* have their own car.
c) *Not one/Not no* student has come late this week!
d) *Some of/Some* restaurants charge extra for bread.
e) Sorry, but I can't hear *either/neither* of you properly.
f) When I got on my bike I noticed that *both tyres/every tyre* were flat.

2 Put one suitable word in each space.

a) I sent letters to ten people, but ....*not*........ ....*one*........ replied!
b) I'm sorry, but there are .... tickets left for the concert.
c) .... I ate for breakfast was a banana.
d) I tried .... the supermarkets, but .... one was closed.
e) I had two phone calls, but there were .... for you, I'm afraid.
f) Both roads lead to the city centre. You can take .... one.

3 Rewrite each sentence so that it has a similar meaning and contains the word in **bold**.

a) All the dogs in the garden were barking.
every
...*Every dog in the garden was barking.*...........................

b) Nobody at all came to the meeting.
single
....

c) Not one of my friends has got a car.
none
....

d) This chair is not comfortable, and nor is this other one.
neither
....

e) There weren't any boys in the class.
no
....

f) We only want to listen to a few CDs.
all
....

g) The two books are interesting.
both
....

4 Complete the second sentence so that it has a similar meaning to the first sentence.

a) These books aren't interesting.

None *of these books is/are interesting.*

b) You have only ten minutes left.

All ....

c) The hotels were both unsuitable.

Neither ....

d) No one replied to my letter.

Not a ....

e) Paul and his brother David are ill.

Both ....

f) Nobody in the team played badly.

All ....

g) The police searched all the houses in the street.

Every ....

h) Not all the questions in the test were easy.

Some ....

5 Underline the correct continuation of each sentence.

a) We looked at two different houses but ...

1 both of them were too small.   2 either of them was too small.

b) Liz invited a dozen guests to her party but ...

1 no turned up.   2 none turned up.

c) Helen and Mark are well behaved, but please let me know if ...

1 both of them misbehave.   2 either of them misbehaves.

d) Michaela feels so tired because she ...

1 didn't sleep for a single moment.   2 slept all for a moment.

e) Write down the number of the car on this list ...

1 each time one passes.   2 all the time one passes.

f) How many presents did you get on your birthday? ...

1 One at all.   2 None at all.

g) There were ten people standing at the bus stop and ...

1 all people had umbrellas.   2 each one had an umbrella.

h) We wrote all our answers on the blackboard but ...

1 no one of us was right.   2 none of us was right.

Adjectives and adverbs

Explanations

Adjectives

Adjectives describe a noun and are used in front of nouns. They have the same form for singular and plural. They do not change for male and female.

Order of adjectives

- When we have more than one adjective, we use this order:

Opinion	*lovely, difficult*
Size	*large, long*
Age	*old, second-hand*
Shape	*round, square*
Temperature	*hot, cold*
Colour	*green, blue*
Material	*wooden, plastic*
Purpose (what it is for?)	**swimming** *pool*
Final noun	*swimming* **pool**

Here are some examples:
> *An old leather football boot.*   (age, material, purpose, noun)
> *A lovely green silk shirt.*   (opinion, colour, material, noun)

It is not advisable to put more than three adjectives together.

- In the 'material' and 'purpose' categories we can have nouns used as adjectives: *plastic, steel, swimming, football.*

Gradable adjectives

- Look at this sequence:

boiling ◄──────────── *hot warm cool cold* ──────────► freezing

Adjectives in the middle of the sequence are called 'gradable'. We can make them stronger or weaker with words like *very, a bit, extremely.*
Adjectives at the end of the sequence are called 'non-gradable'. We cannot make them stronger or weaker because they are already extreme. But we can emphasise them with *absolutely.*
> *It was **absolutely boiling** in Athens last week.*   (NOT ~~very boiling~~)

Adjectives ending -ing and -ed

- Adjectives ending -*ing* describe something that we are reacting to (outside us).
Adjectives ending -*ed* describe our feelings and reactions (inside us).
> *My work was **tiring**.*   *It made me **tired**.*
> *This film is **interesting**.*   *I'm **interested** in the film.*

Others of the same kind are: *excited/exciting, embarrassed/embarrassing, worried/worrying, bored/boring.*

Adjectives with *be,* *become, feel, look*

■ Adjectives can be used on their own, without a noun, after these verbs.

  *This beach **is fantastic!*** *Sue has **become rich**.*

  *I **feel terrible!*** *You **look ill!***

  If we use more than one adjective, note the use of commas and the word 'and':

  *Sue has become **happy and rich**.*

  *Sue has become **happy, rich and famous**.*

one

■ We can use *one* instead of repeating a noun.

  *I like your new coat. It's a really **lovely one!***

Adverbs

■ Adverbs describe a verb. An adverb says how (*quickly*), when (*tomorrow*) or where (*over there*) something happens.

  Many 'how' adverbs are formed by adding *-ly* to an adjective.

  *slow – slow**ly*** *quick – quick**ly*** *careful – careful**ly***

■ Some adverbs have the same form as adjectives. Examples include: *fast, hard, early, late, high, low, right, wrong.*

  *This train is very **fast**.* (adj)

  *This train goes **fast**.* (adv)

  *It was a very **hard** question.* (adj)

  *We worked **hard**.* (adv)

■ Note that the adverb *hardly* is not related to the meaning of *hard*.

  *I could **hardly** stand up.* ('hardly' = almost not)

■ Remember that frequency adverbs come after *be* and auxiliaries, but before other verbs.

  *Katherine **is never** late.* *She **has never arrived** late.*

  *Katherine **never arrives** late.*

Adverbs of degree **(intensifiers)**

■ Adverbs of degree are used with adjectives to describe how much.

  *Peter is **very/really/extremely happy** at his new school.*

  Other adverbs of degree are: *a little, a bit, quite, terribly.*

→ SEE ALSO

Grammar 3: Present time 2

Practice

1 **Put each group of words into the best order.**

a) old a plastic large bag green
   a large old green plastic bag

b) wooden square two tables
   ....

c) red a dress silk beautiful
   ....

d) silver a of jugs antique pair
   ....

e) bowl small a plastic
   ....

f) winding road country long a
   ....

g) boots some old football dirty
   ....

h) cotton long a skirt yellow
   ....

i) squeezed cold juice a freshly glass orange of
   ....

2 <u>Underline</u> **the correct adjective in each sentence.**

a) I can't drink this tea! It's *warm/<u>boiling</u>*!

b) Look at that skyscraper! It's *large/gigantic*!

c) Jill couldn't drive any further that day as she was so *tired/tiring*.

d) I love summer evenings when at last it feels *cool/freezing*.

e) The first part of the film was really *excited/exciting*.

f) That was the best play I've ever seen. It was *good/fantastic*.

g) You look *worried/worrying*. Is anything the matter?

h) We won't go camping until the weather is more *boiling/warmer*.

i) If you feel *bored/boring*, why don't we go to the cinema?

j) I didn't think you were *interested/interesting* in ancient history.

3   Rewrite each sentence so that it has a similar meaning and contains the word in **bold**.

a)   The old couple lived together and were happy.

happily

   The old couple lived happily together.

b)   This has been hard work for you.

worked

   ....

c)   Chris and Paul are slow walkers.

walk

   ....

d)   Georgia is a good pianist.

plays

   ....

e)   Sue is a graceful dancer.

dances

   ....

f)   Kate is ill.

well

   ....

g)   Michael's skating was wonderful.

skates

   ....

h)   Mary is a careful writer.

writes

   ....

i)   Alex didn't sleep well.

slept

   ....

j)   Ann completed the course with success.

successfully

   ....

4 Complete each sentence with one of the words from the box. Use each word once only.

extremely	fast	good	~~happy~~	hard	hardly
ill	quite	terrible	well		

a) When I heard that Suzannah had passed her driving test I was really
...*happy*....... .

b) Jack dances very .... and never steps on people's feet.

c) Alan was so tired that he could .... keep his eyes open.

d) The hotel was .... , but we didn't like the food in the restaurant.

e) Alison was extremely .... and spent a month in hospital.

f) Jonny was driving too .... and was stopped by the police.

g) It's not a wonderful film, but it's .... good.

h) Gina worked very .... and was given an extra holiday.

i) When I realized I hadn't paid for the coat, I felt ....

j) I can't afford to buy that bike because it's .... expensive.

5 Underline the errors in these sentences. Rewrite each sentence.

a) Peter has been working very <u>hardly</u>.
 Peter has been working very hard.

b) My sister bought me a blue lovely woollen sweater.

 ....

c) This book I'm reading is extremely excellent.

 ....

d) David felt badly because he'd shouted at his mother.

 ....

e) Everyone in the team played good.

 ....

f) Too much exercise can make you feel tiring.

 ....

g) Paula felt happily when her exams were over.

 ....

h) Hans has arrived late at school never.

 ....

i) One boxer hit the other really hardly right on the chin.

 ....

j) I'm not really interesting in this car.

 ....

38 Making comparisons

Explanations

Comparatives and superlatives: meaning

Comparatives compare two separate things.

*Mary is a **better player** than Monica.*

Superlatives compare one thing in a group with all the others.

*Sarah is **the best player** in the team.*

Comparatives and superlatives: form

- One syllable

  Comparative adjectives with one syllable are normally formed by adding *-er* to the adjective. In one syllable words ending with one consonant, the final consonant is doubled. Words ending in consonant + *-y* change *-y* to *-i*.

  *long – long**er**   big – big**ger**   dry – dr**ier***

  Superlative adjectives are normally formed by adding *-est* to the adjective.

  *long – the long**est**   big – the big**gest**   dry – the dr**iest***

- Two or more syllables

  Comparative adjectives with two or more syllables are normally formed with *more*.

  *modern – **more modern**   interesting – **more interesting***

  Superlative adjectives are normally formed with *most*.

  *modern – the **most modern**   interesting – the **most interesting***

  Some adjectives with two syllables can be formed in either way.

common	*common**er***	*the common**est***	OR
common	***more** common*	*the **most** common*	

  Other examples include: *quiet, tired, clever, polite, simple.*

- Note from the examples above that *the* is used with superlatives. *The +* superlative can also be used without a noun.

  *Sarah is **the best** swimmer.*
  *Sarah is **the best**.*

Irregular forms

Note the following irregular forms:

good	*better*	*the best*
bad	*worse*	*the worst*
far	*farther/further*	*the farthest/furthest*
little	*less*	*the least*
much/many	*more*	*the most*

And there is a special use of *old* to describe family members that has an irregular form:

old	*elder*	*the eldest*

*This is my **elder** brother. Jane is their **eldest** daughter.*

Adverbs

In general adverbs follow the same rules as adjectives, although many common short adverbs can make comparatives in two ways.

> *Could you drive **slower**, please?*
> *Could you drive **more slowly**, please?*
> *Can you work **quicker**?*
> *Can you work **more quickly**?*

Adverbs that can use both forms like this include: *early, far, fast, hard, late, loud, quick, slow.*

Making comparisons

- *Than* is used with comparatives.
  > *Mary is **better than** Monica.*
  > *Mary is **a better player than** Monica.*

- Note that when we compare actions, we use an auxiliary at the end of the sentence.
  > *Mary plays better than Monica **does**.*   (NOT ... ~~than Monica plays~~)
  > *You've done more work than I **have**.*   (NOT ... ~~than I have done~~)

  We can also say:
  > *Mary plays **better than** Monica.*
  > *You've done more work **than** me.*

- *just as ... as* is used when we compare two equal things.
  > *Mary is **just as good as** Cathy.*
  > *Mary is **just as good** a player **as** Cathy.*

- *not as ... as* is used when we compare two things that are not equal.
  > *Cathy is **not as good as** Mary.*
  > *Cathy is **not as good** a player **as** Mary.*

- As well as saying *more than*, we can also say *less than*.
  > *This game is **more interesting than** the last one.*
  > *I think this game is **less interesting than** that one.*

Intensifiers

We can use adverbs of degree to make comparisons. Adverbs of degree include: *a bit, much, a lot, far.*

> *This house is **much/a lot/far** bigger than that one.*
> *The Italian film was **much more interesting** than this one.*
> *That film was **far less frightening** than this one.*

→ SEE ALSO

Grammar 37: Adjectives and adverbs

Practice

1   <u>Underline</u> the correct word or phrase in each sentence.

a) The fish was *so tasty as/<u>as tasty as</u>* the meat.
b) This book is *the most interesting/the more interesting* I've ever read.
c) This temple is the *eldest/oldest* in Europe.
d) That dress is a lot longer *than/that* the other one.
e) Nothing is *worse/worst* than being stuck in a traffic jam.
f) That skyscraper is one of the *taller/tallest* buildings in the world.
g) The test wasn't *as hard as/hard as* I thought.
h) Actually, today I feel *more bad/worse* than I did yesterday.
i) Our journey took *longer than/the longest* we expected.
j) Could you work *more quietly/more quieter* please?

2   Complete each sentence with a comparative or superlative form of the adjective in bold. Include any other necessary words.

a) The Nile is ...*the longest*............... river in the world.
   long
b) I was disappointed as the film was .... than I expected.
   entertaining
c) Most planes go a lot .... trains.
   fast
d) Yesterday was one of .... days of the year.
   hot
e) I think this book is much .... the other one.
   good
f) The twins are the same height. Tim is .... Sue.
   tall
g) The first exercise was easy but this one is ....
   difficult
h) The Mediterranean is not .... the Pacific Ocean.
   large
i) This classroom is .... the one next door.
   big
j) This is .... television programme I've ever watched.
   bad

3 Complete the second sentence so that it has a similar meaning to the first sentence.

a) David is a better runner than Paul.

Paul is not ......*as good a runner as David (is).*..

b) Nobody in the class is taller than Alison.

Alison is the ....

c) I haven't written as much as you.

You've written ....

d) Jane's hair isn't as long as Sophie's.

Sophie's hair is ....

e) No student in the school is noisier than I am!

I'm the ....

f) This exhibition is much more interesting than the last one.

The last exhibition was not ....

g) This is as fast as the car can go.

The car can't ....

h) Kate ate much less than Andrew did.

Kate didn't ....

4 Put one suitable word in each space.

a) Our team is ......*just*...... ....*as*...... good ....*as*........ your team. They're both the same.

b) This is one of .... famous paintings in the world.

c) Everyone did .... work .... Philip ....

d) You're not a safe driver! You should drive .... slowly.

e) Ann is taller .... Mike but their son Dave is .... tallest in the family.

f) What an awful book. It's one of .... interesting I've ever read.

g) It makes no difference, because this road is .... bad .... that one.

h) Today is .... cold .... yesterday, so I'm wearing my shorts.

5 Correct the spelling of these words where necessary.

a) bigest	...*biggest*...	f) fater	....	k) fiter	....
b) greattest	....	g) smalest	....	l) tighter	....
c) shorter	....	h) longest	....	m) newest	....
d) likeliest	....	i) hardder	....	n) heavier	....
e) tallest	....	j) wettest	....	o) widder	....

6 For each question, complete the second sentence so that it means the same as the first, using no more than three words.

a) Could you not talk so fast, please?

Could you ......*talk more slowly*.........., please?

b) The last film we saw was more frightening than this one.

This film .... as the last one.

c) Nobody in the class cooks better than Sam.

Sam is .... in the class.

d) You ran a lot faster than I did.

I didn't run .... you.

e) Small cars are more economical than large cars.

Large cars are .... small cars.

f) Skating isn't as exciting as skiing.

Skiing is .... skating.

g) Richard doesn't work harder than Alan.

Alan works just .... Richard.

h) Jack isn't as interested in football as his brother is.

Jack's brother .... in football than he is.

i) Bill is the youngest in the family.

Everyone else in the family .... Bill.

j) I haven't eaten as much as you.

You've eaten ....

Explanations

Understanding phrasal verbs

- The term 'phrasal verb' means a normal verb like *get, look, take* followed by one or two prepositions like *back, off, up* etc. Look at these examples:

  1 *Please **take** this note to my teacher.*
  (normal verb meaning: 'to move something from one place to another')
  2 ***Take off** your shoes before you come in.*
  (phrasal verb meaning: 'to remove something')
  3 *We **took off** in the middle of a storm.*
  (phrasal verb meaning: 'when a plane goes up into the air')

  When the preposition is added the meaning of the original verb changes. Sometimes there is still a relationship and you can guess the meaning (see 2 above), sometimes there is a new meaning that is completely different (see 3 above).

- There are different types of phrasal verbs, depending on whether there is one preposition or two, and whether the verb and preposition can be separated. In this book Grammar 38 and 39 cover different types.

- There are many phrasal verbs, and only a few common ones are given in these two units. When you see a new phrasal verb for the first time you should study the context of use, and check the meaning in a dictionary. Phrasal verbs are particularly common in informal writing and speech.

Verbs with three parts

Most of the verbs in the list below need an object, and the object can only come at the end, after both the prepositions:

> *I'm **looking forward to** my holidays.*

With verbs marked with an asterisk * there is no object, and the final preposition is not used.

> *catch up with** (reach someone by going faster)
> *You can rest now and **catch up with** us later.*
> *You're going too fast! I can't **catch up**!*

> *cut down on** (reduce the amount of)
> *Sheila has decided to **cut down on** holidays this year.*
> *You're eating too many sweets. You should **cut down**.*

> *drop in on** (visit for a short time)
> *Let's **drop in on** David while we're in Paris.*
> *The next time you're nearby, please do **drop in**!*

> *get along/on with** (have a friendly relationship with)
> *James doesn't **get on** well **with** his maths teacher.*
> *We work in the same office, but we don't **get on**.*

keep up with* (move at the same speed as)
*You're going too fast! I can't **keep up with** you.*
*Patty finds this class difficult, and can't **keep up**.*

live up to (be as good as someone expects)
*The film didn't **live up to** our expectations.*

look forward to (think you will enjoy)
*I'm **looking forward to** going on holiday this year.*
Note that *to* is a preposition here and so is followed by the *-ing* form of the verb.

look out onto/over (have a view of)
*Our hotel room **looks out onto** the lake.*

put up with (accept without complaining)
*I can't **put up with** all this noise!*

run out of* (have no more of)
*I think the car is about to **run out of** petrol!*
*There isn't any more milk. We've **run out**.*

Verbs with two parts: transitive and inseparable

These phrasal verbs take an object (the word for this is 'transitive'). The object must come after the preposition, not between the verb and the preposition (the word for this is 'inseparable').

call for (come to your house and collect)
*We'll **call for you** about 8.00 so please be ready.* (NOT ~~call you for~~)

call on (visit for a short time)
*I **called on** Professor Jones and wished her a Happy Birthday.*

deal with (take action to solve a problem)
*Could you **deal with** this customer's problem please?*

get at (try to say, suggest)
*Helen couldn't understand what her boss was **getting at**.*

get over (recover from)
*Peter was ill with flu, but he's **getting over** it now.*

head for (go in the direction of)
*The escaped prisoner is thought to be **heading for** London.*

join in (take part in, contribute to)
*When Alex started singing, everyone **joined in**.*

see to (pay attention to, often meaning 'repair')
*The brakes on your car need **seeing to**.*

stand for (tolerate)
*I will not **stand for** so much talking!*

take after (be similar in appearance or character)
*Karen **takes after** her mother. They're very similar.*

Practice

1 Complete each sentence (a–h) with an ending (1–8).

a) If you have any kind of problem, just call me and I'll deal ....*3*.....

b) I've been so busy lately that I've decided to cut ....

c) Ann and Sue are really looking ....

d) Our teacher told us that she would not stand ....

e) Nearly everybody says that Mark takes ....

f) Jackie is very friendly and generally gets ....

g) Half-way through the race, Martin found that he couldn't keep ....

h) We were told that the concert was going to be good but it didn't live ....

1 for cheating in our end-of-term test.

2 on well with the people she works with.

3 with it as soon as I can.

4 after his father's side of the family.

5 down on the amount of time I spend watching television.

6 up with the others any more.

7 up to our expectations at all.

8 forward to seeing you both again in July.

2 <u>Underline</u> the correct preposition in each sentence.

a) Can you explain that again? I don't know what you're getting *by/with/<u>at</u>*?

b) He's a very strict teacher. He doesn't stand *for/up/with* any bad behaviour in class.

c) I enjoyed London, but it didn't really live up *to/with/for* my expectations.

d) I smoke 20 cigarettes a day, but I'm trying to cut *off/through/down*.

e) I think she has got *over/by/down* the break-up with her boyfriend.

f) I'll call *by/in/for* you at eight o'clock, and then we'll go to the party together.

g) I'm going crazy! I can't put *off/up/down* with so much confusion!

h) I'm lucky, I get *on/off/over* really well with my colleagues.

i) If you miss too many lessons, it's difficult to catch *over/up/with*.

j) It's difficult to keep *along/by/up* with changes in bio-technology.

k) My car needs a service – the engine needs seeing *in/to/at*.

l) The printer is working, but it's run *away/out/down* of ink.

3 Complete each sentence with a suitable form of one of the phrasal verbs in the box. Use each one once only.

catch up with	cut down on	drop in on	get on with
keep up with	(not) live up to	look forward to	run out of

a) The book you lent me ...*didn't live up to*...... my expectations.

b) Any time you're in the area, feel free to .... us.

c) Sorry, we have .... orange juice. Would you like some water?

d) Unfortunately Susie doesn't .... her new neighbours.

e) Bill left before I did, but I ran and .... him.

f) I'm really .... my holiday in Italy next week.

g) It was a difficult class, and I couldn't .... the other students.

h) You should .... smoking if you can't stop completely.

4 Rewrite each sentence so that it does not contain the words in *italics*, but does contain a phrasal verb.

a) Brian and his mother *are very similar*.
...*Brian takes after his mother.*......................................

b) *There isn't any* food *left*!
....

c) Mike and Tom *aren't very good friends*.
....

d) Jean is very good at *handling* people's *problems*.
....

e) The handlebars on my bike need *fixing*.
....

f) Julia was very ill, but she's *recovered* now.
....

g) What exactly are you *suggesting*?
....

h) Paul's new school *wasn't as good as he expected it to be*.
....

5 Rewrite each sentence so that it has a similar meaning and contains the word in **bold**.

a) Someone needs to look at the central heating system.

seeing

The central heating system needs seeing to.

b) Let's pay a surprise visit to Julia while we're here.

drop

....

c) We're going in the direction of Paris.

heading

....

d) Our hotel room has a view of the main road!

looks

....

e) Two children started playing, and then the others played too.

joined

....

f) We paid a visit to my aunt on her birthday.

called

....

g) I'm afraid that we haven't got any eggs left.

run

....

h) Monica will come and collect you at 6.30.

call

....

i) Nobody understood what I was trying to say.

getting

....

j) I can't bear so much air pollution!

put

....

Explanations

Verbs with two parts: transitive and separable

These phrasal verbs take an object (the word for this is 'transitive'). This object can come after the preposition or between the verb and the preposition (so the verbs are 'separable').

> We **brought up** this child. We **brought** her **up**.

In general, as in the examples above, object phrases tend to be put after the preposition while pronouns (such as *you, it, him, her, us, them*) are always put between the verb and the preposition.

bring up (look after a child until adult)
*Tom's aunt **brought him up** after his parents died.*

call off (cancel)
*The school **called off** the match because of bad weather.*

clear up (make clean and tidy)
*Could you help me **clear up** the room after the party?*

cut off (be disconnected during a phone-call)
*I'd just got through to Delhi when I was **cut off**.*
This is usually used in the passive.

fill in (complete by writing)
*Could you **fill this form in** with all your details, please?*

give up (stop doing something)
*Paul had to **give up** gymnastics because of injury.*

knock out (make unconscious)
*Bryson **knocked his opponent out** in the second round.*

let down (disappoint, fail to keep a promise)
*Ann said she would help, but she **let me down**.*

look up (find information in a reference book)
*I **looked this word up** in a dictionary and in an encyclopedia.*

pick up (collect in a car)
*The taxi will **pick you up** at 6.30.*

put off (postpone)
*The weather was bad, so they **put off** the match for a week.*

put up (provide accommodation in someone's house)
*A friend in Prague **put me up** for a couple of nights.*

take up   (start a hobby or activity)
*Sam has just **taken up** parachuting.*

try on   (put on clothes to see if they are suitable)
*I **tried the coat on**, but it was too big and the wrong colour.*

turn on/off   (begin or stop operating electrical equipment)
*Don't forget to **turn off** the light before you go to bed.*

wash up   (clean plates, knives and forks etc.)
*After the party, Martin **washed up** all the glasses.*

Verbs with two parts: intransitive

These phrasal verbs do not have an object.

break down   (stop working, especially cars)
*The car **broke down** when we were on the motorway.*

drop out   (stop before you finish)
*Two of the runners **dropped out** half-way through the race.*

get on   (make progress)
*Nina likes her new college, and is **getting on** well.*

get away   (escape)
*One of the burglars was caught, but the other **got away**.*

grow up   (change from a child to an adult)
*I **grew up** in a small town in Peru.*

set off/out   (begin a journey)
*We **set off** early to avoid the traffic.*

take off   (when a plane leaves the ground)
*Our plane **took off** more than three hours late.*

turn up   (arrive, often unexpectedly)
*We invited twenty people, but only five **turned up**.*

→ SEE ALSO

Grammar 39: Phrasal verbs

Practice

1 Complete each sentence with one suitable word.

a) Jess asked if she could help me ...*wash*........ up the dirty dishes.

b) I need a dictionary, so I can .... up this word.

c) If I were you I'd .... off early because Edinburgh is a long way.

d) Our meeting tomorrow has been .... off, I'm afraid.

e) I'm not sure about the size of this coat, so can I .... it on?

f) Robert had to .... in a form, giving all his personal details.

g) You'll never guess who .... up at our school party last week!

h) Six people applied for the job, but one of them .... out.

2 Rewrite each sentence so that it has a similar meaning and contains the word in **bold**.

a) Don't leave the lights on when you leave the school.
   turn
   ....*Turn the lights off when you leave the school.*...........

b) Jack arrived half-way through the lesson.
   turn
   ....

c) You can stay with us for a week.
   put
   ....

d) Marta is doing well in her English class.
   get
   ....

e) Lidia spent her childhood in Uruguay.
   grew
   ....

f) How do you start the computer?
   turn
   ....

g) Carol checked the dates in an encyclopedia.
   look
   ....

h) Surfing is a great sport. When did you start doing it?
   take
   ....

3 Complete each sentence (a–h) with an ending (1–8).

a) It's very cold and wet at the moment so we've put ....*3*....

b) Mary's parents were quite strict and brought her ....

c) Your room is very untidy! Could you clear ....

d) I was talking to Helen when suddenly we were cut ....

e) Zoe tried to persuade her mother to give ....

f) Tim started painting his room this morning and he's getting ....

g) If you like, we could come and pick ....

h) A branch of a tree fell and knocked ....

1   it up please, and put everything away.
2   Peter out for a few moments.
3   off our garden party until next week.
4   up smoking, but she didn't have much success.
5   on very well so far.
6   off and I couldn't get her number after that.
7   you up in our car at about 7.00.
8   up to be very polite and obedient.

1 <u>Underline</u> the correct word or phrase in each sentence.

a) I think my school is *just as good/better* than yours.

b) There are enough apples for one *each/every*.

c) Sharon has been working very *hard/hardly*.

d) Could you give me *an/some* information, please?

e) This is the *best/better* ice-cream in the world!

f) I've been working in this company *for/since* three months.

g) There are *no/none* eggs left in the fridge.

h) The news *is/are* on in a few minutes.

2 Decide which answer (A, B, C or D) best fits each space.

Life on the farm

I was (1) ....D.... by my uncle and aunt and (2) .... on a small farm in the west of England. I think it was better (3) .... living in a city, because (4) .... day I ran about in the open air. (5) .... I went to school, (6) .... I did was play on the farm all day. (7) .... my aunt and uncle worked with the animals, and although they worked very (8) .... , they always explained (9) .... things to me. They didn't have (10) .... money, but they (11) .... well with everyone, and we didn't have (12) .... of the problems of living in the city. I always felt (13) .... on the farm. There was (14) .... noise or pollution, and it was (15) .... peaceful. That's probably why I became a farmer when I was older.

1) **A** lived up to	**B** taken after	**C** grown up	**D** brought up
2) **A** grew up	**B** joined in	**C** turned up	**D** put off
3) **A** as	**B** more	**C** than	**D** the
4) **A** every	**B** in	**C** for	**D** both
5) **A** by	**B** nowadays	**C** in time	**D** until
6) **A** every	**B** each	**C** none	**D** all
7) **A** Either	**B** Both	**C** Neither	**D** All
8) **A** hardly	**B** harder	**C** hard	**D** hardest
9) **A** interests	**B** interesting	**C** interest	**D** interested
10) **A** much	**B** lots	**C** many	**D** too
11) **A** dropped in	**B** got along	**C** kept up	**D** dealt with
12) **A** much	**B** none	**C** no	**D** any
13) **A** happily	**B** a happy	**C** happy	**D** the happy
14) **A** any	**B** no	**C** none of	**D** not
15) **A** too	**B** much	**C** really	**D** as

3   **For each question, complete the second sentence so that it means the same as the first, using no more than three words.**

a) These classrooms aren't very large.

None ....*of these*........................... classrooms are very large.

b) Luca won't leave here before the end of April.

Luca will be here .... the end of April.

c) We don't allow smoking in this cinema.

No .... in this cinema.

d) Can you tell me what you think I should do?

Can you give me .... ?

e) You've been waiting longer than I have.

I haven't been waiting .... you have.

f) It's 4.00 now, and I started waiting here two hours ago.

I've been waiting here .... 2.00.

g) All classrooms must be kept clean.

Each .... must be kept clean.

h) Most of the class walks to school.

Most of the class comes to school ....

i) This is as far as we can go along this road.

We can't go .... along this road.

j) The fire brigade arrived too late to save the burning house.

The fire brigade didn't arrive .... to save the burning house.

4   **Rewrite each sentence so that it contains a form of a phrasal verb using the word in bold. Make any other necessary changes.**

a) You can come and stay with me.

put

...*I can put you up.*................................

b) Carlos can't stand the traffic anymore.

put

....

c) Peter is making good progress at university.

get

....

d) I'll tidy up the room if you do the washing-up.

clear

....

166

e) We're going in the direction of Madrid.

head

....

f) Why don't you search for this word in the dictionary?

look

....

g) Jane is very similar to her father.

take

....

h) Kelly's father is trying to stop smoking.

give

....

5 Look carefully at each line. Some lines are correct but some have a word which should not be there. Tick (✓) each correct line. If a line has a word which should not be there, write the word in the space.

Holiday problems

Last month we decided to drive to Scotland for a	1 ....✓........
few days, for a short holiday. We were the really	2 ...*the*......
looking it forward to a quiet rest in the country.	3 ....
Unfortunately, a lots of things went wrong. First	4 ....
of all, the car was broke down just after we had left	5 ....
home, and we had to phone a garage and then	6 ....
wait by the side of the road for hours ago. By the	7 ....
time the car had been repaired, it was too much late	8 ....
to go on, so we went the home. The next day we set	9 ....
off more early to avoid the traffic, but we had forgotten	10 ....
that it was a public holiday. Every one single person	11 ....
in the country must have had the same idea, so we	12 ....
found ourselves in a long traffic jam. We after decided	13 ....
that the best thing to do was to take after a different	14 ....
road, and look up for a hotel. First we got lost on	15 ....
a narrow country road, and then the car once ran	16 ....
out of the petrol. Finally, we gave up and went home	17 ....
for the second time.	18 ....

6 Put one suitable word in each space, or leave the space blank.

While Lara was visiting (a) ....*the*...... United States, she decided to go by (b) .... plane from (c) .... New York to (d) .... West Coast. She had already stayed with her friends (e) .... two weeks, and they'd told her that (f) .... California was a (g) .... more exciting. 'It's (h) .... warmer, and you'll be able to swim in (i) .... Pacific Ocean!', they said. Lara didn't have (j) .... information about flights, so she went to (k) .... travel agent's next door to (l) .... block of flats where she was staying. She discovered that there were two flights (m) .... next morning, but she couldn't get (n) .... seat on (o) .... of them.

7 For each question, complete the second sentence so that it means the same as the first, using no more than three words.

a) Nobody at all picked up the litter.
Not ....*a single*.................... person picked up the litter.

b) There isn't any cheese in the fridge.
There is .... in the fridge.

c) People who are rich aren't necessarily happy.
The .... not necessarily happy.

d) Jane's drawing is beautiful.
Jane draws ....

e) I haven't seen a worse film than this one.
This is .... I have ever seen.

f) Helen left Paris in July.
Helen stayed in Paris .... July.

8 Put one suitable word in each space.

a) You work ..*much*........ harder ......*than*...... I do.

b) In .... future, people will live longer .... they do now.

c) Alex plays .... guitar in .... rock band.

d) There is .... hot water left, but there isn't ....

e) He could go now he'd answered .... the questions on ....
sides of the form.

f) Jogging isn't .... interesting .... playing tennis.

g) I'll wait here .... 6.00, so try and be here .... then.

h) That was great! It was the .... meal you've .... cooked!

9 <u>Underline</u> the errors in these sentences. Rewrite each sentence.

a) I'm really <u>interesting in the travel</u>.
   ......*I'm really interested in travel.*......................................

b) Kate's brother is doctor.
   ....

c) I ate a food with Jack, and after that I went home.
   ....

d) The milk is good for you.
   ....

e) Can you give me an advice?
   ....

f) I've looked in the box. All is broken, I'm afraid.
   ....

g) They will have finished the new hospital until the end of May.
   ....

h) There's a police waiting outside.
   ....

i) I come to class with the feet.
   ....

j) Your hair are very beautiful.
   ....

Problem check

1 Time words like *for, since* and *ago* are linked to the use of tenses. Check Grammar 4, 5, 6 and 7.

2 The same word can be countable and uncountable with a change of meaning. Which words of this kind do you know? Check with Grammar 33.

3 Compare the uses of articles with articles in your language (if it has articles). Note that the choice of article can depend on meaning and context. Check with Grammar 34 and 35.

4 Avoid using more than three adjectives together. Note the difference between *hard* and *hardly*. Check with Grammar 37.

5 What is the difference between comparative and superlatives? Are they used in the same ways in your language? Check with Grammar 38.

6 Phrasal verbs can have many meanings, so check in a dictionary. Make sure that you know where in the entry for the main verb you can find the phrasal verbs (it is right at the end of the entry, after the various meanings of the main verb used alone).

Explanations

When you learn a new verb, it is advisable to check in a dictionary whether it is followed by the *-ing* form (also called the gerund) or an infinitive with or without *to*. If the infinitive is without *to* it can be called a bare infinitive. Grammar 42 and 43 include some of the most common verbs, but these are only a selection.

Verbs followed by *-ing* or infinitive: little or no change of meaning

■ Some verbs can be followed either by an *-ing* form, or *to* + infinitive, and there is little or no change in meaning. Verbs in this list include:
>*begin, continue, not bear, hate, intend, like, love, prefer, start*

>*When she stood up, the President **began to speak/speaking**.*
>*Some people at the back **continued chatting/to chat**.*
>*I can't **bear listening/to listen** for a long time.*
>*What do you **intend doing/to do** about it?*
>*I don't like watching television. I **prefer reading/to read**.*
>*I think you should **start practising/to practise** now!*

■ There can be a small difference between *like to do* and *like doing*. *To* + infinitive suggests that something is a good idea although you don't necessarily enjoy it. The *-ing* form shows you enjoy something.
>*I **like** to have a short walk after my evening meal.*
>*I **like listening** to the radio.*

■ Note that with 'prefer' we **prefer** one thing **to** another thing. If the things are activities, the *-ing* form is used.
>*Tom **prefers reading to watching** television.*

■ *Hate doing* is more common, except in the fixed expression 'I hate to tell you this, but ...'.
>*I **hate doing** the washing-up!*
>*I **hate to tell** you this, but we've missed the last train!*

■ When we use the modal verb *would* with *like, love, prefer* and *hate* we must use *to* + infinitive.
>*I'd **like to go** to Portugal this summer.*
>*I'd **prefer to do** it myself, if you don't mind.*

Verbs followed by *to* + infinitive

Some verbs can only be followed by the infinitive with *to*. These include:
>*afford, ask, choose, happen, help, manage, offer, refuse, wait, want*

*I can't **afford to go** to the cinema twice in one week.*
*In the end, Laura **chose to study** Economics.*
*Do you **happen to know** the time?*
*Could someone **help me to carry** this? ***
*(Help is also used without to. Could you **help me carry** this?)*
*Jim can't **manage to come** this evening.*
*I **offered to give** her a lift, but she said she'd ordered a taxi.*
*The manager **refused to see** me.*
*There are some people **waiting to** see you.*
*What do you **want to do** this evening?*

**Verbs followed by
to + infinitive, or
that-clause**

■ Some verbs can be followed by the infinitive with *to*, or a *that* clause. It is possible to leave out *that* in everyday speech. These verbs include:
agree, decide, expect, hope, learn, pretend, promise, seem, wish

*We **decided to go** home.*	*We **decided (that) we would** go home.*
*Mike **expects to win**.*	*Mike expects **(that) he will** win.*
*I **hope to see** you later.*	*I **hope (that) I'll** see you later.*
*Helen **pretended to be** ill.*	*Helen **pretended (that) she was** ill.*

■ Note that if we use a *that*-clause we follow the tense rules of reported speech. So, for example, *will* changes to *would* in the past:
*Sarah **agrees to meet** you after school.*
*Sarah **agrees that she will meet** you after school.*
*Sarah **agreed to meet** me after school.*
*Sarah **agreed (that) she would meet** me after school.*

■ There is a small difference between *learn to* and *learn that*.
*At school Graham **learned to speak** French. (learn a skill)*
*At school we **learned that** the Earth goes round the Sun. (learn information)*

■ Note the two forms of *seem*. It + *seem* + *that*-clause is very common.
*You **seem to know** the answer!*
***It seems that you know** the answer.*

■ *Wish* followed by *to* + infinitive has a similar meaning to *want*.
*I **wish to leave** early today.*
Wish followed by a *that*-clause usually includes *would* or *could*.
*I **wish (that) I could** leave early.*
*I **wish (that) my teacher would** let me leave early.*

→ SEE ALSO

Grammar 11: Reported speech 1
Grammar 12: Reported speech 2
Grammar 43: Verbs followed by *-ing* or infinitive 2

Practice

1 <u>Underline</u> the errors in these sentences. Some sentences do not have errors. Rewrite each sentence that has an error and tick (✓) the sentences which are correct.

a) Jim can't afford <u>going</u> to the cinema twice a week.

....*Jim can't afford to go to the cinema twice a week.*...............

b) David wishes leaving the room.

....

c) Are you waiting to use the phone?

....

d) I'd really like going swimming on Saturday.

....

e) Emma pretended leaving, but waited outside.

....

f) James agreed to meet me at the beach.

....

g) My bike seems having something wrong with it.

....

h) The director refused answering Helen's phone call.

....

2 Complete each sentence with a form of one of the verbs from the box. Use each verb once only.

afford	bear	continue	expect	happen
learn	~~love~~	offer	prefer	pretend

a) John really ....*loves*........ spending all day at the beach.

b) I'm completely broke, so I can't .... to go on holiday.

c) Excuse me, but do you .... to know the way to Old Street?

d) We .... our team to win, but they were badly beaten.

e) Carolyn .... to speak French and German when she was at school.

f) Even when the examiner told him to stop, Robert .... speaking.

g) I'm sorry, but I can't .... to listen to this awful music!

h) Last week Chris .... to help me paint my bike.

i) Paul .... to have a bad leg so he didn't have to go to the gym.

j) Sam usually .... playing football to doing homework.

3 Complete the second sentence so that it has a similar meaning to the first sentence.

a) My teacher wouldn't let me leave early.

My teacher refused ...*to let me leave early*......................... .

b) Jill sang without stopping for an hour.

Jill continued ....

c) Apparently you've passed the exam.

It seems ....

d) Richard thinks he's going to do well.

Richard expects ....

e) What are your plans for the summer?

What do you intend .... ?

f) Clearing up my room is something I dislike!

I hate ....

g) Liz said she'd go to the cinema with me.

Liz agreed ....

h) Tina and Brian are getting married.

Tina and Brian have decided ....

i) See you later, I hope.

I hope ....

j) What do you fancy doing this evening?

What do you want .... ?

4 Complete each sentence with one of the words from the box.

agreed	asked	chose	decided	hate
hopes	like	refused	~~seems~~	want

a) Greg often ....*seems*...... to be worried.

b) I .... to tell you this, but we've lost all our money.

c) Do you .... to go for a walk this afternoon?

d) I .... Ann to wait for me, but she didn't.

e) Katrina .... to become a champion skater.

f) The police officer .... to listen to my explanation.

g) Peter .... to work on Saturday instead of on Friday.

h) I'd .... to see you again some time.

i) After a lot of thought, Jim finally .... to spend his holiday in Peru.

j) I asked my teacher for help, and she .... to give me extra lessons.

5 Rewrite each sentence so that it has a similar meaning and contains the word in **bold**.

a) What are you thinking of doing?

intend

...*What do you intend to do?*...

b) I find getting up early unbearable!

bear

....

c) I'll see you in the morning, I expect.

to

....

d) 'I'll be back at 6.00,' said Susan.

promised

....

e) Pat was taught to drive when he was young.

learned

....

f) 'Would you like me to help you?' I asked Joe.

offered

....

g) Ellen didn't have enough money for the ticket.

afford

....

h) 'I won't help!' said Tom.

refused

....

Verbs followed by *-ing* or infinitive 2

Explanations

Verbs followed by *-ing* or infinitive: change of meaning

Some verbs can be followed either by an *-ing* form, or *to* + infinitive, and there is a change in meaning. Study the examples below carefully.

remember and *forget*

We use *remember/forget doing* (or *remember/forget* followed by *that*-clause) for memories of the past (the action happens before the remembering). We use *remember/forget to do* for actions someone is/was supposed to do (the remembering happens before the action).

*I **remember telling** you!*	(tell ← remember)
*Then I **remembered that** you were out.*	(go out ← remember)
***Remember to take** your keys!*	(remember → take)
*I'll never **forget learning** to drive!*	(learn ← forget)
*I **forgot that** I'd promised to phone you.*	(promise ← forget)
*Sorry, I **forgot to post** your letter.*	(forget → post)

mean

We use *mean doing* (or *mean* followed by *that*-clause) when one thing results in or involves another. We use *mean to do* to express an intention.

*Keeping fit **means taking** exercise every day!*	(= involves)
*When I miss the bus, it **means that I have to** walk to school.*	(= involves)
*Jan **meant to watch** the programme, but she forgot.*	(= intended)

stop

We use *stop doing* when we end an action. We use *stop to do* when we give the reason for stopping.

*Jo has **stopped learning** French.*	(= gave up learning)
*We **stopped to look** at the view.*	(= in order to look)

Stop is not followed by a *that*-clause.

try

We use *try doing* when we do something and see what happens. We use *try to do* when we make an effort to do something, but don't necessarily succeed.

*If you have a headache, **try taking** two of these pills.*	(= experiment)
*Peter **tried to lift** the table, but it was too heavy.*	(he failed in this case)

Try is not followed by a *that*-clause.

Verbs followed by *-ing* or infinitive without *to*: change of meaning

■ Some verbs can be followed by an object + *ing*, or an infinitive without *to*. There is a change in meaning. These verbs are sometimes called 'verbs of perception' and include:

feel, hear, listen to, see, watch

■ If we see or hear only part of the action, or it continues, we use the *-ing* form. If we see or hear the whole action from beginning to end, we use the infinitive without *to*.

Compare:

I could **feel** my hands **shaking** with fear!	(continuing action)
I **felt** the building **move**!	(completed action)
We **watched** Joe **eating** his lunch.	(part of the action)
We **watched** Joe **eat** his lunch.	(whole action)

■ These verbs can be used with a *that*-clause with a change of meaning.

I **feel that** this is the time to resign.	(= believe)
We **heard that** you were ill.	(= receive news)
I **saw that** it was too late.	(= realize)

Verbs followed by -ing or noun

Some verbs can be followed either by another verb in an *-ing* form or a noun. These include: *dislike, enjoy, fancy, *can't help, *keep, mind, practise, can't stand.* Those marked * have two meanings.

I **dislike going out** in the rain.
I really **dislike my new boss**.
Everyone **enjoys going** to parties.
I **enjoyed this lesson**.
Do you **fancy going** to the cinema?
I **fancy a swim**!
I **can't help feeling** hungry.

I **can't help myself**!	(= I can't stop)

Keep this. Don't throw it away.

Sue **keeps phoning** me late at night.	(= continues with a bad habit)

Do you **mind waiting**?
Do you **mind cold weather**?
I must **practise speaking** French more often.
Julia **practises the violin** every day.
I **can't stand waking up** early.
I **can't stand hot and spicy food**.

Verbs followed by -ing, or noun, or that-clause

■ Some verbs can be followed either by another verb in an *-ing* form, or a noun, or a *that*-clause. These include: *admit, deny, imagine, suggest.*

The Minister **admitted taking** a bribe.
Paul **admitted that** he was wrong.
Tina **denied stealing** the money.
Both men **denied that** they had done anything wrong.
Imagine travelling to another planet!
Do you really **imagine that** I want to see you again?
I **suggest going** for a pizza.
I **suggest that** we go for a pizza.

■ *Suggest* can also be followed by *should*.

I **suggest that** we **should** go for a pizza.

→ SEE ALSO

Grammar 42: Verbs followed by *-ing* or infinitive 1

Practice

Contrasts with verbs from Grammar 42 are included here.

1 <u>Underline</u> the correct word or phrase in each sentence.

a) Tom suddenly realized he'd forgotten *<u>to lock</u>/locking* his door.

b) On the way back we stopped *to have/having* some tea.

c) Could you stop *to talk/talking*, please.

d) Learning a language means *to be/being* interested in another culture.

e) Ann tried *to open/opening* the window, but it was too high to reach.

f) Please remember *to take/taking* the dog for a walk.

g) Cathy says she'll never forget *to sky-dive/sky-diving* for the first time.

h) I don't really remember *to start/starting* school when I was five.

2 For each question, complete the second sentence so that it means the same as the first, using no more than three words.

a) Would you like to go to the beach?

 Do ....*you fancy*............................ going to the beach?

b) The boy admitted stealing the bike.

 The boy admitted .... stolen the bike.

c) Why don't we wait for the bus?

 .... waiting for the bus.

d) David often interrupts me.

 David .... me.

e) Is it all right if you come back later?

 .... coming back later?

f) Think what being a millionaire would be like!

 .... a millionaire!

g) It's not my fault if I eat a lot.

 I .... eating a lot.

3 <u>Underline</u> the correct verb in each sentence.

a) Helen *enjoyed/<u>chose</u>* to learn French.

b) I really can't *stand/afford* to travel by plane.

c) Do you *mind/want* coming back in half an hour?

d) Tina *suggested/meant* to buy some potatoes, but she forgot.

e) Emily *denied/refused* opening the office safe.

f) Bill *admitted/agreed* making a serious mistake.

g) My parents *disliked/decided* to send me to a different school.

h) I really *like/fancy* a trip to the country.

4   Complete each sentence with a form of one of the verbs in the box.

deny	enjoy	expect	imagine	manage	mean
~~try~~	practise	pretend	refuse		

a) If you ...*try*............ to work a bit harder, I'm sure you'll pass the exam.

b) Kevin .... to have toothache, and left school early.

c) The builders are not sure of the exact date, but .... to start work

.... to call you last week, but she forgot.

..ted by the police .... robbing the bank.

.... speaking to an audience, to gain confidence.

g) .... myself living on a desert island.

..ector six times, but she .... to speak to me.

5   Complete each sentence with one suitable word.

a) Don't ...*forget*....... to buy some milk on your way home.

b) If I'm late, it .... I have to wait until the next lesson begins.

c) I .... throwing the ball, but I didn't break the window.

d) Paul can't .... thinking about his favourite team.

e) Lisa .... forgetting where she put her keys.

f) Gina .... to climb in through the window, but it was locked.

g) I .... playing with my friends when I was little.

h) I can't .... walking home in the rain! It's horrible!

Explanations

Verb + preposition

■ Some verbs are followed by a particular preposition. You can check this in a dictionary. Some common examples are given below.

About
dream   I **dreamed about** Harry last night.
know   Do you **know** a lot **about** economics?
talk   What are you **talking about**?

At
laugh   Don't **laugh at** me.
look   **Look at** that beautiful cherry tree!

For
apologize I must **apologize for** being late.
apply   Jill has **applied for** a new job.
ask   Why don't we **ask for** the bill?
look   I'm **looking for** the bus station.
pay   Sheila **paid for** my ticket.
wait   I'll **wait for** you outside.

In
believe   Do you **believe in** ghosts?
succeed   Helen **succeeded in** collecting £35 for charity.

Of
accuse   Albert was **accused of** spying.
remind   This city **reminds me of** Buenos Aires.
taste   Does your coffee **taste of** soap?

On
depend   I might come. It **depends on** the weather.
rely   You can **rely on** Ann to work hard.

To
belong   Does this **belong to** you?
explain   Could you **explain something to** me please?
lend   Brian **lent his car to** me for the weekend.
             We can also say: Brian **lent me** his car.
listen   You're not **listening to** me!
talk   Ellen was **talking to** her mother on the phone.

■ In questions the preposition usually goes at the end.
  *What are you talking **about**?*
  *Who are you **looking for**?*
  *What are you listening **to**?*

be + adjective +
preposition

Note that in the list below the following adjectives occur twice: *angry, annoyed, pleased, sorry*. One of the prepositions is used when they refer to people and one when they refer to things (this is shown in the list).

About	*angry* (+ things), *annoyed* (+ things), *excited, happy, pleased* (+ things), *right, sorry* (+ things), *upset* *Helen is **excited about** winning the prize.* *I'm **sorry about** your difficulties. Can I help?*
At	*bad, good* *Dora is really **good at** maths.*
For	*famous, late, ready, sorry* (+ people) *Our city is **famous for** its beautiful buildings.* *I was **sorry for** George when he came last in the race.*
From	*different* *This room is **different from** the other one.*
In	*interested* *Are you **interested in** computers?*
Of	*afraid, fond, frightened, full, jealous, tired* *My sleeping bag was **full of** ants!*
On	*keen* *I'm not very **keen on** fried food.*
To	*kind, married, used* *Ellen is **married to** Jack.*
With	*angry* (+ people), *annoyed* (+ people), *bored, pleased* (+ people) *I'm really **angry with** you.*

Practice

1 Complete each sentence with one suitable word.

a) Fiona is very different ...*from*........ her sister.

b) Please try and listen .... my instructions.

c) My home town is famous .... its peaches.

d) Excuse me, but does this umbrella belong .... you?

e) What exactly was Alistair talking .... ?

f) I think we should ask .... some information.

g) Gemma is very keen .... growing her own vegetables.

2 Complete the sentences with one word from list A and one from list B.

A	apologizes	belongs	depends	knows	~~laughs~~	reminds	succeeds
B	about	~~at~~	for	in	of	on	to

a) I don't like him. I think he .....*laughs*......... ....*at*....... me behind my back.

b) I'll be surprised if he .... walking to the top of the mountain.

c) Isabel sends her love and .... not contacting you. She's been really busy.

d) It's difficult to know when the bus will come. It .... the time of day.

e) She's very intelligent. She .... a lot .... economics and things like that.

f) This dictionary isn't mine. I think it .... Jorge.

g) This music .... me .... the time I spent in India.

3 Complete the sentences with one word from list A and one from list B.

A	~~right~~	good	famous	interested	frightened	kind	annoyed
B	~~about~~	at	for	in	of	to	with

a) I was ......*right*........ ...*about*... the train times. It does leave at 16.30.

b) I love science, but I'm not very .... mathematics.

c) Istanbul is .... the beautiful Blue Mosque.

d) Are you .... American movies from the fifties?

e) I'm .... Paul. He should have called me, but he hasn't.

f) Eliza is very .... her dog. She walks it every day.

g) I know it's ridiculous, but I'm quite .... spiders.

4 Rewrite each sentence so that it has a similar meaning and contains the word in **bold**.

a) Dick found his work boring.

bored

Dick was bored with his work.

b) This town is a bit like Glasgow.

reminds

c) Sara has a good knowledge of biology.

knows

d) I'm trying to find the art gallery.

looking

e) I like cream cakes.

fond

f) Sue is Adrian's wife.

to

g) Dina always treats animals kindly.

kind

h) Ugh! This cake has a rubbery taste!

rubber

i) You make Lisa feel jealous!

is

j) Our new house makes me feel excited!

about

5 For each question, complete the second sentence so that it means the same as the first, using no more than three words.

a) You've made me angry.

  I *'m angry with* .... you.

b) I'd like my lunch now.

  I'm .... for lunch.

c) Geography is Richard's best subject.

  Richard is very .... geography.

d) The bad news made me feel upset.

  I .... the bad news.

e) My dog was in my dreams last night!

  I .... my dog last night.

f) Sue is a reliable person.

  You can .... Sue.

g) Jack borrowed my bike for the weekend.

  I lent my .... for the weekend.

h) The dark makes me afraid.

  I'm .... the dark.

6 Complete each sentence with one suitable verb and preposition.

a) We asked our teacher to ...*explain*...... a difficult problem ......*to*...... us.

b) The ring I found .... an old lady in my block of flats.

c) We may come to your party, but it .... our finding a babysitter.

d) When Joe flew to Australia, his aunt .... his ticket.

e) Harry .... to his neighbours .... his bad behaviour.

f) You .... me .... my brother. You're very alike!

g) Tony .... passing his driving test at the first attempt.

h) See you in a minute! I'll .... you outside the cinema.

7 Complete each part sentence (a–g) with one of the endings (1–7).

a) Ellen is not really interested ....4....

b) The hotel was different ....

c) Little Suzie was jealous ....

d) I was really annoyed ....

e) Paul is very keen ....

f) Jane is really good ....

g) I don't think I'm ready ....

1 at making new friends.

2 about losing my new calculator.

3 for another big meal.

4 in learning how to ski.

5 of her new sister at first.

6 from what we expected.

7 on collecting old bottles.

Explanations

Indefinite pronouns

■ Words like *everyone, anything* etc. are called indefinite pronouns. They refer to people, things or places without saying exactly who, what or where they are.

People:	*someone*	*anyone*	*everyone*	*no one*
Things:	*something*	*anything*	*everything*	*nothing*
Places:	*somewhere*	*anywhere*	*everywhere*	*nowhere*
Time:	*sometime*	*anytime*	(all the time)	(never)

■ In the 'People' list we can make a form with *-body* with no change in meaning: *somebody, anybody, everybody, nobody.*

■ Indefinite pronouns are followed by a singular verb, but we refer back to them in a sentence with *they/them/their.*
  Someone is waiting for you. **They** *have been waiting for some time.*
  Someone *phoned, and I told* **them** *you were out.*

someone, anyone etc.

Words with *some-* and *any-* follow the rules given in Grammar 33:

■ *Some* is common in positive sentences and *any* in questions and negatives.
  There's **someone** *at the door.*   **Something** *is worrying me.*
  Does **anyone** *know the answer?*
  There **isn't anybody** *at home.*

■ But we can use *some* in a question if it is an offer or request.
  Can I ask you **something**?

■ And we can use *any* in positive sentences to mean 'it doesn't matter which'.
  We can go **anywhere** *we want during our holidays.*

■ *Some* has the idea of a definite idea, and *any* has the meaning of 'no limit'. Compare:
  Is **someone** *coming to collect you?*   (there must be a particular person)
  Is **anyone** *coming to collect you?*   (anyone at all)
  Have you got **some letters** *for me?*   (There are particular letters I am expecting)
  Have you got **any letters** *for me?*   (I have no idea if you have letters for me or not)

everyone, no one etc.

■ Words with *every-* mean all the people, things or places in a group.
  Everybody likes *Sue.*
  Everything *in the room was red.*

■ *Every one* (two words) has a different meaning. It means *each single one* and is used to give emphasis. In pronunciation, both words have equal stress.
  There were ten chocolates in the box and you've eaten **every one**!

■ *Everything* is used as a single word subject instead of *all*.
  Everything has gone wrong.   (NOT ~~All has gone wrong~~)
  All my plans have gone wrong.

■ Words with *no-* mean no people, things or places.
  No one knows the answer.
  Nobody is at home.
  There is **nothing** to eat.

■ Double negatives are not used.
  No one knows.   (NOT ~~No one doesn't know~~)

Reflexive pronouns: *myself* etc.

■ Reflexive pronouns are used for actions that we do to ourselves.
  I have cut **myself**.   *We enjoyed* **ourselves**.
  Did **you** *cut* **yourself**?   *Have* **you** *hurt* **yourselves**?
  He cut **himself**.   *They introduced* **themselves**.
  She introduced **herself**.

■ Verbs often used in this way include: *cut, enjoy, hurt, introduce, kill*.
  At the end of the play, Cleopatra **kills herself**.
  But other verbs are not normally used with a reflexive pronoun, even though they are in other languages. Examples: *change* (clothes), *complain, decide, dress, feel, meet, relax, remember, rest, sit down, stand up, wake up, wash, worry*.

■ Reflexive pronouns are also used for emphasis.
  Jon cooked all the food **himself**. (no one helped him)

Impersonal *one*

■ In normal conversation we use *you* to refer to 'people in general'.
  As you get older **you** *tend to forget things*.
  You take *the train to the airport from the Central Station*.

  But in formal speech and writing we can use *one* with this meaning. This is considered over-formal by many speakers.
  One takes *the train to the airport from the Central Station*.

■ There is a possessive form *one's*.
  One's luggage *is carried in a special compartment*.

■ If *one* is used as a subject, all later references also use *one*.
  One *takes the train to the airport from the Central Station and* **one** *can reserve* **one's** *seat in advance*.
  If you use *one*, you must continue to use it. Do not mix *one* and *you*.

■ In everyday speech it is more common to use *you* or a passive than to use *one*.
  You *can reserve seats in advance*.
  Seats can be reserved *in advance*.

 SEE ALSO

Grammar 33: Countable and uncountable nouns

Practice

1   <u>Underline</u> the correct word in each sentence.

a) There isn't *anyone/no one* in the garden.

b) Excuse me, could you move? I can't see *anything/something*.

c) There is *anything/nothing* to drink.

d) There's *anyone/someone* to see you outside.

e) You can do *anything/something* you want.

f) *Anyone/Someone* stole the money, but we don't know who.

g) I don't know *anything/nothing* about it.

h) *No one/Someone* would tell me the answer, so I guessed.

i) I've lost my bag and I can't find it *somewhere/anywhere*.

j) I must have put my bag *somewhere/anywhere*, but I don't know where.

2   Complete the second sentence so that it has a similar meaning to the first sentence.

a) There was nothing I could do.
   I couldn't *do anything* .

b) I know Mary better than anyone.
   No one ....

c) No one was on time yesterday.
   Everyone ....

d) I haven't got any work.
   I've got .... to do.

e) There's something I'd like to ask you.
   May I .... ?

f) We're all milk drinkers here!
   Everybody .... milk.

g) When I phoned, there was no reply.
   No one ....

h) Are we going to be driven there?
   Is .... ?

i) I make new friends wherever I go.
   Everywhere ....

j) You had a call this morning.
   Someone ....

3 Complete each sentence so that it includes a suitable form of one of the verbs from the box, and a reflexive pronoun.

> behave   blame   cut   ~~enjoy~~   express   hurt   introduce   talk

a) Have a good holiday, both of you! And ...*enjoy*........ .*yourselves* .

b) Our teacher told us to stop shouting and to ....

c) When I fell off the horse, I didn't ....

d) Beth knows a lot of French, but can't .... easily.

e) Let me .... I'm Susan Perry.

f) The accident wasn't your fault. Don't ....

g) When I .... to .... , other people stare at me!

h) While Tom was picking up the broken glass, he ....

4 Rewrite each sentence so that it has a similar meaning and contains the word in **bold**.

a) The box isn't empty.
something
.....*There's something in the box.*.....

b) All the people were dancing.
everyone
....

c) I feel annoyed.
something
....

d) We haven't got any food.
nothing
....

e) The office is empty.
no one
....

f) Julia is very popular.
everybody
....

g) You can have whatever you like.
anything
....

h) The best place is home.
Nowhere
....

5 Complete each sentence with one suitable word.

a) That's an easy question! *Everybody* knows the answer!

b) Is .... the matter? Can I help you?

c) .... is wrong with the car, and it won't start.

d) There's .... to see you. Shall I ask them to wait?

e) They introduced .... as Helen and Ann.

f) .... never really knows what will happen, does one?

g) .... I've done so far today has gone wrong!

h) .... you could say would make me change my mind, I'm afraid.

i) Did you do it all by ....

j) Yes, I did it by ....

6 <u>Underline</u> the errors in these sentences. Rewrite each sentence.

a) Someone spoke to me, but I can't remember <u>its</u> name.

......*Someone spoke to me, but I can't remember their name.*......

b) All in the garden has been growing a lot lately.

....

c) Carol didn't do nothing yesterday.

....

d) There isn't no one waiting for you.

....

e) Pete and Kate enjoyed themselfs at the party.

....

f) One fills in an application form, and then you wait for an answer.

....

g) We need to do some shopping. There isn't something in the fridge.

....

Possession

Explanations

's (apostrophe s)

- We use apostrophe 's to show that something belongs to a person. We can use the 's form without a following noun if the meaning is clear.

  *This is **Jim's scarf**.*   *This is **Jim's**.*

  *Those are **Helen's gloves**.*   *Those are **Helen's**.*

  *Where is **the director's office**?*

- An apostrophe is sometimes used when something is part of another thing.

  *What is the **book's title**?*

  *What is this **plant's name**?*

- With plural nouns we add the apostrophe only.

  *Those are the **students' coats**.*

- A special use of 's is to refer to someone's home, a shop name or a place name.

  *George bought this melon in the **greengrocer's** / in **Smith's**.*

  *I went to the **doctor's** and the **dentist's** on the same day.*

- If there is no possession, we do not use an apostrophe. Note this common mistake: ~~Apple's sold here~~.

- Note that an apostrophe can also be a short form of *is* or *has*.

  ***It's** a lovely day.*   (*It's* = It is)

  ***It's** got a battery.*   (*It's* = It has)

of and compound nouns

- We use *of* to show that one thing belongs to or with another thing.

  *The end **of the street**.*   (NOT ~~the street's end~~)

  *The last twenty pages **of the book**.*   (NOT ~~the book's last twenty pages~~)

- Compound nouns are formed from two nouns together. The first noun is like an adjective and describes the second noun.

  *I saw the shirt in a **shop window**.*

  *I bought some new **football boots**.*

- Compound nouns are very common in technical descriptions.

  *Loosen the **corner brackets** first.*

- Sometimes a hyphen is used to join the words. Check in a dictionary to see when a hyphen is used.

  *I bought a chocolate **ice-cream**.*

Possessive adjectives

- Possessive adjectives are used before nouns. They are:

  my   your   her   its   his   our   their

- We do not use an article (*the* or *a*) with a possessive adjective.

  *Peter is **my** cousin. He doesn't live in **our** town.*

- We can add *own* to a possessive adjective for emphasis.

  *Paul cooks all **his own** meals.*

  *This isn't **my own** bike. I've borrowed it from a friend.*

Possessive pronouns

- Possessive pronouns are used instead of a possessive adjective and noun. They are:

  mine   yours   hers   his   ours   theirs

- Possessive pronouns stand on their own. They are not used with another noun.

  *This is **my bike**.*   (possessive adjective + noun)

  *This bike is **mine**.*   (possessive pronoun)

- Note that there is no apostrophe in possessive pronouns ending in *s*.

  *Whose keys are these? Are they **yours** or **mine**?*

  ***Yours** are on the table. These are **mine**.*

Double possessive

There are two common situations where we use two possessive forms together. Both are when we describe the relationship between people.

1 *of* and apostrophe

  *Jo is a friend **of my brother's**.*

2 *of* and possessive pronoun

  *I met a cousin **of mine** at the party.*

A common usage of this structure is to describe things owned by people.

  *Do you like this new hat **of mine**?*

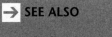

→ SEE ALSO

Vocabulary 6: Compound words

Practice

1   Underline the correct word or phrase in each sentence.

a) Jane met a friend of *her/<u>hers</u>* in the street.

b) Lucy does all *herself/her own* decorating.

c) Are these scissors *your/yours*?

d) The desk next to the window is *my/mine*.

e) Chris and Anna introduced me to a neighbour of *their/theirs*.

f) Excuse me, is this *your/yours* seat?

g) David asks if you've seen that old coat of *his/him*.

h) Pete has borrowed *my/mine* bike.

i) We haven't brought *our/ours* books with us.

j) The dog is black and white, and *its/it's* ears are very long.

2   Put an apostrophe where necessary.

a) Tell Monica its Elenas turn, not hers.
   Tell Monica it's Elena's turn, not hers.

b) Alices younger brothers called Bill.

   ....

c) Tims sandwiches were tastier than ours.

   ....

d) The films beginning is good but its ending is weak.

   ....

e) Are these keys yours or hers?

   ....

f) Barbara fills in the patients record cards at the doctors.

   ....

g) When its raining, everybodys raincoats get wet.

   ....

h) The managers assistant reads all the customers letters.

   ....

i) Your sisters dog runs faster than ours.

   ....

j) Ones our teachers car and the others a visitors.

   ....

3   **Make two compound words from the words listed.**

a) football   cheese   boot   sandwich

  ...*football boot*...   *cheese sandwich*...

b) window   pocket   coat   shop

  ....

c) gate   garden   light   bicycle

  ....

d) department   cottage   store   country

  ....

e) engine   singer   rock   fire

  ....

f) post   sharpener   office   pencil

  ....

g) ground   report   school   football

  ....

h) assistant   shop   station   railway

  ....

4   **For each question, complete the second sentence so that it means the same as the first, using no more than three words.**

a) Naomi is a friend of my sister's.

  Naomi is ...*my sister's*........................ friend.

b) These shoes belong to Sam.

  These .... shoes.

c) I met one of my friends outside the school.

  I met a .... outside the school.

d) This is my favourite programme on television.

  This is .... programme.

e) What are your teachers called?

  What .... names?

f) Have you got a thing for opening tins?

  Have you got .... ?

g) Those bikes belong to our neighbours.

  Those .... bikes.

h) I put my books on the table in the kitchen.

  I put my books .... table.

5 <u>Underline</u> the errors in these sentences. Rewrite each sentence.

a) There are two <u>bus stop's</u> near my house.

......*There are two bus stops near my house.*..........................

b) Our cat sleep's all day in it's bed.

....

c) Have you met the sister of Jane?

....

d) Creature's like these live at the sea's bottom.

....

e) This book is the mine.

....

f) Those are two friends' of my fathers.

....

g) Everybodys drawing's were better than our's.

....

h) Are these your's or mine glove's?

....

i) The house stand's on it's own at the street's end.

....

j) I noticed these shoe's in a window's shop.

....

Linking words

Explanations

This unit includes words and phrases used to organize ideas in speaking and writing. Notice the position of the words in the example sentences. Sometimes a word comes in the middle of a sentence to join two clauses, such as *and*. Other times the word or phrase comes at the beginning of a sentence and is followed by a comma in writing or a pause in speech, such as *First of all, ...*

and, both, too,
as well, also

- *And* is used to join words or parts of sentences. To emphasize the fact that there are two things we can use *both ... and*.
    *Helen put on her coat **and** picked up the suitcase.*
    *Helen picked up **both** her suitcase **and** her umbrella.*

- *Too, as well, as well as* and *also* are used to describe two actions at the same time. Note the positions.
    *Helen picked up her suitcase **and** her umbrella **too**.*
    *Helen picked up her suitcase **and** her umbrella **as well**.*
    *Helen picked up her suitcase **as well as** her umbrella.*
    *Helen picked up her suitcase, her coat **and also** her umbrella.*

For example,
such as

- Note the possible positions of *For example*.
    *Diet varies from place to place. **For example**, in hot countries, people tend to eat more fruit.*
    *In hot countries, **for example**, people tend to eat more fruit.*

- We use *such as* in the middle of a sentence to give examples. It is the same as *like. Such as* cannot be used at the beginning of a sentence.
    *In hot countries, **such as** Greece, people tend to eat more fruit.*

First (of all),
secondly etc.,
finally

- We can use *First (of all)* to begin a list of points in formal speech and writing. For other points we use *Secondly* etc.
    *Television has changed our lives in several ways. **First of all**, it has ... .*
    ***Secondly**, more people ... . **Finally**, it has changed the way that ... .*

- To introduce our final point in formal speech and writing we can say *In conclusion*.
    ***In conclusion**, we can say that television has both good and bad features.*

As well as this,
besides this

These are used in formal speech and writing to show that we are adding a point. The meaning is 'and' but the phrases comes at the beginning of a sentence.
    Television has changed our lives in several ways. First of all, it has ... .
    *Secondly, more people ... . **As well as this/Besides this**, more people ... .*

In fact, actually	*In fact* and *actually* are used to give more detail, or to give surprising information.

> *Dave has several dogs.* **In fact**, *he's got four.*   (more detail)
> *I thought Gina was a doctor but,* **in fact**, *she's a vet.*   (surprise)
> *I thought Gina was a doctor but,* **actually**, *she's a vet.*   (surprise)

In my view, personally	These are used in formal speech and writing to introduce our own ideas.

> *Some people believe that television has killed the art of conversation.* **In my view/Personally**, *I think it gives people something to talk about.*

either, or	■ *Either ... or* is used to describe a choice or an alternative.

> *We can* **either** *go to the cinema,* **or** *stay at home.*
> **Either** *we can go to the cinema,* **or** *we can stay at home.*
> (NOT ~~Or we can go~~ ...)

Note that the structure *Or... or...* does not exist in English. It is possible to begin a sentence with *Or* only when we complete someone else's sentence.

> A: *'We could go to the cinema I suppose ...'*
> B: *'...* **or** *we could stay at home and watch a video.'*

Instead (of)	■ We use *instead (of)* to mean 'in the place of something else'.

> **Instead of** *cooking I ordered a take-away meal.*
> *Jill came to the party* **instead of** *her sister.*

■ At the end of a sentence, *instead* is used without *of*.

> *I didn't cook. I ordered a take-away meal* **instead**.

except	*Except* and *except for* mean 'not including'.

> *They gave presents to everyone* **except** *me.*
> *We have painted all the house,* **except (for)** *the front door.*

even	■ We use *even* to say that something is surprising.

> *Sam studies very hard. He* **even** *gets up at 5.30 to study!*
> **Even** *Sam found the exam difficult.*

■ *Even* is also used to emphasize comparative adjectives.

> *This question is* **even harder than** *the last one.*

Time words with other meanings	The time words *since, yet* and *while* have a completely different meaning and use as linking words. With this use they are more common in writing.

> | *since* meaning 'as' | *I couldn't swim,* **since** *I had a cold.* |
> |---|---|
> | *yet* meaning 'although' | *No one replied to my knock,* **yet** *all the lights were on.* |
> | *while* meaning 'although' | *The first two buses were full,* **while** *the next was completely empty.* |

Practice

1 <u>Underline</u> the correct word or phrase in each sentence.

a) Mrs Davis taught us *except for/<u>instead of</u>* Mr Taylor.

b) We can *either/or* wait here, or phone for a taxi.

c) Helen plays the guitar and *also/too* writes songs.

d) In Scandinavian countries, *for example/such as* Finland, they have very cold winters.

e) Everyone in the team played badly *also/except* Sam.

f) All the shops were closed, *since/yet* it was a public holiday.

g) Jack studies *and/both* geography and history.

h) The Peakworth tent is strong and waterproof, *since/yet* light to carry.

2 Rewrite each sentence so that it has a similar meaning and contains the word in **bold**.

a) Debra visited both the castle and the museum.

too

Debra visited the castle and the museum, too.

b) Jill was the only person who came late.

except

....

c) Although I said it was raining, it isn't!

fact

....

d) Karen hurt her leg, so she couldn't play tennis.

since

....

e) My opinion is that smoking is bad for you.

view

....

f) I ate the chocolate cake and the apple pie.

as well as

....

g) Daniel played in goal, in his brother's place.

instead

....

h) Finally, I'd like to thank the head teacher, Ann Coles.

in

....

3 Decide which answer (A, B, C or D) best fits each space.

Nowadays there are many good reasons for using bicycles (1) ....*C*.... cars to travel in city centres. (2) .... , bicycles are (3) .... silent and clean, (4) .... are easy to park. (5) .... , using a bicycle (6) .... keeps people fit. However, city centres must (7) .... have cycle lanes (8) .... be free of private cars completely. Some large cities, (9) .... Amsterdam in the Netherlands, are already organized in this way. (10) .... , a combination of the use of bicycles with very cheap or free public transport solves the problem of traffic jams and makes the city centre a more pleasant place.

1) **A** but   **B** except for   **C** instead of   **D** such as
2) **A** As well   **B** First of all   **C** In fact   **D** Personally
3) **A** both   **B** and   **C** too   **D** as well
4) **A** also   **B** for example they **C** except   **D** and as well as this
5) **A** And   **B** Yet   **C** While   **D** Secondly
6) **A** and   **B** both   **C** also   **D** too
7) **A** in conclusion **B** either   **C** besides this   **D** both
8) **A** such as   **B** yet   **C** also   **D** or
9) **A** such as   **B** as well   **C** in my view   **D** while
10) **A** personally   **B** finally   **C** for example   **D** actually

4 Complete each sentence with a word or phrase from the box. Use each word or phrase once only.

| actually | as well as this | both | either |
| ~~except~~ | instead | personally | such as |

a) Everyone ......*except*.................. Julia remembered to bring their dictionaries.

b) We've repaired the roof, and .... we've repainted the whole house.

c) .... , I don't think that there are aliens or flying saucers.

d) I managed to lose .... my passport and my wallet.

e) I was going to go to the cinema, but I went to the theatre ....

f) People think that Tim is shy, but .... he's very talkative.

g) Some illnesses, ... the common cold, do not have a cure.

h) We're going to .... go camping, or stay with some friends.

5 Complete the spaces (a–j) with the words (1–10).

(a) ....5...... I'd like to thank everyone who has helped with the school play.
(b) .... the actors, and the stage hands, have worked very hard, and
everyone who made the costumes worked hard (c) .... I would (d) ....
like to thank all those who have sold tickets. This year we had an (e) ....
larger audience than last year, and (f) .... Tuesday evening, every single seat
was sold. This year the play ran for a week (g) .... for two days. We did not
have a lot of time for rehearsals, and (h) .... the play was a great success.
(i) .... , I feel that we should congratulate all the actors for their wonderful
performance. (j) .... , I'd like to give Judy Walker, the director, this present
from everyone at the school.

1 even
2 yet
3 as well
4 except for
5 first of all
6 in conclusion
7 also
8 personally
9 both
10 instead of

Capital letters and punctuation

Explanations

Capital letters

■ Capital letters (also called upper-case letters) are used:

to begin a sentence	*This is a beautiful place.*
for names of people	*Jim, Helen*
for addressing people	*Mrs Jones, Uncle Peter, Mum*
for personal pronoun *I*	*I saw Ellen last night.*
for titles of books etc.	*'War and Peace' is a great book.*
for names of places	*France, Hungary*
for calendar information	*Wednesday, March, New Year's Day*

■ In book and film titles, small words like *and*, *a/the* and prepositions do not usually have capitals, unless they are at the beginning.
   'Four Weddings and a Funeral' is a funny film.

■ Some words can be written with capitals, or in lower-case. These are:

names of the seasons	*in Spring, in spring*	
decades	*the Fifties, the fifties*	
jobs	*Sanderson was a good president.*	(general use)
	Paul met President Brunswick.	(job title)
compass points	*I live in the north of Scotland.*	(description)
	Sally works in the Far East.	(place name)

Full stop (.)

■ Full stops are used at the end of a sentence. They are also used in abbreviations to show that letters in a word are missing.
   e.g.   etc.
Full stops are often left out after the abbreviations Mr and Mrs.

Comma (,)

■ A comma in writing represents a brief pause in speech. It is also used in lists, except for the last two items where we use *and*.
   I bought some bananas, some oranges and some potatoes.
If the last two items of the list are long then we do use a comma.
   All day we cleaned the floors, washed the walls, and tidied the house.

■ Linking words at the beginning of a sentence are followed by commas.
   First of all, this can be dangerous.
Linking words in the middle of a sentence have commas before and after.
   Ann, on the other hand, did not agree.

■ Commas are used with non-defining relative clauses.
   Tony, who is usually late, turned up at 10.30.

■ Commas are used in direct speech.
   Jim said, 'I'll be late.'

But they are not used after reporting verbs in reported speech.
Jim said he would be late.

■ Commas cannot be used to join sentences directly, without any other changes. Look at this example.
Two men were walking down the street. They were carrying a box.
These two sentences cannot be joined simply by changing the full stop to a comma.
~~Two men were walking down the street, they were carrying a box~~.
But there are other ways to combine the sentences. For example:
Two men were walking down the street, carrying a box.
Two men carrying a box were walking down the street.

Semi-colon (;)

■ We can join two sentences with related meanings using a semi-colon.
Road users annoy pedestrians; pedestrians annoy road users.
A semi-colon is also used to separate long items in a list.
Students are asked not to leave bicycles by the entrance; not to leave bags in the sitting room; and not to leave coats in the dining room.

Colon (:)

■ A colon introduces items in a list.
There are two rules: one, don't do it; two, don't get caught.
It can also introduce an explanation of the previous part of the sentence.
Finally, we had to stop: we were tired and it was dark.

Speech marks (' ')
(" ")

■ Speech marks (also called quotation marks) are used with direct speech. Punctuation goes inside. They can be single or double.
'It might rain later,' I explained.
"Why are we leaving so early?" Helen asked.

■ Titles of books, films, plays etc. are put inside single quotation marks. Punctuation is put outside in this case.
We went to a performance of Ibsen's 'Ghosts'.
However, in printed text, the titles of books, films, plays etc. are usually put in italics.

Question mark (?)
and exclamation
mark (!)

■ Question marks only occur after the question.
What's the time?

■ Exclamation marks are used in informal writing, but are not considered appropriate in formal writing.
You'll never guess what! I've just got engaged!

 SEE ALSO

Grammar 25: Relative clauses
Grammar 47: Linking words

Practice

1 <u>Underline</u> the sentence which is punctuated correctly.

a) 1 <u>'Would you mind telling me where we are?' Petra asked.</u>
   2 'Would you mind telling me, where we are Petra asked?'
   3 'Would you mind telling me, where we are,' Petra asked?

b) 1 I agreed, that a cottage in the mountains, would be better.
   2 I agreed that a cottage in the mountains would be better.
   3 I agreed that a cottage, in the mountains would be better.

c) 1 Angela who arrived after I did, asked me when the play finished?
   2 Angela, who arrived after I did, asked me when the play finished.
   3 Angela, who arrived after I did asked me, when the play finished.

d) 1 Peter told me, not to wait and said 'I'll see you later.'
   2 Peter told me not to wait and said, 'I'll see you later.'
   3 Peter told me not to wait and said I'll see you later.

e) 1 In the end I went home, I was wet and hungry, and felt ill.
   2 In the end I went home; I was wet and hungry; and felt ill.
   3 In the end I went home: I was wet and hungry and felt ill.

f) 1 I bought some flour, some eggs, two lemons and some sugar.
   2 I bought some: flour, some: eggs, two: lemons and some sugar.
   3 I bought some flour some eggs two lemons, and some sugar.

2 Rewrite each sentence putting in any necessary capital letters.

a) we're meeting uncle david on tuesday evening at eight.
We're meeting Uncle David on Tuesday evening at eight.

b) last february i met mrs wilkinson for the first time.

c) tim lives in the south of france near cannes.

d) we saw a great film at the abc called 'the remains of the day'.

e) we went to a party at mrs harrisons' house on new year's eve.

f) julia's reading 'a portrait of a lady' by henry james.

3   **Rewrite each group of words so that it contains the punctuation listed.**

a) First of all who is going to carry the suitcase asked Emilie
   (one full stop, one comma, one question mark, speech marks)
   'First of all, who is going to carry the suitcase?' asked Emilie.

b) Kate said she'd be on time but I didn't believe her
   (one full stop, one comma)

   ....

   ....

c) James said that he'd missed the train got lost and been arrested
   (one full stop, two commas)

   ....

   ....

d) When the bell rang our teacher stood up and said Stop writing please
   (one full stop, three commas, speech marks)

   ....

   ....

e) On the other hand we could go to the cinema couldn't we said David
   (one full stop, two commas, one question mark, speech marks)

   ....

   ....

f) Good morning Alan said Tina how do you feel today
   (one full stop, one comma, one question mark, speech marks, one capital
   letter)

   ....

   ....

g) If I were you I'd ask for some help or perhaps start again
   (one full stop, two commas)

   ....

   ....

h) The old stadium was eventually demolished very few people went there and
   it was becoming dangerous
   (one full stop, one comma, one colon)

   ....

   ....

Spelling and pronunciation 1

Explanations

Adding -ing to verbs

- One-syllable words which end in one vowel and one consonant double the last consonant.

    *swim/**swimming***   *put/**putting***

    Compare these words which do not double the consonant:

    shoot/shooting   *lift/lifting*

- Two-syllable words which end in one vowel and one consonant double the last consonant when the stress is on the second syllable.

    *begin/**beginning***   *control/**controlling***

    Compare these words with the stress on the first syllable.

    *wonder/**wondering***   *threaten/**threatening***

    One exception to this rule in British English is *travel/travelling*.

- Words which end in one vowel, one consonant and -*e* drop the final -*e*.

    *write/**writing***   *leave/**leaving***

Words ending in -ful

The suffix -*ful* has only one *l*.

     beautiful   *successful*

When -*ly* is added to make an adverb, the *l* becomes double.

     *beautifu**lly***   *successfu**lly***

-ie or -ei?

There is a useful rule: *i* before *e* except after *c*.

     field   *niece*

     but   ***receive***

But note that this rule only works when the sound is 'ee' /iː/. For example in this word the sound is different and *e* comes before *i*:

     reign

Silent letters

- Many words contain letters which do not form a sound. These are sometimes referred to as 'silent letters'. The silent letters are underlined.

bt/mb	*dou__b__t plum__b__er thum__b__*
kn	*__k__nee __k__nife __k__now*
ps	*__p__sychology __p__sychiatrist*
sc	*des__c__end as__c__end*

- *q* and *u*

    The letter *q* is always followed by *u*.

    ***q**uestion*   *s**q**uid*   *ac**q**uire*

Practice

Words commonly spelled wrongly are also included here.

1 **Correct the spelling where necessary.**

a) decideing ......*deciding*.............. g) thier ....

b) swiming .... h) beatiful ....

c) foto .... i) reciept ....

d) qestion .... j) begining ....

e) whistle .... k) phychiatrist ....

f) knowen .... l) sucesfull ....

2 **Use the letters in brackets to make a word which fits the space.**

a) Sue said she'd (nehop) .....*phone*.................. me but I haven't
(iredvece) ...*received*.................. a call yet.

b) When the referee blew the (stewlih) .... the players left
the (edlif) ....

c) Ellen (feclyslusucs) .... completed the course in nuclear
(shipscy) ....

d) I didn't (wonk) .... how to cut the string without a
(inkef) ....

e) The police arrested the (itfeh) .... as he was
(negvial) .... the bank.

f) Jim asked a (siqontue) .... , but his teacher wasn't
(nilsigent) ....

g) At the (nigengibn) .... of the film, I had a poor
(wive) .... of the screen.

h) These ancient (mulcosn) .... are
(yitbuelfual) .... made.

3 **Write each verb with an -*ing* ending.**

a) control ...*controlling*........... g) upset ....

b) thicken .... h) hook ....

c) grip .... i) write ....

d) choose .... j) improve ....

e) fly .... k) swim ....

f) make .... l) ride ....

4 Correct the spelling in this letter.

Dear Becky,

I'm sory that I haven't writen to you for so long. I'm afriad I've been very bussy at shool, and I haven't had much time for writeing leters. Last week I finised my examenations, so now I'm geting redy to go on holyday.

I was wundering wether you wood like to come to stay for a fiew days? You cann meat my freinds, and we coud all go swimeing. The wheather is realy good now hear in Italy, and I'm shure you will engoy yourshelf.

Best wishes,

Silvia

5 Correct these words commonly spelled wrongly.

a) tommorow ...*tomorrow*....................

b) Wensday ....

c) advertisment ....

d) neihbour ....

e) thrugh ....

f) greatfull ....

g) neccessarry ....

h) dissappointed ....

i) wheather ....

j) rember ....

k) libary ....

l) anser ....

6 <u>Underline</u> the silent letter/s in these words.

a) de<u>b</u>t
b) exhibition
c) high
d) knife
e) lamb
f) psychologist
g) receipt
h) what
i) yacht

j) autumn
k) answer
l) daughter
m) half
n) light
o) salmon
p) whole
q) would
r) writing

Explanations

Same sound, different spelling

In English one particular sound can be spelt using different letters. In each group below the sound underlined is the same.

Vowels

c*o*mpany br*o*ther l*o*ve tr*ou*ble r*u*bbish bl*oo*d

r*oa*d m*o*st h*o*me th*ou*gh l*o*w

*ea*rth f*u*rther w*o*rd h*u*rt

w*ai*t gr*ea*t l*a*te w*ei*ght

n*o*w sh*ou*t dr*ow*n pl*ou*gh

Consonants

rela*ti*on *sh*ock *s*ure con*sci*ous deli*ci*ous

*ch*urch furni*t*ure wa*tch*

lei*s*ure mea*s*ure confu*si*on

Same pronunciation, different spelling and meaning

Different words can have exactly the same pronunciation. Common examples are:

court/caught	*stair/stare*	*sore/saw*	*allowed/aloud*
lesson/lessen	*find/fined*	*waste/waist*	*fare/fair*
warn/worn	*wait/weight*	*no/know*	*two/too*

Words which look similar

Some words may have only a letter or two difference to other words, but they have a completely different meaning. Be especially careful with these commonly confused words:

later/latter	*quiet/quite*
recent/resent	*accept/except*
through/thorough	*formerly/formally*
insure/ensure	*lose/loose*

Words with a syllable which is not pronounced

Some words are particularly difficult to spell because they seem to have a syllable which is not pronounced. The examples below show how many syllables are actually pronounced in speech:

temperature (3 syllables)	*library* (3 syllables)
Wednesday (2 syllables)	*vegetable* (3 syllables)
people (2 syllables)	*interesting* (3 syllables)

Nouns and verbs with c and s

Noun	*advice*	*practice*
Verb	*advise*	*practise*

How to improve spelling

- Use a dictionary to check the pronunciation of new words.
- Relate the spelling of new words to words you already know.
- Make lists of the words you usually spell wrongly. Test yourself or ask friends to test you.
- Read widely to give you experience of the way words are spelled.

Practice

Words commonly spelled wrongly are also included here.

1 **Find pairs of words with the same sound <u>underlined</u>.**

a)	dirt	1	c<u>o</u>mpany
b)	pl<u>u</u>m	2	mea<u>s</u>ure
c)	h<u>ea</u>rt	3	furni<u>t</u>ure
d)	ca<u>tch</u>	4	w<u>or</u>d
e)	ph<u>o</u>ne	5	r<u>u</u>le
f)	<u>s</u>ure	6	br<u>ow</u>n
g)	d<u>ou</u>bt	7	t<u>oa</u>st
h)	f<u>oo</u>d	8	confu<u>si</u>on
i)	cau<u>t</u>ion	9	p<u>a</u>rk

2 **<u>Underline</u> the correct word in each sentence.**

a) Please stop looking at me like that! It's very rude to *stair/<u>stare</u>*.

b) I think you should *practice/practise* diving every day.

c) The doctor gave Martin a *through/thorough* examination.

d) Could you give me some *advice/advise* about language courses?

e) We wanted to go by train, but we couldn't afford the *fair/fare*.

f) Could you wait a moment? I'm not *quiet/quite* ready.

g) Reading *allowed/aloud* is hard unless you have time to check first.

h) Sorry I didn't come to your party, but I just felt *two/too* tired.

i) You can have model J6 or model J8, but the *later/latter* is more expensive.

j) The back of the chair is nearly falling off – it's really *lose/loose*.

3 **Tick (✓) if a pair of words rhymes.**

a)	sweet/eat	..✓..	i)	chose/bruise	......
b)	worse/horse	......	j)	low/go	......
c)	worn/torn	......	k)	abroad/afford	......
d)	lose/loose	......	l)	quite/diet	......
e)	tea/bee	......	m)	friend/leaned	......
f)	thought/short	....	n)	blood/food	......
g)	later/latter	......	o)	weight/height	......
h)	word/heard	......			

4   **Correct the spelling in this letter.**

Dear Silvia,

Thanks for your leter and your invittation to Italy! I've never traveled abraod before, and I'm realy looking forwerd to staying with you and your familly. I've spokken to my parrents and they've aggreed. They say they're going to phone soon to discus the arangements.

I've dicided to have some Italian lesons so that I can practice when I come to Italy. I'd like you to write some simple sentences for me. Please note my new adress. We moved last weak and now I've got a much biger bedroom.

best wishes,

Becky

5   **Correct these words commonly spelled wrongly.**

a) vegtable   ...*vegetable*...

b) langage   ....

c) qeueu   ....

d) recieve   ....

e) peple   ....

f) beatiful   ....

g) intresting   ....

h) biscit   ....

i) cieling   ....

j) difrent   ....

k) knowlige   ....

l) indipendant   ....

6   **There is another word with exactly the same pronunciation as the word given. Write it in the space.**

a) ate   ...*eight*...   h) nun   ....

b) been   ....   i) peace ....

c) Czeck   ....   j) pear   ....

d) flour   ....   k) right ....

e) hole   ....   l) rose   ....

f) mussel ....   m) sew   ....

g) no   ....   n) stare ....

1 <u>Underline</u> the correct word or phrase in each sentence.

a) Paula keeps talking about that new bike of *hers/her/her's*.

b) I asked my teacher for help, but she refused *to help/helping* me.

c) David isn't interested *at/for/in* collecting stamps.

d) Sue couldn't swim *although/as* she had a bad cold.

e) It's really dark. I can't see *anything/something/nothing*.

f) I really enjoy *to spend/spending* time with you!

g) Ann is not very good *at/by/for* French.

h) Helen hasn't told me *anything/nothing* about the trip.

2 Decide which answer (A, B, C or D) best fits each space.

An unfortunate misunderstanding

Last year we (1) ....B.... to have an expensive holiday, so we (2) .... to visit some friends, Brian and Ann, who (3) .... to live by the sea. They (4) .... to put us up for two weeks, and as we always (5) .... seeing them, it (6) .... to be a good idea. They asked us if we (7) .... sleeping on the sofa, and said that they would (8) .... to make us comfortable. We (9) .... to get there by bus, and when we arrived we could (10) .... Brian and Ann sitting in the garden. They (11) .... to be glad to see us, but it was obvious that they hadn't (12) .... to see us. They said that we had (13) .... to tell them when we were arriving, and they (14) .... asking us how long we were going to stay. We (15) .... feeling embarrassed, so the next day we went home.

1) A continued	B couldn't afford	C liked	D promised
2) A fancied	B tried	C wished	D decided
3) A meant	B kept	C hoped	D happened
4) A offered	B admitted	C enjoyed	D intended
5) A denied	B imagined	C enjoyed	D preferred
6) A began	B seemed	C imagined	D expected
7) A minded	B suggested	C wanted	D remembered
8) A practise	B mean	C learn	D try
9) A suggested	B tried	C managed	D started
10) A watch	B see	C keep	D wait
11) A intended	B pretended	C expected	D suggested
12) A preferred	B forgotten	C promised	D expected
13) A forgotten	B denied	C seemed	D chosen
14) A loved	B wanted	C kept	D couldn't stand
15) A imagined	B minded	C couldn't help	D seemed

3 **For each question, complete the second sentence so that it means the same as the first, using no more than three words.**

a) Jeff was the only student who forgot the test.

Everyone remembered the test ....*except Jeff*.................. .

b) Roberta knows this town better than anyone.

No .... this town better than Roberta.

c) These two pairs of gloves belong to the twins.

These are .... gloves.

d) Andy wouldn't carry my bag.

Andy .... my bag.

e) Peter is reliable.

You can .... Peter.

f) Serena is one of my brother's friends.

Serena is .... my brother's.

g) The snow began yesterday evening.

It .... yesterday evening.

h) Do you think you could close the window?

Would you mind .... the window?

4 **Look carefully at each line. Some lines are correct but some have a word which should not be there. Tick (✓) each correct line. If a line has a word which should not be there, write the word in the space.**

Winning a million

Life changed completely for Carol Miles when she won	1 ....✓......
£1,000,000 in the lottery. 'I decided that to buy a ticket	2 ....*that*......
while I was waiting for take the bus. I didn't get excited	3 ....
about it, because I didn't expect me to win. In fact, I	4 ....
completely forgot it to check my numbers, until a	5 ....
friend reminded for me to do it. You can imagine how	6 ....
surprised I was!' Carol had often been dreamed about	7 ....
being rich, but she has got discovered that having lots	8 ....
of money doesn't always mean being happy. 'I can't	9 ....
enjoy for anything now. When I go out with my friends,	10 ....
for example, they either expect me to pay or the bills,	11 ....
or they're angry with me when I offer to pay it. Some	12 ....
people they are jealous of my good luck, I think, and	13 ....
accuse me of thinking only about money. Nobody seems	14 ....
to have understand. I thought I would enjoy myself, but	15 ....
everyone has started to treat me with differently, except for	16 ....
one friend of mine who has asked me to lend it him £10,000!'	17 ....

5 Complete each sentence with one suitable word.

An afternoon at the bus station

Hannah had been waiting (a) ...*for*............ a colleague of (b) ....
father's to collect her from the bus station for more than an hour, and she was
tired (c) .... waiting. There was (d) .... else there, and it had
(e) .... raining. A friend of (f) .... had lent her an umbrella
to take on her trip, but she (g) .... to be getting wet. Perhaps her
father was angry (h) .... her, she thought, or had simply
(i) .... to collect her. Her mobile phone wasn't working and there
wasn't (j) .... a phone-box in the bus station. Why did
(k) .... always go wrong when she travelled by bus? (l) ....
the bus was crowded and she felt very uncomfortable, or it (m) ....
stopping and the journey lasted for hours. Suddenly she (n) .... a car
stopping outside. (o) .... was waving at her. It was her father!

6 Rewrite this letter, correcting the spelling and adding any necessary capital
letters and punctuation.

17 Harford Street,
Bilsworth,
BK3 4JG
Tel: 08143 6783

dear david

   it was grate too here from you after so long i enjoied hearing all youre knews
i didn't reallize that you'd spent a year abbroad you must have had a realy good
time in greece ive dicided to go their next sumer praps we coud go twogether

   ive had a fantastick year at colidge the work is harder than the work we did at
scool but its more intresting im studing bussiness administration and computer
sience at the momment ive also maid lots of new freinds

   im thinkeing of comming to bristol for a few days to vissit my sister woud
you like to meat you coud show me the sites and we coud talk abowt our old
scooldays

   why dont you give me a ring and we coud discus it it woud be wunderfull to
see you agane
best wishes
ellen

7 Put one suitable word in each space.

a) ...*Instead*... ...*of*............... going out to lunch, we stayed at home.

b) There were a dozen oranges in the bowl but you've eaten ....
.... one.

c) I thought it was Wednesday today, but .... it's
Tuesday!

d) .... , I would like to thank everyone who has given
help.

e) Ted is a friend .... brother's, but isn't a friend of
....

f) Joe bought two shirts and a jacket ....

g) I really like this new coat of .... Where did you buy it?

h) Kate fell over and cut .... on a piece of broken glass.

i) I suppose it depends .... whether you believe .... UFOs
or not.

j) The test was so hard that .... our teacher didn't know the answers.

Problem check

1 What is the difference between these pairs of sentences? Check with Grammar 43
if you are not sure.
a) I tried to take an aspirin.
I tried taking an aspirin.
b) I remember to do my homework.
I remember doing my homework.
c) The boys stopped having a rest.
The boys stopped to have a rest.

2 The same verb or adjectives can be followed by different prepositions. Check
these meanings in a dictionary:
a) You remind me of my brother.
Can you remind me about the test?
b) We're pleased with him.
We're pleased for him.
We're pleased by him.

3 Only use *one* in formal speech and writing. Don't mix *one* and *you*.

4 Remember that using an apostrophe can mean that a letter is missing (*it's = it is*)
or it can show possession (*Ann's hat*).

5 The best way to improve your punctuation and spelling is through wide reading.
Make lists of words you often spell wrongly.

VOCABULARY
1
Dealing with vocabulary

When you find a new word

If you are reading and you find a word you do not know, do not immediately use a dictionary. Ask yourself:

- Is this an important, useful word?
- Do I need to know the exact meaning?

If the word seems important, and you have time, then of course use a dictionary and add the word to your vocabulary notebook.

If the word seems unimportant, or you are reading just for pleasure, or you don't have time, then you can:

- leave it and come back later
- try to guess the meaning of the word from the context
- compare the new word with other words that look similar, then guess
- ask someone

Making the most of your dictionary

Choose a dictionary which has all the information you need. To use a dictionary effectively you need to know:

- how to find words in alphabetical order
- what the abbreviations in each entry mean
- how to look for words if you don't find them at first (e.g. look further down in the same entry to find other words in the family or the collocation you are looking for)
- when to carry it with you
- when to use it and when not to use it (you might get bored if you use it too much)

Keeping a vocabulary notebook

Many people, when they find a new word, just write the translation at the side of the page and do nothing more. But this is not the best way to learn a word: first it is hard to remember words in isolation, and second you need extra information about how the word is used, not just its basic meaning. So it is a good idea to keep a vocabulary notebook where you can review and revise new words. For each word in the book you might want to include:

Definition
Grammatical class (e.g. noun)
Pronunciation
Translation
Collocation (words which combine with the main word)
An example sentence that shows how the word is used
Frequency (many dictionaries have a system to show how common it is)
Formal or informal

If you put the words in a notebook it will be easier to remember them. But if you organize the words inside the book then it is even better. Here are some ideas:

- Record words in alphabetical sections.
- Make sections for different large topic areas like 'Families and Friends', 'Hobbies and Interests', 'Places'.
- Make a 'Lexical set'. This is a small group of words based on one specific topic.

  Garden

  lawn   hedge   shed   flowerbed

You can write this as a word spider:

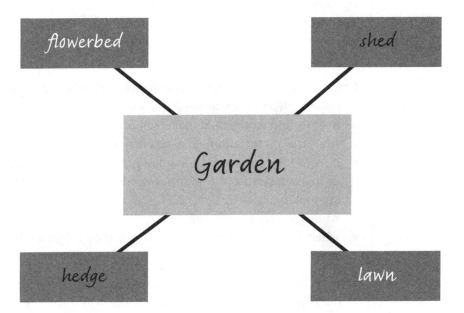

- Make a 'Word family'. This is a group based on word formation.

beauty	noun
beautiful	adjective
beautify	verb

- Make sections for idioms and special expressions.
- Make sections for words that are useful to you personally, or that interest you, or that cause you problems.

Word formation 1

Words can be formed by adding a prefix to the beginning or a suffix to the end.
There are many prefixes and suffixes are included in this unit and in Vocabulary 3.
Examples of prefixes: *un-, dis-, im-, mis-*

> *un-* + *certain* **uncertain**   *dis-* + *appear* **disappear**
>
> *im-* + *possible* **impossible**   *mis* + *understand* **misunderstand**

Examples of suffixes: *-ness, -ful, -less, ship*

> *happy* + *-ness* **happiness**   *care* + *-ful* **careful**
>
> *end* + *-less* **endless**   *friend* + *-ship* **friendship**

Words of two or more syllables ending in *-y* change *-y* to *-i*. See Grammar 49.

1   **Add a word from the box to the prefix in each sentence to make a negative word.**

advantage	agree	appear	employed	fortunately
~~interesting~~	patient	understanding		

a) I didn't read all of the book because I found it un.*interesting* .

b) Cycling has one dis......................... . It makes you feel hot and sweaty.

c) Sue had a ticket for the theatre, but un......................... she fell ill that night.

d) Terry can't stand waiting in queues, because she's very im......................... .

e) My brothers always dis......................... when it's time to do the washing-up.

f) After Jack lost his job, he was un......................... for three months.

g) Oh, I completely dis......................... with you. I think it was a great film.

h) Because of a mis......................... , half the class went to the wrong classroom.

2   **Complete the word in each sentence with a prefix from the box.**

out-	over-	under-	re-

a) My alarm clock didn't go off, and so I ...*over*..... slept this morning.

b) Pete packed some shirts and socks, some .... wear, and his jeans.

c) It's very cold this morning, so wear your .... coat.

d) Our team was completely .... played by the team from Wales.

e) I've decided to .... write my letter, because I made too many mistakes.

f) Steve .... cooked the meat, and it was burnt in places.

g) I have to go to the library today and .... new my ticket.

h) The staff went on strike because they were .... paid and overworked.

3 Complete the word in each sentence with a suffix from the box. Make any other necessary changes to the word.

-er	-let	-ess	-hood	-ship	-ful	-ery

a) After two years of friend....*ship*.... , Kate got to know David really well.

b) If you don't speak the language you feel more like a foreign................ .

c) Sarah spent a very happy child............... on a small island.

d) I asked a steward............... what time the plane arrived, but she didn't know.

e) Every teenage............... knows that parents worry a lot.

f) Don't forget to add a spoon............... of sugar, and some milk.

g) We live in a beautiful neighbour............... on the outskirts of the city.

h) Tina picked up a hand............... of snow, and threw it in my face.

i) Under the floor there was a rumbling sound of machine............... .

j) The college sent Sue a small book............... describing its courses.

4 Complete each sentence with a noun made from the verb given.

a) There are over one million ...*inhabitants*......... in this city.
   inhabit

b) Greg often suffers from .... in the school holidays.
   bore

c) This is the tallest .... in the whole of the country.
   build

d) Some students can't find suitable ....
   accommodate

e) I was upset by Carol's .... to help me.
   refuse

f) It took Richard years to become a successful ....
   act

g) Every .... in this company has received a pay rise.
   employ

h) You need a lot of .... to write a good story.
   imagine

i) Don't forget to turn off the .... before you leave.
   cook

j) I saw an interesting .... in the local paper.
   advertise

5 Complete each sentence with a noun ending in *-ness* made from a word in the box. Make any necessary changes.

dark	friendly	happy	lonely	~~short~~	sick
silly	thin	tired	thorough		

a) The *shortness* of the journey surprised me, as I thought it would be longer.

b) Sue was impressed by the .... of everyone in her new school.

c) We knew it was going to rain because of the .... of the sky.

d) Old Mrs Holt's .... was cured when she was given a pet cat.

e) The doctor told Peter that his .... was a result of overwork.

f) Wendy's teacher was impressed by the .... of her work.

g) We wished the bride and groom .... in their new life together.

h) Joe's teachers began to grow tired of his .... in class.

i) I felt rather cold when I arrived because of the .... of my clothes.

j) Jean took a travel .... pill, and then she felt much better.

6 Complete the word in each sentence with a suffix from the box.

-less	-ly	-y	-ish	~~ic~~	-al	-ous

a) Everyone thanked the fire-fighters for their hero*ic*........ efforts.

b) Paul received most of his music........... education from his mother.

c) The government is going to provide more houses for home........... people.

d) Lisa's mother........... qualities made her a favourite with the children.

e) This road is extremely danger........... when the weather is bad.

f) It was very fool........... of you to leave all the doors and windows open.

g) On rain........... days, we spend a lot of time indoors watching television.

Word formation 2

1 <u>Underline</u> the correct word in each sentence.

a) By 11.00 I felt so <u>*tired*</u>/*tiring* that I went to bed.

b) I heard the film was good, but it was very *disappointed/disappointing*.

c) Being alone in an old house at night can be *frightened/frightening*.

d) Julie was so *embarrassed/embarrassing* that her whole face turned red.

e) Jim gets *bored/boring* if he has to study too much.

f) It's very *confused/confusing* to be taught in so many classrooms.

g) Andy said that the twenty-mile walk was *exhausted/exhausting*.

h) Are you *interested/interesting* in going to the beach tomorrow?

i) I was really *surprised/surprising* when my boss gave me the day off.

j) Why don't you go away and stop being so *annoyed/annoying*!

2 Complete the word in *italics* in each sentence with a prefix or suffix from the box. Make any other necessary changes to the word.

-age	dis-	-ful	im-	un-	-y	-ness

a) I suppose Paul might help us, but it seems *likely*. ....*unlikely*...............

b) Fred can't fill his pool because there's a water *short*. ....

c) I found most of the maths questions completely *possible*. ....

d) Jan has taken up *photograph* as a hobby. ....

e) Thanks for those notes. They were really *use*. ....

f) I *like* winter sports so I never go skiing. ....

g) When it's time for bed I start feeling *sleep*. ....

h) This is a really *usual* stamp. I've not seen one like it before. ....

i) I really like Dan. He's always so happy and *cheer*. ....

j) I'm writing to thank you for the *kind* you showed me. ....

3 Complete each sentence with a word formed from the word in **bold**.

a) It's ....*unusually*.............. cold today, considering it's still summer.
   usual

b) Actually, I found Tony's book was .... interesting.
   surprise

c) .... , my father used to go to school with your father.
   interest

d) The police managed .... to find the missing children.
   success

e) Jean's compositions are always .... written.

   beautiful

f) I'm .... ashamed of your behaviour!

   thorough

g) This question is .... difficult, isn't it!

   awful

h) Mike tried .... to phone Cathy several times.

   success

i) These instructions seem .... complicated.

   necessary

j) Someone had .... left the front door open.

   obvious

4   Complete each word with a word formed from the word in **bold**.

a) I can't sit on this chair. It's really un..*comfortable*... .

   comfort

b) Ann has left home and is in............................ of her parents.

   depend

c) These old envelopes are re............................ so we can save money.

   use

d) Not being chosen for the team was a great dis............................ .

   appoint

e) Maria and Louis have a really good ....ship.

   relate

f) Being un............................ means that you share with others.

   self

g) Not taking exercise is rather un............................ .

   health

h) David has a really un............................ temper, and gets angry easily.

   control

i) These trousers won't get smaller. They're un............................ .

   shrink

j) They didn't give Gary the job as he was in............................ .

   experience

5 Complete each sentence with a word formed from the word in **bold**.

a) Harry asked for a .....*receipt*......... and the cashier gave him one.
receive

b) Nina wants to be a .... and join the government.
politics

c) No one knows the exact .... of the water here.
deep

d) You have to have a lot of .... to go fishing.
patient

e) .... is a serious matter, and you have to think about it.
marry

f) Tom sent in his .... for the job the next day.
apply

g) Helen's mind is filled with all kinds of unusual ....
know

h) There was no .... for the crash of the airliner.
explain

6 Complete each sentence with a word formed from the word in **bold**.

a) The ...*theft*............ of the diamonds baffled the police.
thief

b) Most people have no real .... in ghosts.
believe

c) Tina had no .... that anything was wrong.
suspect

d) We measured the .... of the room with a ruler.
long

e) Our teacher was really .... when she found out.
anger

f) George won a medal for ....
brave

g) Looking in the mirror too much is an example of ....
vain

h) Do you think you have the .... to pass the test?
able

Collocations and fixed expressions 1

1 Complete each sentence with a word from the box. Each word is used THREE times.

do	make	have	take	give

a) ...*Have*........ a nice day!

b) At the weekend I like to relax and just .... nothing.

c) Can I .... a chat with you sometime about Anna?

d) Hello? Is that the doctor's surgery? I'd like to .... an appointment.

e) I'll .... you my answer by the end of the week.

f) I'm going to have an early night to make sure I .... a good performance tomorrow.

g) If you have a headache you can .... an aspirin.

h) Sometimes it's difficult to .... any progress with English.

i) Sorry, I can't come out tonight, I have to .... my homework.

j) That was a lovely meal. I'll .... the dishes in a moment.

k) We always .... a lot of fun when we go clubbing on Fridays.

l) We can't wait any longer. We have to .... action.

m) Would you like me to .... you a lift to the station?

n) You can catch a taxi or .... the bus.

o) You should dress well for your interview to .... a good impression.

2 Match each group of adjectives (a–j) with a noun (1–10).

a) an ambitious/a clever/a three-point   1 sofa

b) a sudden/a violent/a loud   2 sister

c) a powerful/a notebook/a desktop   3 control

d) a comfortable/a three-seater/a leather   4 plan

e) a neat/a suspicious/a software   5 computer

f) complete/strict/quality   6 improvement

g) a considerable/a dramatic/a short-term   7 rent

h) a serious/a deadly/an infectious   8 explosion

i) an elder/a much-loved/an unmarried   9 disease

j) monthly/affordable/unpaid   10 package

INTERMEDIATE LANGUAGE PRACTICE

3 Complete each sentence with a verb from list A and a noun from list B.

A	appear clear control fight ~~protect~~ rent return take
B	behaviour call flat minute screen ~~skin~~ space survival

a) You should use suntan lotion when you go to the beach to ....*protect*.... your ....*skin*......... .

b) I need to .... a .... on my desk for my new computer.

c) I hate it when I'm using my computer and error messages .... on the ....

d) I left a message on her answering machine but she didn't .... my ....

e) It's going to be expensive to live in London. I'll have to .... a .... and pay for all my food.

f) Belgium are losing by two goals to nil against Brazil. Now they have to really .... for ....

g) Could you give me a hand? It will only .... a ....

h) The problem with modern society is that parents don't .... the .... of their children.

4 In each sentence one of the adverbs in *italics* does NOT make a common collocation with the verb in **bold**. Cross out the wrong collocation.

a) 'I'm back,' she **said** ~~*especially*~~/*simply/calmly*.

b) I *particularly/strongly/properly* **dislike** restaurants where the waiters are rude.

c) The government **acted** *firmly/completely/immediately* against the threat of terrorism.

d) She **spoke** *briefly/greatly/warmly* about her grandmother.

e) He went to the police and **confessed** his crime *openly/really/voluntarily*.

f) The price of oil **rose** *highly/sharply/dramatically* last month.

g) The sun was **shining** *brightly/directly/perfectly* onto the old town square.

h) Ronaldo was *deliberately/largely/suddenly* **pushed** in the penalty area.

i) He held the rope and **pulled** *deeply/hard/gently*.

j) He always **spends** his money *strongly/carefully/wisely*.

5 Complete each sentence with one noun from list A and one noun from list B.

A | ~~bank~~ | bargain | meat | sea | space | stomach | student
B | ~~account~~ | ache | dish | floor | loan | price | shuttle

a) I can't spend much money this weekend. My ...*bank* ...*account*... is in the red.

b) Only forty euros for a top-name sports shoe! That's a real ....

c) They say that in the future we'll be able to go to the moon for our holidays by ....

d) There's a lot of volcanic activity on the .... that we don't normally see.

e) I'll need to get a .... from the bank to help me complete my university studies.

f) I went to Sandra's house last night and she made us all a lovely ....

g) I think I'm going to go home now. I've got a bit of a ....

6 Complete each sentence with a verb phrase from the box.

~~afford to~~ designed to forget to hard to hope to likely to
slow to teach me how to try not to willing to

a) Don't break it. I can't ......*afford to*........ buy a new one.

b) The weather is changing. It's getting much colder and we're .... have snow tomorrow.

c) I'd love some more chocolate cake. It's .... resist.

d) What do you .... gain by your actions?

e) It's the first time I've tried ice-skating. Please .... laugh!

f) Can you .... play chess as well as you?

g) The government was .... react to the threat of war.

h) Don't .... ask him about his mother. She's been ill recently.

i) These exercises are .... strengthen your stomach muscles.

j) She's a great music teacher – she's .... share her love of Mozart with us all.

Collocations and fixed expressions 2

1 **Complete the expression based on the word *time* in each sentence, using a word from the box.**

~~high~~	in	lose	on	pass	spare	tell	time

a) Come on John! It's ...*high*......... time you started doing some work!

b) What do you most enjoy doing in your .... time?

c) I don't go sailing often, but I enjoy doing it from time to ....

d) When I have to wait at the airport, I do a crossword to .... the time.

e) When Carol was given her first watch, she learned to .... the time.

f) Sally is never late. She's always .... time for her lessons.

g) Thank goodness the doctor hurried. She saved Jim's life just .... time.

h) Hurry up. We've no time to .... The train leaves in five minutes!

2 **Complete the sentences with the most suitable verb from the box.**

burst	caught	got	had	lost	~~made~~	paid	spent	told	took

a) Peter's father ...*made*....... lots of money by selling old cars.

b) Sophie .... a party last week and most of her friends came.

c) I .... some very good photos of our dog with my new camera.

d) Dave .... a lot of money on rebuilding his motorbike.

e) The ending of the film was so sad that many people .... into tears.

f) According to the story, George Washington always .... the truth.

g) Kelly .... into trouble at school for playing a joke on her teacher.

h) You didn't understand because you .... no attention to the instructions.

i) I .... a cold last week so I couldn't play in the football match.

j) We .... our way completely and had to ask for directions.

3 Complete each sentence with a word from the box.

| alone | breath | difference | leaf | mad | ~~mess~~ | secret | temper |

a) I made a complete ....*mess*........ of one exam, and had to take it again.

b) When I swim underwater I can hold my .... for two minutes.

c) Peter told the boy to leave his little brother ....

d) Can you tell the .... between butter and margarine?

e) The loud music from the house next door drove Mary ....

f) When I stepped on Helen's foot again, she tried not to lose her ....

g) I'll tell you, but only because I know that you can keep a ....

h) Bob wanted to change his ways and turn over a new ....

4 The words in *italics* are in the wrong sentences. Find the correct sentence for each one.

a) Now that my summer holidays have begun I feel as free as *houses*.
   ...*a bird*........

b) Without my glasses I'm as blind as *a pig*. ....

c) After our search, suddenly David turned up as large as *rain*! ....

d) As cool as *a bat*, the robber asked for all the money in the bank!
   ....

e) Our dog eats too much, and is getting as fat as *a picture*. ....

f) Little Sarah looked as pretty as *a cucumber* in her new dress. ....

g) Take this medicine, and in a few days you'll be as right as *life*. ....

h) Don't be frightened of being on this plane. It's as safe as *a bird*.
   ....

5 Complete the expressions in *italics* in each sentence with a word from the box.

| down | ~~life~~ | round | soul | sound | then | time | wide |

a) It's extremely important. In fact, it's a *matter of* ......*life*........ *and death*.

b) Ann is great fun, and is always *the life and* .... *of the party*.

c) The police have been searching *far and* .... for the stolen jewels.

d) We were completely lost, and drove *round and* .... for hours.

e) I've told you .... *and again* not to write tests in pencil!

f) The two missing explorers have been found *safe and* ....

g) That man has been walking *up and* .... outside the house all day.

h) I don't see Paul very often, but I visit him *now and* ....

6 Replace each phrase in *italics* with one of the expressions in the box.

get ready	~~have an early night~~	have fun	have nothing to do
take a day off	take it easy		

a) I'm really tired. I'm going to *go to bed before it gets late.*
    ....*have an early night*....................

b) I think we should *prepare ourselves* for the trip as early as we can.

    ....

c) I felt ill last Tuesday, so I decided to *stay at home and not go to work.*

    ....

d) Let's go out tonight and *enjoy ourselves.*

    ....

e) I *don't have any work* this evening, so we can go to the cinema.

    ....

f) I've been working very hard, so I'm going to *relax and have some rest.*

    ....

Compound words

1 **Complete each compound word with a word from the box.**

ache	clip	cut	glasses	lace	~~path~~	post	table

a) Make sure you walk on the foot...*path*........ , because the road is dangerous.

b) I need to fix these two sheets together. Have you got a paper .... ?

c) As I was doing up my shoe, my shoe.................... broke.

d) On our first day at school, we copied down our time.................... .

e) Tom had a hair.................... yesterday and his friends made fun of him.

f) It's really sunny today, and I've forgotten my sun.................... .

g) Could I have a couple of aspirins? I've got a terrible head.................... .

h) The bus swerved to avoid a dog and hit a lamp ....

2 **Complete each sentence with a compound noun made from two words from the box.**

air	alarm	birthday	central	clock	conditioning	~~fiction~~	heating
machine	party	report	school	~~science~~	stick	walking	washing

a) I love .....*science*......... ....*fiction*......... films with robots in them.

b) Old Mr Low has a bad leg and always leans on his ....
....

c) David's teachers wrote lots of good things in his ....
....

d) As soon as the .... rings, I jump out of bed.

e) When it's hot, I turn on the ....-.......................... and it cools
the room.

f) Julia invited all her friends from school to her ....

g) This house has .... and there is a radiator in
every room.

h) If you have any dirty clothes, just put them in the ....
....

3 **The compound nouns in *italics* are in the wrong sentences. Find the correct sentence for each one.**

a) I couldn't unscrew the *pocket money*, so I couldn't drink my cola.
.....*bottle top*....................................

b) On my way to school, I saw a fantastic bike in a *bathroom mirror*.
....

c) My bike had a flat tyre, and I didn't have my *television screen* with me.
....

d) As the girls were leaving, they saw their teacher at the *bottle top*.
....

e) When I saw my face in the *school entrance*, I knew I really was ill.
....

f) During my favourite serial, a newsflash appeared on the *door handle*.
....

g) Paul's parents gave him a small amount of *bicycle pump* every week.
....

h) Susie was too small to reach the *shop window*, so she knocked.
....

4 **Match each situation with an object from the box.**

bottle opener	coffee maker	dishwasher	fire extinguisher	food mixer
~~hairdrier~~	lawn mower	pencil sharpener	stain remover	water heater

a) Comb it first and then use this. ....*hairdrier*............

b) Just put all the dirty plates in here. ....

c) I've dropped ink all over my white trousers. ....

d) Use this in an emergency. ....

e) I've just broken mine, and I can't write. ....

f) I'm really thirsty but I can't open this lemonade. ....

g) That grass really needs cutting. ....

h) It's much quicker preparing a cake with this. ....

i) If you need a bath, I'll turn it on. ....

j) If you'd like a cup, I've just put it on. ....

5 Make a compound word which describes the person in each sentence, using one of the words in *italics*, and a word from the box.

bather	~~dreamer~~	fighter	keeper	lifter	maker	manager	sitter

a) Someone who spends all *day* lost in pleasant thoughts.   ...*day-dreamer*...

b) Someone who owns or runs a *shop*.   ....

c) Someone who is lying in the *sun* to get a tan.   ....

d) Someone who looks after a *baby* while you're out.   ....

e) Someone who exercises with objects of great *weight*.   ....

f) Someone who is a member of the *fire* brigade.   ....

g) Someone who is in charge of the branch of a *bank*.   ....

h) Someone who is away from home on *holiday*.   ....

6 Complete each compound word with a word from the box.

about	bringing	coat	~~come~~	doors
ground	pour	set	skirts	stairs

a) Jane has a high in...*come*.......... , but she works very hard to earn it.

b) I'm sorry I said that. I hope you're not up..................... .

c) You have to turn left at the next round..................... .

d) Kevin fell down..................... and hurt his ankle.

e) It's cold today, so you'd better wear your over..................... .

f) That child is so polite. She obviously had a good up..................... .

g) It's a lovely day. Why don't we have lunch out..................... ?

h) They live in a small house on the out..................... of the town.

i) It's easy to travel in London if you use the Under..................... .

j) On our way home we got soaked in a terrific down..................... .

Money and shopping

1 Replace the words in *italics* with one of the phrases from the box.

in a sale	pay you back	save up	in debt	~~second hand~~
be well-off	annual income	can't afford it		

a) Kate's car was *owned by someone else before her.*

   second-hand

b) We're not going on holiday this year, because we *are short of money.*

   ....

c) Don't worry, next week I'll *give you the money you lent me.*

   ....

d) We decided to *put money aside* so we could buy a small boat.

   ....

e) I don't want to end up *owing a lot of money* to the bank.

   ....

f) What exactly is the amount of your *earnings every year?*

   ....

g) I bought my DVD-player *when the prices were reduced.*

   ....

h) Mary used to *have a lot of money*, but she's quite poor now.

   ....

2 Complete the sentence with a compound noun formed from two words in the box. One word is used twice. Some compounds are written as one word.

assistant	bag	book	carrier	card	cash	credit	cut
department	desk	~~money~~	~~pocket~~	price	shop	store	

a) Most parents give their children some ...... *pocket money* .... to spend.

b) Perhaps you left your wallet at the .... when you paid.

c) Jane buys all her CDs cheap in a/an .... store.

d) I bought the new novel by Richard Francis in my local ....

e) You can buy nearly anything in a big ....

f) The .... who served me helped me buy what I wanted.

g) When I go abroad I always take a .... with me.

h) I brought my shopping home in a strong ....

3   Underline the correct word or phrase in each sentence.

a) Dora <u>earns</u>/gains/wins more money in her job than I do.

b) The factory workers asked for a rise in their income/reward/wages.

c) Paul borrowed/lent/loaned some money from me but didn't pay it back.

d) I'm sorry, but we don't accept credit cards, only cash/coins/money.

e) Is it all right if I pay with cheque/by cheque/from cheque?

f) We don't exchange goods unless you still have the bill/cheque/receipt.

g) I'm afraid I've only got a £50 note. Do you have change/money/rest?

h) I still debt/owe/own the bank more than £5000.

4   Complete the shopping situations (a–h) with a remark (1–8).

a) I can't decide whether to buy it or not, so I think ....6....

b) Have you got a pair like this in red? ....

c) Can I pay by credit-card? ....

d) Can I help you? No thanks, ...

e) That's £45, please. ....

f) Thanks very much for your help. ....

g) There isn't a price label on this shirt. ....

h) This computer looks difficult to use. ....

1   Not at all, madam. It's a pleasure.

2   I'm just looking.

3   Could you explain how it works?

4   How would you like to pay?

5   We're out of stock at the moment. Sorry.

6   I'll leave it.

7   Sorry, we only accept cash or cheques.

8   How much is it?

5   Complete each phrase with a suitable word from the box.

bar	box	bunch	carton	loaf	~~packet~~	tin	tube

a) a ...*packet*... of biscuits

b) a .... of toothpaste

c) a .... of tomatoes

d) a .... of milk

e) a large .... of tissues

f) a .... of chocolate

g) a .... of bananas

h) a .... of bread

6   Decide which answer (A, B, C or D) best fits each space.

Shopping in the street

When I (1) .....C..... shopping, I enjoy visiting street (2) .... and looking for
(3) .... I wander around looking at each (4) .... , and asking about
(5) .... Many (6) .... on sale are less (7) .... than those in high-street
shops, though the (8) .... is not always as good. It also depends on how
much you want to (9) .... Clothes are often (10) .... , but it is difficult
to (11) .... them on. It's always (12) .... looking at second-hand books,
because you can (13) .... a lot of money in this way. Fresh fruit and
vegetables are usually good (14) .... , and there is always an excellent
selection. The main problem is whether you can carry home lots of (15) ....
bags!

1) A like	B make	C go	D do
2) A markets	B trades	C shops	D sales
3) A values	B cheaper	C special	D bargains
4) A counter	B table	C stall	D department
5) A costs	B prices	C values	D figures
6) A produces	B shopkeepers	C offers	D goods
7) A expensive	B cost	C priced	D cheaper
8) A expense	B package	C kind	D quality
9) A spend	B use	C make	D cash
10) A fashion	B cheaper	C worn	D logical
11) A purchase	B carry	C try	D wrap
12) A worth	B more	C been	D time
13) A borrow	B spend	C save	D count
14) A health	B value	C time	D taste
15) A hand	B papers	C more	D heavy

8 Living space

1 **Complete each sentence with a word from the box.**

carpet	curtains	~~cushion~~	drawer	pillow	radiator	sofa	socket

a) Is that chair comfortable, or would you like to use a ...*cushion*... ?

b) Mark couldn't use his computer as there wasn't a .... in the room.

c) This house has central heating, and there's a .... in every room.

d) I was so tired that I fell asleep as soon as my head touched the ....

e) Could you draw the .... ? Someone is staring through the window.

f) My bedroom has a fitted .... which covers the whole floor.

g) The knives and forks are in the second .... on the left.

h) Come over here and sit next to me on the ....

2 **Complete each part sentence (a–h) with one of the endings (1–8).**

a) Please sit down and make yourself .....4....

b) Many of our language students share ....

c) I like Do-It-Yourself, but I've decided to have ....

d) Alan seems to have so many clothes that he can never find ....

e) If you can't find the house you can always ask for ....

f) Susan lives on the tenth floor of ....

g) If you're short of money you can buy ....

h) As we live in a semi-detached house, we hear ....

1 room for all of them in the wardrobe.

2 a block of flats on the south side of the city.

3 directions at the bus-station.

4 at home, while I make some tea.

5 accommodation in the villages nearby.

6 the decorating done by a local firm.

7 a lot of noise through the wall from the family next door.

8 furniture from the street market near the cathedral.

3 Each sentence contains an inappropriate word or phrase. <u>Underline</u> this word, and then replace it with a word or phrase from the box.

bookcase	chimney	fence	floor	gate	~~window~~	step	towel

a) Unfortunately the ball hit the house and broke a <u>glass</u>.
   window

b) I washed my hands in the bathroom and dried them with a cloth.
   ....

c) There was a small wooden door leading into the field.
   ....

d) As I sat down at the kitchen table, I knocked my cup onto the ground.
   ....

e) In the corner of Joe's room was a small library for his books.
   ....

f) All round the garden there was a high wooden wall.
   ....

g) On the roof-tops Tina could see a tall fireplace pouring out smoke.
   ....

h) The floor of the kitchen is a bit lower, so mind the stair.
   ....

4 <u>Underline</u> the correct word in each sentence.

a) Will you be <u>*at home*</u>/*at house* later this evening?

b) Paul's room is at the top of the *stairs/steps* opposite the bathroom.

c) Can you remember to clean the *wash-basin/sink* in the bathroom?

d) The rooms downstairs are so low I can touch the *roof/ceiling*.

e) Tony is a keen *cooker/cook* and always uses an electric *cooker/cook*.

f) You'll find plates in the *cupboard/wardrobe* next to the fridge.

g) Ann was sitting *at/to* her desk, but Chris was sitting *in/on* an armchair.

h) I won't be long. I'm just going upstairs for *a bath/a bathe*.

i) Lisa didn't like doing *homework/housework*, so she paid a cleaner.

j) Under the house there's a *cave/cellar* where we keep our old things.

5 Complete the sentences with a compound word formed from two words in the box. One word is used twice.

| arm | ash | basin | ~~bed~~ | bin | book | case | chair | dish | down |
| dust | flower | hole | key | ~~room~~ | stairs | tray | wash | washer | |

a) It's very cold in my ....*bedroom*..... , and I find it hard to sleep.

b) Sarah spent all afternoon sitting in a large .... in front of the TV.

c) I left my socks soaking in the .... in the bathroom.

d) Do you think you could put all your rubbish outside in the .... ?

e) There's a beautiful .... full of roses right outside my window.

f) Don't worry about the washing-up. We'll put everything in the

....

g) I can't open the front door. Something is stuck in the ....

h) If you really insist on smoking, please use this ....

i) Can you come .... ? There's someone at the door for you.

j) In this .... are the dictionaries and an encyclopedia.

6 Complete each sentence with a verb from the box in a suitable form. You can use a verb more than once.

| drop | finish | get | look | move | ~~put~~ | take | turn |

a) I've got nowhere to stay tonight. Can you ......*put*........ me up?

b) We've bought a new house but we can't .... in until next month.

c) Adrian doesn't .... on with his neighbours, because they're so noisy.

d) Jan likes cooking, but she says it .... up a lot of her time.

e) Don't forget to .... off the television before you go to bed.

f) Helen has done most of the decorating and plans to .... it off tomorrow.

g) I have a large room, and it .... out onto a beautiful garden.

h) Karen and Mike live next door and they often .... in for a chat.

Personal matters

1 <u>Underline</u> the correct word in each sentence.

a) When her bicycle was stolen, Jill became extremely *angry/nervous*.

b) Peter felt *ashamed/embarrassed* when he had to make a speech.

c) I always write thank-you letters, just to be *gentle/polite*.

d) You never do anything to help me! You're so *lazy/tired*.

e) Penny never does anything silly. She's very *sensible/sensitive*.

f) The children had to stay in the house all day and felt *bored/tired*.

g) Jackie doesn't worry about anything and is always *cheerful/sympathetic*.

h) Mr Jackson is very *annoyed/bad-tempered* and often shouts at people.

i) When he heard about the accident, Alan was very *damaged/upset*.

j) I've got an important exam tomorrow and I'm a bit *jealous/nervous*.

2 Complete each sentence with one of the verbs from the box. Use each verb once only.

cheer	complain	cry	nod	shake his head	shout	~~smile~~	whistle

a) Please look at the camera and ...*smile*............... . Say 'cheese'!

b) If you agree with what I say, just ....

c) The food in the restaurant was terrible so we decided to ....

d) I had to .... Ann's name three times before she heard me.

e) The little boy fell over and then started to ....

f) At the end of the President's speech, the crowd began to ....

g) Paul hardly ever says 'no'. He tends to .... instead.

h) When I try to .... I put my lips together but I can't do it!

3 Complete each sentence with a word formed from the word in *italics*.

a) You can't *rely* on Joe. He's very ...*unreliable*.......... .

b) Carla has very little *patience*. She's very ....

c) Jack shows no *interest* in this subject. He's ....

d) Pat is lacking in *honesty*. She's ....

e) Bill doesn't act like a *friend*. He's ....

f) Lisa doesn't have much *experience* of this work. She's ....

g) Peter never acts *politely*. He's ....

h) The official did not *help* us very much. She was ....

i) Graham doesn't *consider* other people. He's ....

j) Ann refused to *co-operate* with the police. She was ....

4 Complete each sentence with an adjective from the box. Use each adjective once only.

ashamed	annoyed	~~disappointed~~	exhausted
fascinating	glad	jealous	terrified

a) When her team lost the cup final, Sue felt very *disappointed* .

b) I was .... when Jack accepted my invitation to dinner but didn't come.

c) Mark was .... when he saw smoke coming from the plane's engine.

d) Thanks for your letter. I'm .... to hear that you're feeling better.

e) David was .... to tell his parents that he had been sent to prison.

f) After running for fifteen kilometres, Zara felt completely ....

g) Helen felt .... when she saw her boyfriend talking to another girl.

h) Mrs Hobson told us about her life. She's a .... person.

5 Replace the words in *italics* in each sentence with one of the phrases from the box.

are fond of	fancy	fed up with	get on my nerves
give up	let me down	~~longing for~~	put me off

a) I'm *really looking forward to* a few weeks' holiday!
 longing for ....

b) Sarah has decided to *do without* eating chocolate.
 ....

c) I wanted to study biology, but my teacher *discouraged me*.
 ....

d) Sports programmes on television really *annoy me*.
 ....

e) Do you *feel like* going to the cinema this evening?
 ....

f) Why can't you tell the truth? I'm *tired of* your excuses!
 ....

g) Terry and I *like* going for walks in the country.
 ....

h) George agreed to help me, but then *disappointed* me.
 ....

6 Complete each sentence with a word from the box.

conscience	death	hand	heart	~~mood~~
tears	temper	thanks	trouble	voice

a) The children were happy because their teacher was in a good ....*mood*........ .

b) .... to Mr Dawson, our car was repaired in time for our holiday.

c) Ruth was helpful, and went to a lot of .... to make us comfortable.

d) Harry was leaning out of the window and shouting at the top of his

....

e) When Alice heard the bad news, she burst into ....

f) Neil is a very kind person. His .... is in the right place.

g) If you do something bad, it will be on your .... for a long time.

h) I was really angry, and lost my .... , and shouted at people.

i) We need some help. Could you give us a .... ?

j) The first time I saw a horror film, I was scared to ....

7 Match positive and negative words and put them in the columns below.

cheerful	clever	lazy	tense	~~kind~~	generous	mean
miserable	relaxed	stupid	hard-working	~~unpleasant~~		

Positive

....*kind*....................

....

....

....

....

....

Negative

....*unpleasant*..........

....

....

....

....

....

1 Complete each sentence with a word from the box.

alike	children	couple	elder	engaged	friendship
housewife	~~husband~~	single	twin		

a) Jane got married to her ...*husband*. , Bob, four years ago.

b) Jane's friends think that she and Bob are the perfect ....

c) They haven't got any .... yet, but they want a large family.

d) Jane's .... sister, Mary, was born half an hour before she was.

e) Jane and Mary look .... but are not exactly the same.

f) Mary isn't married. She says she prefers to be ....

g) She says she believes in .... , but doesn't believe in marriage.

h) Diana is Jane and Mary's .... sister. She calls them her 'little sisters'.

i) Diana has been .... for three years, but hasn't got married yet.

j) She has a career and doesn't like the idea of being a ....

2 Complete each sentence with a noun formed from a verb in the box.

acquaint	celebrate	die	engage	greet	marry	~~relate~~	resemble

a) All Sue's friends and ...*relations/relatives*... came to her party.

b) I occasionally meet Terry, but he's more an .... than a friend.

c) When Paul arrived, he received a warm and friendly ....

d) Six months after their .... , Michael and Lisa got married.

e) There was a great .... in the village when their team won the cup.

f) In an ideal .... , husband and wife share each other's problems.

g) Dina and her mother look alike. There is a strong .... between them.

h) Tim cried when he heard about the .... of his old dog.

3 Underline the correct word in each sentence.

a) Children are not allowed to see this film. It's for _adults_/old only.

b) By the time the vet arrived, the injured cat was already _dead/died_.

c) Unfortunately it rained on Nick and Helen's _wedding/marriage_ day.

d) David and Diana have two sons and one _daughter/girl_.

e) I think we should try to understand the problems of _aged/old_ people.

f) There should be more facilities for _youth/young_ people in this town.

g) More than fifty _relatives/parents_ were invited to Jack's party.

h) It's my _anniversary/birthday_ today. I'm eighteen years old.

4 Complete each part sentence (a–j) with an ending (1–10).

a) I've started going
b) When little Tina is grown
c) I wonder if you could put
d) Carol doesn't really get
e) Everyone says that Tom
f) Let's have some friends
g) Do you think you could look
h) Why don't we all get
i) Ellen and Laura were brought
j) If I have time I'll drop

1 takes after his father.
2 together again next Friday evening?
3 up by an aunt after their parents died.
4 in on Steve for a chat.
5 after my dog while I'm away?
6 out with George's younger sister.
7 round for dinner on Friday.
8 on well with her mother-in-law.
9 up she wants to be an astronaut.
10 us up for a few days next week?

5 Match each sentence (a–h) with a sentence (1–8) which helps to explain the meaning of the word in _italics_.

a) We've got a new _neighbour_ called Helen Willis. ....5....

b) This is Sue. She's a _colleague_ of mine. ....

c) Andrew is going to be our _best man_. ....

d) At the end of the evening I thanked our _host_. ....

e) I'm sure that Mary will be a wonderful _bride_. ....

f) Next week I'm going to stay with my _grandparents_. ....

g) I've always got on well with my _sister-in-law_. ....

h) Georgina is the ideal _guest_. ....

1 I was happy that he'd invited me to his party.
2 Even before she married my brother we'd become good friends.
3 She always offers to help in the house when she stays with us.
4 We both work in the same department at the bank.
5 She moved into the house next door yesterday.
6 They're both in their seventies, but they live a very full life.
7 When John and I get married, he'll stand next to John.
8 She's a dressmaker, and has designed her own wedding dress.

6 Complete each sentence with a word or phrase from the box. Use each word or phrase once only.

after	against	away	~~in~~	on	on and off	out	over

a) It would be nice to meet again. I'll get ....*in*........... touch with you next week.

b) I'm afraid Sonia isn't here. She went .... for the weekend.

c) I keep leaving and coming back. I've lived here .... for several years.

d) Matthew brought up the children .... his own after his wife died.

e) The baby was called Clare, ... its grandmother.

f) Peter is .... at the moment but he'll be back in half an hour.

g) Ann decided to get married .... the wishes of her parents.

h) After their final quarrel, Carrie told Luke their relationship was ....

7 Who are these people?

a) your mothers' parents ...*grandparents*...........

b) your mother's brother ....

c) your mother's sister ....

d) your husband's son from a previous marriage ....

e) the sister of the person you marry ....

f) your brother's (or sister's) male child ....

g) your brother's (or sister's) female child ....

h) a child with no brothers and sisters ....

i) someone from another country ....

j) someone you have not met before ....

1 <u>Underline</u> the correct word in each sentence.

a) The trousers are the right length, but the *stomach/<u>waist</u>* is too small.
b) I like this watch, but the strap is too small for my *palm/wrist*.
c) The hand has four fingers and a *thumb/toe*.
d) When Robert is nervous he tends to bite his *nails/joints*.
e) This bag has a strap and I can carry it on my *neck/shoulder*.
f) Gina twisted her *ankle/elbow* and she can't walk very easily.
g) Paul dropped the stone on his foot and broke two *toes/fingers*.
h) When you're worried lines appear on your *eyebrows/forehead*.

2 Decide which answer (A, B, C or D) best fits each space.

Clothes

Choosing clothes can be difficult. Some people want to be (1) ....*C*.... , but they don't want to look exactly (2) .... everybody else. Not all clothes are (3) .... for work or school, perhaps because they're not (4) .... enough, or simply not (5) .... It is easy to buy the (6) .... size, and find that your trousers are too (7) .... , especially if you're a little bit (8) .... Very (9) .... clothes make you feel (10) .... , but when they have (11) .... in the washing machine, then you have the same problem! If you buy light (12) .... clothes, then they might not be (13) .... enough for winter. If your shoes are not (14) .... , and if you aren't (15) .... for the cold, you might look good, but feel terrible!

1) A of fashion	B fashioned	C fashionable	D fashion
2) A alike	B like	C similar	D same
3) A fitted	B suitable	C comfort	D equal
4) A formal	B strict	C uniform	D suited
5) A comforting	B comfort	C comforted	D comfortable
6) A false	B mistake	C wrong	D error
7) A straight	B close	C stiff	D tight
8) A slim	B overweight	C thin	D enormous
9) A loose	B lose	C loosened	D lost
10) A thin	B slim	C narrow	D spare
11) A lessened	B reduced	C decreased	D shrunk
12) A of cotton	B in cotton	C cotton	D cottoned
13) A warm	B cold	C hot	D cool
14) A tight	B enclosed	C firm	D waterproof
15) A worn	B clothed	C dressed	D fitted

3 Complete each sentence with a verb from the box. Use each verb once only.

| disguise | dress up | ~~fit~~ | go with | look | put on | suit | wear |

a) This dress doesn't ...*fit*............. me. It's far too big.

b) The children decided to .... as astronauts for the party.

c) Sue always seems to .... trousers. She says they're more comfortable.

d) I like your new haircut. It makes you .... younger.

e) It's a nice pullover, but the colour doesn't .... you.

f) The escaped prisoner managed to .... himself as a policeman.

g) I got up late and had only a few minutes to .... my clothes.

h) I don't think that yellow socks .... a black suit.

4 Match the words from the box with the definitions.

| blouse | cap | dress | shorts | skirt | ~~sleeve~~ | sock | suit |

a) part of an item of clothing for covering the arm
   ...*sleeve*......

b) woman's or girl's clothing that covers the body from shoulders to knee or below

   ....

c) jacket together with trousers or skirt made from the same material

   ....

d) a soft covering for the head worn by young people, and in some sports

   ....

e) trousers that end above or at the knee

   ....

f) item of clothing for women or girls that hangs from the waist and covers all or part of the legs

   ....

g) item of clothing for women or girls covering the upper half of the body

   ....

h) soft item of clothing that covers the lower leg and foot inside the shoe

   ....

5 Complete each expression in *italics* with one of the parts of the body from the box.

| arms | eye | face | foot | hair | hand | head | heart | leg | ~~tongue~~ |

a) The word is on the *tip of my* .....*tongue*...., but I just can't remember it.

b) Crossing the mountains on my own was a ....-*raising* adventure.

c) I know this is hard to believe, but you must .... *the truth*.

d) It is now over thirty years since man first *set* .... *on* the moon.

e) After his long trip Tom's parents *welcomed him with open* ....

f) Peter knows the songs *by* .... and doesn't need to look at a book.

g) Try to stay calm, and don't *lose your* .... , and everything will be fine.

h) Have I really won the prize, or are you only *pulling my* .... ?

i) Lisa needs some help with her suitcase. Could you *give her a* .... ?

j) I waved at Ann, hoping *to catch her* .... , but she didn't see me.

6 Label the drawing with the words in the box.

| ankle | bottom | ~~cheek~~ | chest (man)/bust (woman) | chin | elbow |
| heel | hip | knee | neck | shoulder | thigh | waist | wrist |

a _cheek_

b

c

d

e

f

g

h

i

j

k

l

m

n

12 Everyday problems

1 Complete each sentence with a verb from the box.

blocked	collapsed	~~crashed~~	exploded
flooded	injured	sank	trapped

a) Yesterday a lorry ......*crashed*...... into a bus at the traffic lights.

b) The falling roof tiles .... several passers-by, though not seriously.

c) The old wooden building .... in a high wind.

d) A terrorist bomb .... at the railway station last week.

e) The river burst its banks and .... the town during the night.

f) Rocks and mud from the mountain .... the main road yesterday.

g) The storm at sea .... several small fishing boats.

h) The rising water .... two families in their homes for six hours.

2 <u>Underline</u> the correct word or phrase in each sentence.

a) The doctor gave Sue a *prescription/recipe* for some medicine.

b) Tim's mother used a thermometer to take his *fever/temperature*.

c) It took Julie a long time to *get over/get off* her illness.

d) The cut on Katrina's leg took a long time to *cure/heal*.

e) I couldn't run because I had a *hurt/pain* in my leg.

f) I bought these sea-sickness pills from the *chemist's/physician's*.

g) David was ill with *a flu/flu* for two weeks.

h) Dick couldn't speak because he had a *throat ache/sore throat*.

3 Complete each sentence with a word from the box.

ambulance	~~bandage~~	blood	hospital
operation	patient	surgeon	ward

a) A long white ......*bandage*...... was wound around my arm.

b) This .... was built only two years ago, but is already too small.

c) The .... in the bed next to mine was a man with a broken leg.

d) The doctor told Jim that he would have to have a/an ....

e) David's bed is in a small .... with two others.

f) Joanna was operated on by the best .... in the city.

g) Some people feel faint when they see ....

h) Stephen was hurt in an accident and a passer-by called a/an ....

4 Complete each sentence with a compound noun made from two words from the box.

air	bus	car	centre	city	failure	hour	~~jam~~
park	parking	pollution	power	rush	shortage	stop	
strike	ticket	~~traffic~~	train	water			

a) The roads were crowded and I was stuck in a ...*traffic*... ...*jam*......... for hours.

b) The .... is bad in this city. It's getting hard to breathe!

c) All the lights went out because there was a ....

d) I left my car in the wrong place and the police gave me a ....

e) I couldn't use the railway yesterday because there was a ....

f) I had to pay a fortune to leave my car in a multi-storey ....

g) I waited at the .... for hours but all the buses were full.

h) There is always a lot of traffic during the ....

i) It doesn't rain a lot here, and at the moment there is a ....

j) The Government has decided to ban all cars from the ....

5 Match the beginnings of the sentences (a–j) with the endings (1–10).

a) Fire-fighters managed to put ..6..   1 fire accidentally.

b) After a few minutes a fire ......   2 fire to the house deliberately.

c) It was believed that someone set ......   3 spark from a passing train.

d) Luckily Paul carried a fire ......   4 into flames.

e) The fire was started by a ......   5 heat inside the burning car.

f) Metal melted from the intense ......   6 out the fire after two hours.

g) I could hardly breathe because of the ...... 7 thick cloud of smoke.

h) The old theatre caught ......   8 -extinguisher in his car.

i) The wooden hut was burnt to ......   9 a heap of ashes.

j) In seconds the building burst ......   10 engine arrived at the blaze.

6 Match each sentence (a–h) with a sentence (1–8) which has a similar meaning.

a) They arrived too late to see her. ....3....

b) They didn't think it was safe. ....

c) They asked her to come next week instead. ....

d) They argued with her. ....

e) They were injured. ....

f) They didn't know where they were going. ....

g) They asked someone to tell them the way. ....

h) They've cancelled their party. ....

1 They asked for directions.

2 They had a row with her.

3 They missed her.

4 They were hurt.

5 They put her off for a week.

6 They felt it was dangerous.

7 Their party is off.

8 They'd lost their way.

7 Match the beginnings of the sentences (a–i) with the endings (1–9).

a) All the surfaces in the living room are ....3....

b) The bathroom door ....

c) The sink is ....

d) The bread has ....

e) The cola has ....

f) You're wearing your pullover ....

g) The table cloth is ....

h) That shirt needs ironing, it's very ....

i) My life is ....

1 back to front.

2 blocked.

3 dusty.

4 creased.

5 gone flat.

6 gone stale.

7 in a mess.

8 stained.

9 won't lock.

Travel and holidays

1 Decide which answer (A, B, C or D) best fits each space.

Holidays

Most people enjoy going (1) ....*C*..... for their holidays, and having the opportunity to (2) .... in an interesting city or a seaside (3) .... If you speak (4) .... languages, you can make new friends, and (5) .... home some interesting (6) .... as presents. But before you can do that, you have to (7) .... your destination, and that is often a problem! If you fly, then you may find that your flight has been (8) .... (9) .... by train can also be difficult, since trains are often (10) .... in the summer, and you might have to reserve a (11) .... in advance. Whichever way you (12) .... , you can have problems with your (13) .... , and it is often difficult to find good (14) .... Apart from this, you might not be able to afford the (15) .... !

1) A out	B forward	C abroad	D foreign
2) A remain	B pass	C spend	D stay
3) A resort	B post	C too	D one
4) A strange	B stranger	C foreigner	D foreign
5) A fetch	B take	C go	D get
6) A memories	B souvenirs	C memoirs	D recollections
7) A reach	B arrive	C go	D travel
8) A waited	B reversed	C delayed	D booked
9) A Journeys	B Travels	C Voyages	D Passes
10) A filling	B occupied	C overdone	D crowded
11) A post	B chair	C seat	D position
12) A voyage	B travel	C trip	D tour
13) A baggages	B luggage	C goods	D sacks
14) A staying	B homes	C lodges	D accommodation
15) A fare	B fair	C far	D fur

2 Complete each sentence with a word from the box. Use each word once only.

after	~~down~~	for	off	in	out	up

a) The car broke .....*down*...... in the mountains, and we couldn't find a garage.

b) James had to set .... at dawn to catch the early train.

c) Sue's bike passed me, and I had to ride fast to catch .... with her.

d) I arrived at the airport, checked .... , and then had some coffee.

e) We were heading .... Paris, but we were not in a hurry to get there.

f) Jill ran .... of money after a week, and had to go home.

g) Our next-door neighbours looked .... our dog while we were away.

3 Complete each sentence with a word formed from the word in **bold**.

a) They told me to ask at the ...*information*..... desk.
inform

b) The plane gathered speed as it roared along the ....
run

c) The .... of our plane has been delayed.
depart

d) The plane made a bumpy .... and I felt ill.
land

e) The clerk asked me if I had made a ....
reserve

f) I got a seat because of another passenger's ....
cancel

g) We arrived late at the .... , and missed the plane.
air

h) We fastened our seatbelts and prepared for ....
take

4 Complete each part sentence (a–j) with one of the endings (1–10) and make a compound word.

a) I sent my friend a post .....7.....   1 suit with you to the beach.
b) I fastened my seat ....   2 table turned out to be wrong.
c) We stayed on a small camp ....   3 belt, and waited for takeoff.
d) I always forget my guide ....   4 port, you must tell the police.
e) Don't forget to take your swim ....   5 hiking can be dangerous.
f) If you lose your pass ....   6 side when I was little.
g) We stayed in a quiet guest ....   7 card of the town where I stayed.
h) The train time ....   8 book when I visit old cities.
i) I used to like going to the sea ....   9 house down by the river.
j) Nowadays I'm afraid that hitch ....   10 site just outside the town.

5   Underline the correct word in each sentence.

a) In Greece we visited several <u>ancient</u>/antique temples.

b) Whenever Lucy travels by boat she feels *seasick/dizzy*.

c) Brighton is a *popular/touristic* seaside town.

d) Holidays in the mountains are always more *relaxed/relaxing*.

e) We always eat the *local/topical* food when we're abroad.

f) On my summer holidays I like getting *suntanned/sunburnt*.

g) It may not be easy to find accommodation at *reasonable/logical* prices.

h) After cycling all day, Bill was completely *exhausted/tired*.

i) The owner of the hotel gave us a *hospitable/warm* welcome.

j) Jack likes spending most of his holiday in the *open/plain* air.

6   The words in *italics* are in the wrong sentences. Find the correct sentence for each one.

a) We spent two weeks in a lovely seaside *station*.
   ...*resort*..........

b) Jim stayed the night in a small bed and *hostel*.
   ....

c) Karen was exhausted after her fifteen-mile *holiday*.
   ....

d) Martin and Carol had a great time on their camping *cards*.
   ....

e) As it was cheaper, I bought a return *stop*.
   ....

f) We managed to find some petrol at a remote filling *village*.
   ....

g) The bus made an overnight *breakfast* in a town near the border.
   ....

h) The family rented a cottage in a country *walk* for the summer.
   ....

i) If you're a student, you can save money by staying in a youth *ticket*.
   ....

j) David never carried cash on holiday. He always takes credit *resort*.
   ....

Interests and free time

1 <u>Underline</u> the most suitable word in each sentence.

a) United managed to <u>*beat*</u>/*win* City in the last minute of the match.
b) At the end of the play, everyone in the theatre *exploded/applauded*.
c) If you want to *enter for/sign on* the competition, you'll need a form.
d) The cycling club is *doing/holding* a meeting next Thursday.
e) The youth orchestra has *acted/performed* all over Europe.
f) I'm *doing/going* fishing next week. Do you want to come?
g) The final score was 2–2, so Rovers *drew/equalled* the game.
h) David *passes/spends* an hour every day playing computer games.
i) Did you *enjoy/please* yourself at the folk festival?
j) We were late and so we *lost/missed* the beginning of the film.

2 Match each word from the box with one of the explanations.

athletes	audience	cast	competitors	fans
group	members	~~spectators~~	team	viewers

a) People who watch a sporting performance.
   ...*spectators*............

b) People who exercise and take part in games of speed and strength.

   ....

c) People who support a sport, or a famous person.

   ....

d) People who together take part in a sport.

   ....

e) People who all belong to the same club.

   ....

f) People who play rock music together.

   ....

g) People who listen to or watch a play or performance.

   ....

h) People who watch television.

   ....

i) People who act together in a play.

   ....

j) People who are all trying to win the same prize.

   ....

3 **Complete each sentence with a word from the box.**

| exhibition | line | medal | ~~prize~~ | queue |
| rod | screen | ticket | tyre | whistle |

a) Helen won first ...*prize*............ in the competition.

b) When Steve won the race, he was given a gold ....

c) We had to wait in a .... before we could get into the cinema.

d) Rachel had to push her bike after she got a flat ....

e) There was so much shouting that no one heard the referee's ....

f) I've got a spare .... for tomorrow's concert. Do you want to come?

g) Have you seen the new .... of paintings at the National Gallery?

h) I'm going fishing tomorrow. I've just bought a new ....

i) Kate was the first runner to cross the finishing ....

j) We didn't enjoy the film because we were too close to the ....

4 **Complete each sentence with a word from the box.**

| drop | go | join | ~~knock~~ | live | make | stand | turn |

a) Lenny 'The Fist' Smith, the boxer, said he would ....*knock*...... out his opponent.

b) Carol won the match because the other player failed to .... up.

c) The singer asked the audience to .... in and all sing together.

d) It was a reasonable film, but it didn't really .... up to my expectations.

e) Tom and Sue used to .... out together.

f) From my seat, I couldn't .... out what was happening on the stage.

g) The referee made it clear that he would not .... for bad behaviour.

h) Peter had to .... out of the race after his car broke down.

5 Match each activity (a–h) with a place (1–8).

a) Sunbathing and wearing swimming costumes. ....8.....   1 a stage

b) Watching elephants dancing. ....   2 a running track

c) Doing keep fit exercises. ....   3 a party

d) Crossing the finishing line. ....   4 a funfair

e) Taking a dog for a walk. ....   5 a circus

f) Celebrating someone's birthday. ....   6 a park

g) Riding a ghost train or a big wheel. ....   7 a gym

h) Speaking clearly so the audience can hear. ....   8 a beach

6 Decide which answer (A, B, C or D) best fits each space.

Music

What kind of music do you (1) ....B.... ? Some people like going to (2) ....
concerts, and listening to (3) .... The (4) .... wear very formal clothes,
and the (5) .... is silent until the end of the (6) .... Perhaps you're a
rock music (7) .... Rock concerts are often held at football (8) .... or in
parks. (9) .... of the audience dance to the music, or sing the songs.
(10) .... music is (11) .... at weddings and parties in many countries, and
some people (12) .... their own music at home. Nowadays we (13) ....
music in shops and lifts, and many people (14) .... their own music with
them, or even (15) .... to music when they study. Music is everywhere!

1) A listen	B enjoy	C have	D preferring
2) A classic	B classics	C classical	D classified
3) A a group	B an orchestra	C a band	D a record
4) A musicians	B actors	C musicals	D instruments
5) A spectators	B people	C guests	D audience
6) A happening	B action	C music	D performance
7) A fan	B enthusiasm	C reader	D friend
8) A matches	B stadiums	C pitches	D pools
9) A Members	B Selections	C Persons	D Those
10) A Historical	B Nation	C Traditional	D Ancient
11) A acted	B formed	C done	D played
12) A do	B get	C make	D take
13) A listen	B hear	C perform	D understand
14) A carry	B wear	C lift	D play
15) A hear	B have	C follow	D listen

1 **Decide which answer (A, B, C or D) best fits each space.**

A house in the country

The house is situated among beautiful (1) ....B.... , two miles from the nearest village, surrounded by (2) .... On a (3) .... a short distance from the house is a (4) .... , and a small (5) .... flows past the end of the garden, which also contains a small (6) .... The name of the house, Rose Cottage, is on the garden (7) .... , from which a (8) .... leads to the (9) .... door. On the (10) .... floor there is a large (11) .... room, a dining room, a kitchen, and (12) .... and toilet. (13) .... there are three bedrooms. There is also a garage next to the house. The village has a post (14) .... , a small shop and a pub, and there is a railway (15) .... three miles away.

1) A view	B scenery	C sights	D looks
2) A grass	B flats	C earth	D fields
3) A mountain	B peak	C hill	D summit
4) A wood	B greenery	C jungle	D forest
5) A river	B channel	C stream	D canal
6) A sea	B bath	C water	D pond
7) A gate	B door	C opening	D entrance
8) A road	B path	C way	D pavement
9) A forward	B front	C first	D further
10) A bottom	B back	C ground	D earth
11) A lounge	B seating	C saloon	D living
12) A bathroom	B bath	C basin	D washing
13) A Over	B Up	C Upstairs	D Higher
14) A shop	B centre	C place	D office
15) A station	B stop	C post	D base

2 <u>Underline</u> **the most suitable word in each sentence.**

a) We arranged to meet in the centre of town in the main *place/<u>square</u>*.

b) Their cottage is in the heart of some beautiful *country/countryside*.

c) The children spent all day playing on the sandy *beach/seaside*.

d) I dropped my ice-cream on the *earth/ground*, so I couldn't eat it.

e) This *footpath/pavement* leads across the fields to the village.

f) There was a wonderful *scenery/view* from my hotel room.

g) You can't stop here. *Car-park/Parking* is not allowed in this street.

h) Helen decided to leave the *country/land* and work abroad.

3 Complete each sentence with a word from the box.

block	centre	crossing	hall	junction
part	place	~~station~~	traffic	zone

a) The police officer asked me to come with him to the police ...*station*.... .

b) When you reach the road .... turn right.

c) The mayor's office is in the town ....

d) Margaret lives on the top floor of a .... of flats.

e) Cars have to stop for you if you use a pedestrian ....

f) Which .... of town do you live in?

g) You can buy fresh fish in the market .... every Friday.

h) Take the first turning on the left after the next set of .... lights.

i) The centre of town is now a traffic-free .... and cars are banned.

j) A new shopping .... has been opened on the edge of the town.

4 Replace the words in *italics* with one of the words from the box.

capital	crowded	international	isolated
local	neighbouring	~~rural~~	urban

a) It's much healthier to live in a *country* area, far away from the city.
...*rural*...

b) Sue has just moved to a *nearby* town.
....

c) We lived in the middle of nowhere in an *out of the way* cottage.
....

d) Paris is the *most important* city of France.
....

e) There is not a lot of *world* news in this newspaper.
....

f) I do my shopping at the *neighbourhood* shops, not in the town centre.
....

g) At weekends the town centre is always *full of people*.
....

h) There is far too much pollution nowadays in *city* areas.
....

5 Complete each compound noun with a word from the box.

| about | bridge | ~~ground~~ | path | park | roads | side | skirts |

a) Our children spend a lot of time having fun at the local play..*ground*..... .

b) When you reach the cross.................... , take the road to Linton.

c) You have to turn left when you reach the next round.................... .

d) We can't leave the car here. We'll have to look for a car.................... .

e) Follow this foot.................... until you reach the main road.

f) There was an old woman selling fruit at the road.................... .

g) Paula lives on the out.................... of the town, where the countryside begins.

h) You can cross the railway line by walking over a foot.................... .

6 Match the words from the box with the explanations.

| bridge | bungalow | caravan | ~~castle~~ | cottage |
| semi-detached house | | terraced house | | tower |

a) A strong building made in the past to defend people against enemies.
...*castle*...

b) A small house on wheels which is pulled by a car.
....

c) A house which is one of a pair of houses joined together.
....

d) A house with only one floor.
....

e) This carries a road or railway over a river.
....

f) A house which is part of a row of houses all joined together.
....

g) A small house in the country.
....

h) A tall building standing alone, or as part of a castle or church.
....

16 Food and drink

1 <u>Underline</u> the correct word in each sentence.

a) Would you like a *bread/<u>roll</u>* with your soup?

b) The first *course/plate* consisted of cold fish and salad.

c) That was a really lovely *food/meal*. Please let me pay for you.

d) I felt so thirsty that I drank two *cans/tins* of Corky Cola.

e) Nowadays many people buy *frozen/iced* food instead of fresh food.

f) Could you give me the *receipt/recipe* for this cake? It's delicious!

g) This pie is fantastic! It's really *tasteful/tasty*.

h) Helen is a really good *cook/cooker*.

i) Can I have a *fork/spoon* so I can stir my coffee?

2 Complete each sentence with a suitable verb from the box.

add	bake	boil	chop	fry	grate	mix	peel	~~roast~~	squeeze

a) John decided to .....*roast*........ the beef in the oven for two hours.

b) Put all the ingredients in a bowl and .... them together well.

c) First .... the onions into small pieces.

d) I wanted to .... some cakes this morning, but I didn't have time.

e) Taste the soup, and .... salt and pepper if necessary.

f) .... the potatoes, and then cut them into large pieces.

g) These vegetables taste great if you .... them for a minute in hot oil.

h) .... some cheese, and sprinkle it over the pasta.

i) .... a lemon and sprinkle the juice over the salad.

j) .... the rice in salted water for ten minutes.

3 Complete each phrase with a suitable word from the box.

bacon	biscuits	butter	chips	fork	~~salt~~	saucer	vinegar

a) pepper and ...*salt*..........

b) knife and ....

c) egg and ....

d) bread and ....

e) fish and ....

f) oil and ....

g) cup and ....

h) tea and ....

4 **Complete the phrase with a suitable word from the box.**

bar	carton	cup	glass	jar	loaf	pinch	~~slice~~

a) a ...*slice*......... of bread or cake   e) a .... of bread

b) a .... of chocolate   f) a .... of water

c) a .... of jam   g) a .... of salt

d) a .... of tea   h) a .... of milk

5 **Match each description with the name of a kind of food from the box.**

cheese	chop	~~grape~~	lamb	lettuce	onion	pie	plum

a) Green or purple fruit which grows in bunches.
    ..*grape*........

b) Small vegetable with a strong smell and taste.
    ....

c) Plant with large green leaves used in salads.
    ....

d) Meat from a young sheep.
    ....

e) Meat, vegetables or fruit baked in pastry.
    ....

f) Small sweet fruit with red or yellow skin, and a stone in the centre.
    ....

g) Solid food made from milk.
    ....

h) Piece of pork or lamb with a bone, cut from the ribs of the animal.
    ....

6 **Complete each sentence with a word from the box.**

bill	book	dessert	~~menu~~	takeaway	tip

a) We weren't sure what to have, so we asked for the ....*menu*........ .

b) Tony finished his meal, paid the .... , and left the restaurant.

c) After two courses we felt full, so we didn't have any ....

d) We had a very tasty Indian .... for the main course.

e) This is a popular restaurant and you have to .... a table.

f) The service was excellent so we left a large .... on the table.

7   Complete each sentence with *a* or *some*, or leave the space blank.

a) I'd like ....*a*............ chicken, please, a large one for roasting.

b) Could I have .... bread, please?

c) Do we have time for .... snack before our bus leaves?

d) Would you like to come to .... lunch with me on Thursday?

e) There's .... milk jug in the cupboard near the fridge.

f) George has decided to go on .... diet, starting next week.

g) I'm going to have .... cheese and tomato sandwich.

h) For breakfast I eat .... toast and marmalade, and drink a glass of milk.

i) Do you like .... yoghurt? Personally, I can't stand it!

j) Tim managed to eat .... chicken, but felt too ill to eat anything else.

8   Label the vegetables using the words from the box.

asparagus	aubergine (Br)/eggplant (Am)	bean broccoli
cabbage	carrot cauliflower celery	courgette (Br)/zucchini (Am)
leek	~~lettuce~~ mushroom onion	pepper

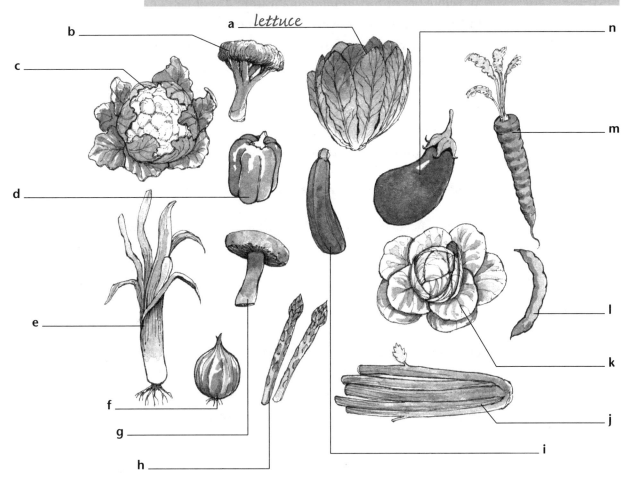

a   *lettuce*

259

1 <u>Underline</u> the correct word in each sentence.

a) Penny took three exams and managed to _pass/succeed_ them all.

b) Most people would prefer a _job/work_ which was near home.

c) Tim had to _learn/teach_ fifty children how to swim.

d) I can't come to the cinema tonight. I'm _reading/studying_ for a test.

e) Rita did very well, and was given maximum _grades/marks_.

f) Every Friday, the building workers are given their _salary/wages_.

g) It's hard reading _aloud/loudly_ when you don't understand the words.

h) The manager told David to make an _application/invitation_ for the job.

i) Ann works in advertising and _earns/wins_ a very high salary.

j) Would you like to come into my _bureau/office_? We can talk there.

2 Complete each sentence with a word from the box.

business	date	~~heart~~	phone	practice	rules	time	work

a) Before her history exam, Laura learnt a list of dates by ...._heart_...... .

b) The manager will be with you in a moment. He's on the ....

c) I haven't spoken Spanish for ages and I'm a bit out of ....

d) Ever since Tim lost his job he's been out of ....

e) Bringing your mobile phone to the class is against the .... !

f) This factory isn't very modern. Most of the machines are out of ....

g) Our maths teacher is always late. He's never on ....

h) Mrs Smith isn't here at the moment. She's away on ....

3 Complete each sentence with a word from the box.

get	hand	keep	~~look~~	pick	stand	take	write

a) If you don't know the answer, ..._look_.......... it up in the back of the book.

b) My boss wouldn't let me .... time off to go to a football match.

c) Stop talking, and .... on with your work!

d) George finds it hard to .... up with the rest of the maths class.

e) Carol stayed in France and managed to .... up the language.

f) If you speak so fast I can't .... down what you're saying.

g) Don't forget to check over your work before you .... it in.

h) Mrs Wood is going to .... in for your teacher while he's away.

4 Complete each sentence with a word formed from the word in **bold**.

a) Nowadays it's very important to get a good ...._education_...... .
   educate

b) Our company helps .... people to find new jobs.
   employ

c) Paul has good ideas, but writes very ....
   care

d) Helen has become a .... businesswoman.
   succeed

e) I hope to leave school with some useful ....
   qualify

f) Mr Dale was my .... for ten years, and paid me well.
   employ

g) According to the .... , the French lesson starts at ten.
   time

h) Cathy has three jobs, so she has a high ....
   come

i) John's .... of history is amazing for a boy of his age.
   know

j) All the .... in this company are given free meals.
   employ

5 Match each sentence (a–j) with a sentence (1–10) which has a similar meaning.

a) She was given the sack. ....7.....   1 She was given a better job.

b) She got a rise. ....   2 She answered an advertisement.

c) She got a promotion. ....   3 She decided to leave.

d) She retired. ....   4 She did the job carefully.

e) She did it for a living. ....   5 She didn't have a job.

f) She resigned. ....   6 She earned her money that way.

g) She was unemployed. ....   7 She was dismissed.

h) She applied for the job. ....   8 She wanted a better job.

i) She was ambitious. ....   9 She was old and stopped work.

j) She was conscientious. ....   10 She was given more money.

6 Decide which answer (A, B, C or D) best fits each space.

The wrong age for school!

Are the years you (1) ....D.... at school the best years of your life? Personally, I found most (2) .... rather uninteresting. We had to sit at our (3) .... in silence and (4) .... attention. The teachers used to (5) .... on the blackboard and (6) .... us difficult questions. We also had to (7) .... lots of homework, and (8) .... it in on time. We had to wear a school (9) .... , and we had to obey lots of (10) .... I (11) .... school as soon as I could and started (12) .... I read books at the public (13) .... , and later I decided to (14) .... college. I really enjoyed studying because I was older and knew that I wanted some (15) .... When I was at school, I was just the wrong age!

1)	A go	B have	C pass	D spend
2)	A lectures	B lessons	C them	D class
3)	A chairs	B desks	C posts	D parts
4)	A pay	B make	C have	D follow
5)	A read	B sit	C write	D talk
6)	A make	B do	C get	D ask
7)	A answer	B do	C take	D finish
8)	A write	B hand	C pass	D complete
9)	A uniform	B robe	C dress	D cloth
10)	A ways	B rules	C laws	D time
11)	A passed	B qualified	C examined	D left
12)	A job	B labour	C employee	D work
13)	A bookshop	B shelves	C library	D university
14)	A go	B attend	C study	D follow
15)	A qualifications	B examinations	C papers	D grades

1 <u>Underline</u> the correct word in each sentence.

a) Before we set off, we listened to the *climate/<u>weather</u>* forecast.

b) Paula saw a flash of *lightning/thunder* and then heard a deep boom.

c) The traffic had to slow down because of the thick *fog/vapour*.

d) There won't be much rain. It's only a short *shower/stream*.

e) Spring is my favourite *season/term* of the year.

f) Last summer was very hot, and there was a real *heatwave/temperature*.

g) Look at those clouds! There's going to be a *blast/storm*.

h) On a hot day in summer, I look forward to the *chilly/cool* evening.

i) We were caught in the rain and got *damp/soaked* to the skin.

j) In the morning there was half a metre of *ice/snow* blocking the road.

2 Choose the word which best matches the description.

a) Large white water bird with a long neck.   duck/swan

b) Four legged animal with horns, good at climbing.   goat/sheep

c) Sea animal with a shell and five pairs of legs.   crab/frog

d) Insect with large beautifully coloured wings.   bee/butterfly

e) Small reptile with four legs and a long tail.   lizard/snake

f) Small flying insect which drinks blood from the skin.   fly/mosquito

g) Small long-eared animal that lives in a hole.   mouse/rabbit

h) Animal with long legs and neck and orangey skin.   camel/giraffe

i) Eight-legged creature which catches insects.   bat/spider

j) Young animal which barks, often a pet.   kitten/puppy

3 Complete each sentence with a word from the box.

bark	berry	blossom	~~branch~~	leaf	root	thorn	trunk

a) Sue managed to reach the ...*branch*.... of a tree and climb up to the window.

b) I felt ill after I ate a red .... from a bush in the woods.

c) The wall was cracked by the .... of a tree growing underneath it.

d) In the autumn, every .... on the tree turns yellow and then falls off.

e) Liz hurt herself on a .... while she was picking some roses.

f) The .... of this tree can be removed and used as a kind of paper.

g) In spring all the apple trees are covered in white ....

h) An oak tree has a very broad .... , sometimes two metres thick.

4 Choose the best ending (1–8) for each sentence (a–h).

a) In cities the air is hard to breathe because of car ......8......   1 waste
b) The earth's climate is changing because of ....   2 pollution
c) Not having enough of something is called a ....   3 recycling
d) Air, sea and land can suffer from ....   4 global warming
e) Throwing things away unnecessarily is called ....   5 rubbish
f) A mixture of smoke and fog is called ....   6 exhaust fumes
g) Things which we throw away are called ....   7 shortage
h) To avoid wasting things we can use ....   8 smog

5 Decide which answer (A, B, C or D) best fits each space.

The threat to the Environment

Nowadays people are more aware that wildlife all over the world is in (1) ....A..... . Many (2) .... of animals are threatened, and could easily become (3) .... if we do not make an effort to (4) .... them. There are many reasons for this. In some cases, animals are (5) .... for their fur or for other valuable parts of their bodies. Some birds, (6) .... as parrots, are caught (7) .... , and sold as pets. For many animals and birds, the problem is that their habitat – the (8) .... where they live – is (9) .... More (10) .... is used for farms, for houses or industry, and there are fewer open (11) .... than there once were. Farmers use powerful chemicals to help them grow better (12) .... , but these chemicals pollute the environment and (13) .... wildlife. The most successful animals on earth – human beings – will soon be the only ones (14) .... , unless we can (15) .... this problem.

1) A danger	B threat	C problem	D vanishing
2) A marks	B more	C species	D forms
3) A disappeared	B vanished	C empty	D extinct
4) A harm	B safe	C protect	D serve
5) A hunted	B chased	C game	D extinct
6) A like	B such	C or	D where
7) A lively	B alive	C for life	D for living
8) A spot	B point	C place	D site
9) A exhausting	B departing	C escaping	D disappearing
10) A earth	B land	C soil	D area
11) A spaces	B air	C up	D parts
12) A products	B fields	C herbs	D crops
13) A spoil	B harm	C wound	D wrong
14) A survived	B over	C missing	D left
15) A answer	B calculate	C solve	D explain

6 Complete each sentence with a pair of verbs from the box with opposite meanings.

clean up	cut down	~~destroy~~	let	plant
pollute	prevent	~~protect~~	recycle	throw away

a) People should be encouraged to ...*protect*......... the environment, rather than ....*destroy*........ it.

b) We should try to .... disasters happening, not just .... them happen.

c) Everyone should try to .... beaches, and not .... them.

d) It would be a good idea to .... more trees, not to .... trees.

e) We can use things again if we .... rather than .... them.

7 Complete the sentences with the pairs of words from the box.

~~country/city~~	farm/cottage	fence/hedge	hills/mountains
paths/tracks	stream/river	town/village	crops/weeds

a) Elderly people often move away from the ...*city*............... to live in the ...*country*......... .

b) I've often walked over the .... , but I don't like climbing ....

c) A boat can sail up a .... , but a .... is too small.

d) If you go for a walk, stay on the .... If you follow any of the animal .... you might get lost.

e) Farmers try to get rid of all the .... and increase the quantity of .... they grow.

f) I come from a little .... The nearest big .... is Bedford.

g) One field has a wooden .... , the other has a .... made of bushes.

h) In the middle of the .... was a lovely old .... with a garden.

Tools and technology

1   **Underline** the correct word in each sentence.

a) In the UK it's a 'mobile phone', but in the US it's a <u>cell phone</u>/*pocket phone*.
b) In Britain most private cars run on *gas/petrol* or diesel.
c) Ann's friends bought her an *electric/electrical* mixer for her birthday.
d) Peter had to push his bike when he got a flat *tyre/wheel*.
e) This car has got a really powerful *engine/machine*.
f) When the machine is on, a little red *light/torch* comes on.
g) The noise of the workmen banging in *nails/screws* was disturbing.
h) The radiators will have to be fitted by a *heater/plumber*.

2   Match the words from the box with the explanations.

| ~~answering machine~~   camera   dishwasher   photocopier |
| mobile phone   sewing machine   vacuum cleaner |

a) Use this if you can't stay in to take your calls.   ...*answering machine*...
b) Use this to make calls when you're out and about.   ....
c) Use this to do your own dressmaking.   ....
d) Use this to get rid of dust and dirt.   ....
e) Use this to take a snapshot for your album.   ....
f) Use this to deal with dirty cutlery and crockery.   ....
g) Use this if you need several pages all the same.   ....

3   Complete each phrase in *italics* with a verb from the box.

| blow   break   cut   go   plug   ~~ring~~   run   turn   warm   wear |

a) I'm sorry I can't talk now, but I'll ...*ring*......... *back* in half an hour.
b) The police think that a car bomb was used to .... *up* the building.
c) These tyres are strong, and won't .... *out* for ages.
d) Jane's old car used to .... *down* all the time.
e) You can .... *in* the computer to the socket by the window.
f) If you don't pay the electricity bill they will .... *you* off.
g) I think it's time to .... *off* the television and go to bed.
h) Whenever there is a thunder storm, all the lights .... *out*.
i) It's not necessary to .... *up* the engine first, although it's so cold.
j) If you leave the radio on all night the battery will .... *out*.

4 Complete the sentences about computers with a word from the box.

button	cursor	~~hard disk~~	highlight	icon
print out	memory	modem	website	

a) The computer stores large amounts of information on its ....*hard disk*... .

b) When a program is running, it is using the computer's ....

c) A small picture that represents a program is called an ....

d) The flashing symbol that shows where text will appear is the ....

e) When you've finished writing text you often want to ....

f) You can click the left or right mouse ....

g) Organizations use the internet to provide information about themselves – they put the information on their ....

h) You connect the computer to the internet via a ....

i) Hold down the left mouse button and drag the cursor across any text that you want to ....

5 Replace the group word in *italics* in each sentence with an example word from the box.

~~car~~	cello	electric	toothbrush	oven
frying pan	gun	ladder	saw	

a) The police discovered the *vehicle* more than twenty miles away.
...*car*...........................

b) My sister bought me this *gadget* to clean my teeth as a present.
....

c) The builders left their *equipment* outside the house.
....

d) The cost of the kitchen includes an *electrical appliance*.
....

e) This *kitchen utensil* is lightweight and non-stick.
....

f) I had to use a *tool* to cut the floorboards in half.
....

g) One of the robbers was carrying a *weapon*.
....

h) This *instrument* is rather heavy to carry.
....

6   Complete each sentence with a word from the box.

battery	~~handle~~	key	lock	plug	socket	switch	wire

a) Lisa turned the door ....*handle*..... , opened the door and entered the room.

b) My watch stopped working because the .... had run out.

c) The television won't work in this room, as there isn't an electric

   ....

d) Bill pressed the light .... , but none of the lights was working.

e) To wind up this old clock you need a special kind of ....

f) Mary put the key in the .... , but it wouldn't turn.

g) I've bought an electric kettle, but the lead hasn't got a .... on it.

h) The electric bell didn't work because the .... had been cut.

7   Match each sentence with the necessary object from the box.

binoculars	compass	hairdrier	iron	lawnmower
~~pump~~	razor	scissors	thermometer	tin-opener

a) There is no air in either of these tyres.

   ...*pump*.....................

b) Do you fancy some tinned beans for lunch?

   ....

c) The grass in the back garden is awfully long.

   ....

d) Sam has been letting his beard grow but now he's going to shave.

   ....

e) When it's long like this you need more than a towel.

   ....

f) I've got to cut the ends off the legs of my new jeans.

   ....

g) Do you think I've got a temperature?

   ....

h) It's difficult to see wild animals when they're so far away.

   ....

i) Jean was completely lost, and needed to know where north was.

   ....

j) You can't go out with all those creases in your shirt.

   ....

VOCABULARY

20

Everyday objects

1 <u>Underline</u> the correct word in each sentence.

a) I have to do some sewing. Do you have a *pin/<u>needle</u>*?

b) You need special *glue/sticker* when you make model aeroplanes.

c) I always carry a *carving knife/penknife* in my pocket.

d) Paul keeps his papers together with a *rubber band/rubber ring*.

e) Sheets of paper can be fastened together with a *paper clip/zipper*.

f) I wrapped up the parcel using brown paper and *rope/string*.

g) Helen took the *cutters/scissors* and started trimming Mary's hair.

h) Oh bother! One of my shirt *bottoms/buttons* has fallen off.

i) As David was tying his *shoelace/shoestring*, it broke.

j) Little Susie usually ties up her hair with a red *ribbon/strip*.

2 Match each sentence with the necessary object from the box.

diary	dictionary	envelope	correction fluid	file
notepad	~~notice~~	ruler	sharpener	stamp

a) It's important to let everyone know what time the meeting starts.
...*notice*...............

b) Hang on a minute, I'll just write down those details.
....

c) Oh dear, I've written my name in the wrong place.
....

d) Write down the date of the next match so you don't forget.
....

e) I've written my letter but I've got nothing to put it in.
....

f) I keep losing the sheets I wrote my homework on.
....

g) How long is this piece of paper exactly?
....

h) What a nuisance! My pencil has broken.
....

i) My letter's ready for the post. How much will it cost?
....

j) I'm not really sure what this word means.
....

3 The words in *italics* are in the wrong sentence. Find the correct sentence for each one.

a) You can hang your coat on the *fireplace* behind the door.
...*hook*...................

b) It's time for lunch. Can you put the *doormat* on the table?
....

c) I've bought a beautiful *hook* with long leaves for your room.
....

d) Don't forget to put all the rubbish from the kitchen into the *broom*.
....

e) Cathy pulled back the *plant* and looked out at the street.
....

f) You can sweep the floor with the *curtains* in that cupboard.
....

g) My mother insists that we all wipe our feet on the *tablecloth*.
....

h) Some logs were blazing and crackling in the *dustbin*.
....

4 Complete each sentence with a word from the box.

alarm	~~comb~~	gown	hanger	mirror	pillow
slippers	table	toothpaste	towel		

a) My hair is in an awful mess. Have you got a ....*comb*........... ?

b) When I get up I put on my dressing .... and go downstairs.

c) It's sometimes a shock to see your own face in the ....

d) Helen always sits at her dressing .... and brushes her hair.

e) When I'm in the house I take off my shoes and put on my ....

f) I want to clean my teeth but I can't find any ....

g) Every morning at 6.30 the .... clock goes off and I wake up.

h) You can wash your hands here, and there's a .... behind the door.

i) I can't get to sleep unless I have a really comfortable ....

j) You can put your coat in the wardrobe on a coat ....

5   **Match the words from the box with the explanations.**

street sign	hedge	kerb	lamp post	pavement
~~pedestrian crossing~~	gate	subway		

a) This is a safe place to go from one side of the street to the other.
   ...pedestrian crossing..

b) This has a light at the top in the street.
   ....

c) This is where people walk in the street.
   ....

d) This is a kind of wall made of a living plant.
   ....

e) This closes the opening in an outside wall.
   ....

f) This is a line of stones between the footpath and the road.
   ....

g) This helps you know where you want to go.
   ....

h) This is a way of crossing under the road.
   ....

21 People

1 <u>Underline</u> the correct word in each sentence.

a) Mrs Grant is a good *employee/<u>employer</u>* and pays her staff well.

b) Excuse me, but are you the *ower/owner* of this bike?

c) Tom works in a local garage as a car *engineer/mechanic*.

d) I want to borrow some money, so I'm seeing the bank *boss/manager*.

e) Little Jimmy has got a new *professor/teacher* at his primary school.

f) Helen joined the army as an *officer/official*, and is now a captain.

g) The house really needed decorating so I called a *painter/wallpaper*.

h) Please ask the *cash/cashier* for a receipt.

i) Have you thought about getting a job as a *waiter/table server*?

j) I waited for my letters, but the *poster/postman* was late as usual.

2 Match a person from the box with each problem.

| carpenter | dentist | electrician | ~~gardener~~ | guide |
| hairdresser | optician | photographer | plumber | vet |

a) The lawn is really long and there are weeds everywhere.
   ...*gardener*........

b) I want to visit as much of the old city as possible in an afternoon.
   ....

c) The taps don't work, and there is water all over the floor.
   ....

d) I want to have a special portrait made for my eighteenth birthday.
   ....

e) One of my fillings has come out, and I've got terrible toothache.
   ....

f) I want to use the wood from these shelves to make a bookcase.
   ....

g) When I turn on the television, all the lights go off.
   ....

h) I can't see to read very well and I think I need glasses.
   ....

i) Benny hurt one of his paws when I was taking him for a walk.
   ....

j) It's far too long at the back and too curly at the front.
   ....

3 **Complete each sentence with a word from the box.**

assistant	flatmate	employee	guest	host
~~member~~	partner	supporter	team-mate	

a) Peter has just become a/an ....*member*.. of the fishing club.

b) I started this business with my .... , Dora, about ten years ago.

c) I've got a new .... to help pay the rent. She moved in last week.

d) We provide every .... in the hotel with whatever he or she needs.

e) At the end of the party, Bill thanked his .... and then left.

f) Any .... who wishes to work at weekends should see the manager.

g) I've been a/an .... of Hull City FC for as long as I can remember.

h) Mary was my .... last year in the basketball tournament.

i) This job is a lot for one person, so we think you need a/an ....

4 **Match each word from the box with an explanation.**

celebrity	~~coward~~	expert	favourite	fool
genius	liar	miser	optimist	pessimist

a) Someone who does not have any courage.
...*coward*......

b) Someone who hates spending money and becomes rich by keeping it.
....

c) Someone who says that a bottle is half full.
....

d) Someone who is very well known in the media.
....

e) Someone who is loved more than any other.
....

f) Someone who has special knowledge or training.
....

g) Someone who does something silly or mistaken.
....

h) Someone who has very great ability or special talent.
....

i) Someone who says that a bottle is half empty.
....

j) Someone who does not tell the truth.
....

5 Complete each sentence with a group word from the box.

audience	cast	~~crew~~	crowd	group
queue	society	staff	team	trio

a) The ...*crew*........ of the ship cheered as the new captain came on board.

b) Paula has just joined the dramatic .... at school.

c) The head teacher thanked the .... for working so hard.

d) There was a long .... of people waiting in the post office.

e) A huge .... had assembled outside the president's palace.

f) The members of the .... play the violin, the piano and the cello.

g) A small .... of us went on a trip to Rome last summer.

h) When the music stopped, the .... applauded for ten minutes.

i) Last year Helen was the captain of the basketball ....

j) When the play ended all the .... came on stage and took a bow.

6 Complete each sentence with a word formed from the word in **bold**.

a) This city has over half a million ...*inhabitants* .
   inhabit

b) Margaret has decided to have a career as a ....
   politics

c) Every .... in this country has the right to vote.
   city

d) Eric studied hard to become a rock ....
   guitar

e) After the crash, Carla was the only ....
   survive

f) David's mother is a famous ....
   science

g) At nineteen, Tony became a professional ....
   crime

h) I've always wanted to be a jazz ....
   music

i) It'll take Kate years to become a ....
   law

j) Jack was my .... in the tennis match.
   oppose

Formation rules

1 Tenses

Present simple
I/you/we/they like.
Do you like?
You don't like.

She/he/it likes.
Does she like?
He doesn't like.

Present continuous
I am going.
She/he/it is going.
Are you going?
I am not going.
She isn't going.

You/we/they are going.

Am I going?
Is she going?
You aren't going.

Present perfect
I/you/we/they have left.
Have they left?
They haven't left.

She/he/it has left.
Has she left?
He hasn't left.

Present perfect continuous
I/you/we/they have been waiting.
Have you been waiting?
We haven't been waiting.

She/he/it has been waiting.
Has she been waiting?
He hasn't been waiting.

Past simple
1 I/you/she/he/it/we/they started. (regular)
   Did you start?
   You didn't start.
2 I/you/she/he/it/we/they went. (irregular)
   Did you go?
   You didn't go.

Past continuous
I/he/she/it was going.
Was he going?
She wasn't going.

You/we/they were going.
Were you going?
You weren't going.

Past perfect
I/you/she/he/it/we/they had left.
Had he left?
They hadn't left.

Future perfect
I/you/she/he/it/we/they will have finished.
Will they have finished?
They won't have finished.

2 Reported Speech

'I always drink milk.'	He said (that) he always drank milk.
'I'm leaving.'	She said she was leaving.
'I'll be back soon.'	He said he would be back soon.
'I've forgotten it.'	She said she had forgotten it.
'I took it.'	He said he had taken it.
'I was reading.'	She said she had been reading.
'I had left by then.'	He said he had left by then.
'I must go.'	She said she had to go/must go.
'I can help.'	He said he could help.
'I would like to help.'	She said she would like to help.

3 Passive Tenses

Active	**Passive**
He helps.	He is helped.
He is helping.	He is being helped.
He has helped.	He has been helped.
He helped.	He was helped.
He was helping.	He was being helped.
He will help.	He will be helped.
He will have helped.	He will have been helped.

4 Infinitives

Present:	to like
Present passive:	to be liked
Past:	to have liked
Past passive:	to have been liked

5 Participles (*-ing* forms)

Present:	liking
Present passive:	being liked
Past:	having liked
Past passive:	having been liked

Irregular verbs

Infinitive	Past simple	Past participle
be	was/were	been
beat	beat	beaten
become	became	become
begin	began	begun
bend	bent	bent
bite	bit	bitten
blow	blew	blown
break	broke	broken
bring	brought	brought
build	built	built
burn	burnt/burned	burnt/burned
burst	burst	burst
buy	bought	bought
catch	caught	caught
choose	chose	chosen
come	came	come
cost	cost	cost
cut	cut	cut
deal	dealt	dealt
dig	dug	dug
do	did	done
draw	drew	drawn
dream	dreamt/dreamed	dreamt/dreamed
drink	drank	drunk
drive	drove	driven
eat	ate	eaten
fall	fell	fallen
feed	fed	fed
feel	felt	felt
fight	fought	fought
find	found	found
fly	flew	flown
forbid	forbade	forbidden
forgive	forgave	forgiven
freeze	froze	frozen
get	got	got
give	gave	given
go	went	gone
grow	grew	grown
hang	hung	hung
have	had	had
hear	heard	heard
hide	hid	hidden
hit	hit	hit
hold	held	held
hurt	hurt	hurt
keep	kept	kept
know	knew	known
lay	laid	laid
lead	led	led

learn	learnt/learned	learnt/learned
leave	left	left
lend	lent	lent
let	let	let
lie	lay	lain
light	lit	lit
lose	lost	lost
make	made	made
mean	meant	meant
meet	met	met
pay	paid	paid
put	put	put
read	read	read
ride	rode	ridden
ring	rang	rung
rise	rose	risen
run	ran	run
say	said	said
see	saw	seen
sell	sold	sold
send	sent	sent
set	set	set
shake	shook	shaken
shine	shone	shone
shoot	shot	shot
show	showed	shown
shut	shut	shut
sing	sang	sung
sink	sank	sunk
sit	sat	sat
sleep	slept	slept
speak	spoke	spoken
spell	spelt/spelled	spelt/spelled
spend	spent	spent
stand	stood	stood
steal	stole	stolen
stick	stuck	stuck
swim	swam	swum
take	took	taken
teach	taught	taught
tear	tore	torn
tell	told	told
think	thought	thought
throw	threw	thrown
understand	understood	understood
wake	woke	woken
wear	wore	worn
win	won	won
write	wrote	written

Grammar index

279

Grammar answers

In some cases more than one answer is acceptable.

Grammar 1

1. a) *12* b) 4 c) 2 d) 3
   e) 8 f) 10 g) 13 h) 1
   i) 5 j) 6 k) 7 l) 11
   m) 14 n) 9

2. a) *2* b) 4 c) 5 d) 1
   e) 8 f) 7 g) 3 h) 6

3. a) *2* b) 1 c) 2 d) 3

Grammar 2

1. a) *do you go*
   b) are you waiting
   c) doesn't know
   d) I'm having
   e) do you leave
   f) is happening
   g) do you know
   h) I'm having

2. a) *does Sue live*
   b) you know Jim
   c) are you doing at the moment
   d) you sitting here
   e) we change trains here
   f) are you wearing two pullovers

3. a) *Naomi and Bill aren't watching television.*
   b) Peter doesn't like chocolate cake.
   c) I'm not using this pencil at the moment.
   d) The children aren't having lunch in the kitchen.
   e) I don't get up early on Saturday.
   f) Elena isn't writing a novel.

4. a) *Do you like*
   b) does the sun rise
   c) are you reading
   d) I'm having
   e) don't watch videos
   f) It's snowing
   g) are you talking
   h) goes
   i) Do you wear
   j) She's building

5. a) writing i) using
   b) digging j) waiting
   c) taking k) washing
   d) deciding l) riding
   e) swimming m) flying
   f) having n) studying
   g) lying o) going
   h) reading

Grammar 3

1. a) 2 b) 1 c) 1 d) 2
   e) 2 f) 1 g) 2 h) 2

2. a) *I don't believe*
   b) has
   c) I'm leaving
   d) are you doing
   e) You're being
   f) I'm driving
   g) are we eating
   h) tastes
   i) are you going
   j) I don't understand

3. a) *hate*
   b) are you going
   c) do you wear
   d) think
   e) doesn't usually sit
   f) are you looking at
   g) Does this bus stop
   h) am not taking

4. a) 1 b) 7 c) 2 d) 5
   e) 6 f) 8 g) 4 h) 3

5. a) *do you usually do*
   b) only eats
   c) Do you know
   d) are you staring
   e) Do you speak
   f) is staying
   g) You're putting
   h) Are they speaking

Grammar 4

1. a) *was washing, rang*
   b) did you feel
   c) got, received
   d) went swimming
   e) bit, screamed
   f) sang, ate
   g) fell, happened
   h) was washing-up, broke
   i) see, missed
   j) were you doing, phoned

2. a) *I didn't enjoy the concert.*
   b) Did you eat all the bread?
   c) John spent a lot.
   d) I didn't feel well yesterday.
   e) Anna bought a car.
   f) Did they win the prize?
   g) Paul speaks Greek.
   h) I didn't pay all the bills.

3. a) *while* f) ago
   b) Last week g) when
   c) when h) in
   d) at i) When
   e) While j) ago

4. a) 3 b) 1 c) 6 d) 5
   e) 2 f) 7 g) 8 h) 4

5. a) *woke up, told*
   b) was waiting, arrived
   c) wanted, chose
   d) was studying, phoned
   e) found, was looking for
   f) was watching, arrived
   g) went out, was lying
   h) went, did you eat

Grammar 5

1. a) *When we <u>had eaten</u> lunch, we <u>sat</u> in the garden.*
   b) While I <u>was looking</u> for my keys, I remembered <u>I'd left</u> them at home.
   c) Anna <u>used to play</u> badminton when she <u>was</u> at school.
   d) When I got into bed, I <u>fell</u> asleep immediately.
   e) When I <u>finally/'d finally found</u> the house, I <u>knocked</u> at the door.
   f) After Jill <u>gave/had given</u> Nick his books, she went home.
   g) Maria <u>used to live/lived</u> in Sweden when she was a child.
   h) I <u>used to get up</u> early when I went sailing.
   i) The Vikings <u>sailed</u> to North America a thousand years ago.
   j) Juliet was sure <u>she'd seen</u> the tall man before.

2. a) *was waiting, noticed, hadn't been*
   b) went, found, had stolen
   c) met, thought, had seen
   d) got off, was walking, realized, had left
   e) had bought, didn't have
   f) said, hadn't arrived

3. a) had broken g) didn't know
   b) wanted h) had flown
   c) had stolen i) had been
   d) thought j) took place/
   e) had done had taken
   f) needed place

4. a) *used to have*
   b) would/used to read
   c) would/used to meet
   d) didn't use to like
   e) used to write
   f) used to live
   g) used to be
   h) would/used to cheer

5. a) *had taken*
   b) didn't use
   c) didn't have/he hadn't
   d) used to play

e) get up
f) we'd missed
g) would/used to spend

6 a) *When I'd washed and got ready, I went out to meet my friends.*
b) I knew much more about the job when I'd visited their offices.
c) When I'd looked at the new dress for ages, I asked how much it cost.
d) I felt much more independent when I'd passed my driving test.
e) Anne went on holiday when she'd saved enough money.
f) When the team had finally won the match, they ran round the pitch to celebrate.

Grammar 6

1 a) *Have you cut*
b) 've had
c) has never seen
d) has stolen
e) haven't slept
f) 've just broken
g) hasn't won
h) Have you ever eaten

2 a) *'ve been married*
b) 've been
c) 've written
d) 've never eaten
e) 've loved
f) 've broken

3 a) since e) yet h) So far
b) always f) for i) often
c) ever g) never j) already
d) just

4 a) *'ve worked here*
b) haven't been/'ve never been
c) My pen has
d) have left
e) 've just seen
f) haven't finished
g) you been
h) 've left
i) haven't spoken
j) Anna/she woken

Grammar 7

1 a) *I've lived here*
b) left
c) has just stolen
d) I've decided
e) I lost
f) It's started
g) We've visited
h) I've been standing
i) has been
j) We went

2 a) lost, 've just lost
b) work, 've decided
c) 've been, 've come
d) Have you seen, left
e) had, caught
f) 've never eaten, ate

g) hope, 've cooked
h) have taken up
i) reached, weren't
j) has had, 's gone

3 a) *Have you seen, 've been looking forward*
b) 've been studying, haven't finished
c) 've been phoning, 's gone
d) Have you heard, has robbed
e) 've broken, has written

4 a) *'ve been living here*
b) has gone
c) 've been learning
d) haven't finished
e) just left
f) haven't been
g) haven't eaten/'ve never eaten
h) forgotten

5 a) so f) teaching
b) since g) yet
c) been h) has
d) met i) practising
e) recently j) taught

6 a) *My penfriend has been writing to me for years.*
b) We started this course three weeks ago.
c) 'What have you been doing all day?' 'I've been writing letters.'
d) When did you arrive in this city?
e) Have you ever been to India?
f) Paula has been staying in a hotel by the sea.
g) I've been feeling ill for three weeks/I felt ill three weeks ago.
h) I've lived/I've been living in this city since I was born.
i) I've been waiting here for ages. Where have you been?
j) Tony has left his books on the bus.

Grammar 8

1 a) *2* b) 2 c) 1 d) 1
e) 2 f) 1

2 a) *is joining/is going to join*
b) won't be
c) 's going to snow
d) 'm going out
e) 're going to knock
f) will probably ride
g) is going to give/is giving
h) 'm going to go
i) 're going to hit
j) will probably win

3 a) *'m having a party*
b) going to rain
c) our team will
d) won't be
e) is going to finish
f) 'll meet you
g) are we meeting/going
h) will visit/will come to visit

4 a) *I'm going swimming next Saturday. Would you like to come?*

b) ✓
c) The boat is turning over! I think it's going to sink!
d) ✓
e) The weather forecast says it's definitely going to be sunny tomorrow.
f) ✓
g) Sorry, I won't see you tomorrow. I have to go to London.
h) Bye for now. I'll see you later this evening.

5 a) *I'm going to study engineering in France.*
b) I'm going to have a party next Friday.
c) We're going to the doctor's, so we can't come.
d) Kelly will probably get the job.
e) Martin's wife is going to have another baby.
f) Sarah isn't going to get married yet.
g) I think it'll snow tomorrow.
h) The score will be 3–0.

Grammar 9

1 a) *will be lying*
b) rings
c) We'll be moving
d) does your train leave
e) you leave
f) will you be working
g) I'll be
h) won't stop

2 a) 5 b) 2 c) 1 d) 6 e) 3 f) 4

3 a) ✓
b) you grow
c) ✓
d) you give
e) arrives, I'll let
f) be using
g) she'll have left.
h) I'll do it.

4 a) *Shall we play tennis?*
b) I'm going to study Arabic in Cairo.
c) I'll be home by midnight.
d) I'll meet you later.
e) Will you go to the shops for me?
f) We won't make too much noise.
g) Shall I help you with those bags?
h) We'll come back later if you like/Shall we come back later?

5 a) *'ll have finished*
b) meet next/again, I'll phone
c) I check the spelling
d) let me share her
e) we have
f) leave/go until I
g) the lesson has finished
h) you be doing

Grammar 10

1
a) *I used to ride*
b) Shall I
c) Have you seen her
d) have you been working
e) I haven't finished
f) I was washing
g) are you staring
h) I'm having
i) stops
j) did you last go

2
a) *do you do*
b) ran
c) was sitting
d) don't understand
e) realized
f) 'm studying
g) was reading
h) know
i) 'm staying
j) did you do

3
a) *arrived, Steve had*
b) I help
c) do you usually
d) has been playing
e) I'll
f) was eating/having
g) is staying
h) haven't seen
i) you doing

4
1) C   2) A   3) D   4) D
5) B   6) A   7) C   8) C
9) D   10) B   11) B   12) D
13) A   14) C   15) A

5
a) *before*   f) never
b) since   g) lately/recently
c) all week   h) at/by
d) yet   i) for
e) As soon as   j) By the time

6
1) *been*   7) ✓   13) ✓
2) ✓   8) are   14) been
3) ✓   9) been   15) ✓
4) have   10) will   16) have
5) had   11) shall   17) be
6) ✓   12) have

7
a) *it had stopped ringing*
b) I haven't played it before.
c) When did Pete write to you last?
d) Do you ever go to the cinema?
e) I went to the beach every day.
f) She's playing basketball.
g) I've been waiting here for ages!

8
a) *Have you finished yet?*
b) I'll see you tomorrow!
c) Did you have a nice time?
d) Do you know what I mean?
e) Are you coming out for a drink later?
f) Have you been waiting long?

Grammar 11

1
a) *Sally said that she'd lost her keys.*
b) Chris said/told me that he must leave early.
c) Maria and Tony said they would see us tomorrow.
d) Tom said, 'I'm coming to your party.'
e) Sue said that she'd written a letter to Lisa.
f) Steve told us/said that he was arriving at 8.00.
g) 'I've bought a new bike,' Pam told us.
h) 'What's the matter?' Ellen asked.

2
a) *I've finished*
b) I'll be back at 6.00
c) I'm going to go shopping
d) I want to make a phone call
e) I've forgotten my homework
f) I have to be back by 3.30
g) I'll let you know
h) I'm going to be late

3
a) 3   b) 5   c) 2   d) 1
e) 4

4
a) *told*   d) told/saying
b) spoke, said   e) told/tell
c) said, told   f) told/spoke

5
a) *wouldn't be there because she was having a party*
b) 'd lost the map and (he) didn't know the way.
c) she finished the book, she was going to watch television
d) was doing some homework but he wouldn't be long
e) 'd got up late and (had) missed the bus

Grammar 12

1
a) *whether, was*
b) when, would
c) if/whether, had
d) if/whether, took
e) where
f) If/whether, had

2
a) *Are you having lunch or going out*
b) What did you do yesterday
c) Do you often go sailing
d) How many German books have you read
e) Are you going to change schools
f) Who do you sit next to in class

3
a) *if/whether I was staying there all summer*
b) what 'procrastinate' meant
c) if/whether I'd done my homework
d) when her birthday was
e) if/whether I'd remembered to lock the door
f) why I'd turned off the television

4
a) *Mike promised Sue he would be at her house before 8.00.*
b) Chris invited Jean to (go to) the cinema.
c) Patsy advised Dave not to eat too much.
d) Nick suggested going for a walk.
e) Carol apologized for breaking the window.
f) Bill offered to do the washing-up.
g) Tina's mother congratulated her on passing her driving test.
h) Pat refused to open his mouth.

Grammar 13

1
a) *we're, will be*
b) lived, we'd see
c) take, we'll arrive
d) don't hurry, we'll be
e) were, would be able to
f) don't wear, you'll feel
g) studied, would get
h) had, I'd ride
i) lend, I'll let
j) had, I'd give

2
a) *fall in, will get*
b) were/was, 'd go
c) knew, 'd tell
d) run, 'll catch
e) rains, 'll go/could go
f) had, 'd join

3
a) *would*   f) Would
b) unless   g) would
c) would   h) If
d) Unless   i) would
e) Would   j) unless

4
a) 8   b) 6   c) 9   d) 10
e) 1   f) 3   g) 4   h) 2
i) 5   j) 7

5
a) *had, 'd be able*
b) take, 'll feel
c) ate, would live
d) became, 'd buy
e) leave, will give
f) follow, 'll come
g) used, wouldn't be
h) touch, won't bite
i) leave, 'll give
j) owned, wouldn't visit

Grammar 14

1
a) *What would you do if you had wings?*
b) If I were you, I'd leave now.
c) How would you feel if you lived on Mars?
d) If I were you, I'd buy a bike.
e) What would you do if you were rich?
f) What would you say if Jim came with us?
g) If I were you, I'd take the bus.
h) What would you do if you owned a robot?

2
a) *had phoned, would have given*
b) took, might feel
c) had driven, wouldn't have crashed

d) had come, would have enjoyed
e) I'd known, would have sent
f) helped, might be
g) had scored, could have won
h) wore, wouldn't get

3 a) *had left early, wouldn't have missed*
   b) 'd bought more milk, would have had
   c) 'd taken/'d remembered to take a map, wouldn't have got lost
   d) 'd gone to bed, would have woken up
   e) had made a shopping list, wouldn't have forgotten to buy/would have remembered to buy
   f) 'd realized you were tired, I wouldn't have asked you to go
   g) had sailed across the Atlantic, would have reached
   h) 'd turned left at the station, wouldn't have lost

Grammar 15

1 a) *hadn't sunbathed*
   b) could stay
   c) could swim
   d) had
   e) could see
   f) didn't sit
   g) had
   h) enjoy
   i) could
   j) I'll

2 a) 2   b) 2   c) 1   d) 2
   e) 1   f) 2   g) 2   h) 1
   i) 1   j) 1

3 a) *had brought*
   b) had bought
   c) went
   d) knew
   e) had taken
   f) hadn't bought
   g) had finished
   h) spoke/could speak

4 (Suggested answers)
   a) *I had a sandwich*
   b) you have a good
   c) 'd been here/'d come here/ 'd visited it
   d) lived
   e) danced/could dance

5 a) hadn't wasted
   b) weren't
   c) were
   d) could
   e) had
   f) didn't have to
   g) hadn't moved
   h) wasn't

Grammar 16

1 a) *by someone*
   b) –
   c) by a doctor
   d) –

e) –
f) by the postman
g) by the police
h) by someone

2 a) was questioned
   b) is watched
   c) will be finished
   d) has been elected
   e) is being rebuilt
   f) has been closed
   g) is written
   h) was stolen
   i) will be met
   j) was won

3 a) *Many pet dogs <u>are lost</u> every year.*
   b) The injured man <u>was taken</u> to hospital.
   c) A new bridge <u>is being built</u> across the river.
   d) All the food at the party <u>was eaten</u>.
   e) Nothing <u>will be decided</u> before next Saturday.
   f) The match <u>is being played</u> on Friday evening.
   g) The robber unlocked the door <u>with</u> a false key.
   h) This book <u>was written</u> by Sam's father.

4 a) *has been discovered*
   b) will be opened
   c) was painted by
   d) will be announced
   e) is being redecorated
   f) have been arrested
   g) are sold by
   h) is being built

5 a) *The casino has been closed.*
   b) The match has been postponed.
   c) English is spoken all over the world.
   d) The new swimming-pool has been opened.
   e) This purse was left in the classroom yesterday.
   f) Traffic has been banned from the city centre.
   g) A new government has been elected.
   h) The flat was broken into last week.

Grammar 17

1 a) *cut*
   b) taken
   c) sent
   d) serviced
   e) broken
   f) offered
   g) were you born
   h) repaired
   i) was given
   j) was made

2 a) *had his*
   b) was lent to me by
   c) had one of my teeth taken
   d) was born

e) sold a rock concert ticket
f) his house broken into
g) were you
h) was given this ring by my
i) is being kept
j) will be sent

3 a) *I'm having my car serviced tomorrow.*
   b) I had my bike stolen yesterday.
   c) We had our house painted last year.
   d) I'm having my tooth taken out tomorrow!
   e) I've just had my hair cut.
   f) We're having our new carpet fitted tomorrow.
   g) Ann has just had her portrait painted.

4 a) *is believed to be living*
   b) is supposed to fall
   c) is expected to win
   d) is thought to be planning
   e) is said to be making
   f) is reported to disagree

Grammar 18

1 a) *might*   f) may not
   b) can't be   g) can't be
   c) must be   h) must be
   d) could be   i) could be
   e) might   j) can't come

2 a) *can swim really*
   b) might
   c) can't be
   d) must work
   e) can't come
   f) might (be able to) see you tomorrow
   g) your teacher can't come
   h) must be very hot
   i) can I open
   j) must be

3 a) S   b) D   c) S   d) D
   e) S   f) D   g) S   h) S
   i) D   j) D

4 a) *You ought to see a dentist.*
   b) We don't have to go to school tomorrow.
   c) That can't be John, because he's in Paris.
   d) Ann could/might/may be at home.
   e) You'd better wear a warm coat today.
   f) I may be late.
   g) I don't think (that) you should/ought to go skiing.
   h) You can't leave your bike here.

5 a) *have*   f) had
   b) should   g) can't
   c) must   h) have
   d) may/might   i) able
   e) must/should j) ought

6 a) I think you'd better/you should take more exercise.
   b) The plane should land soon.

c) You can't use a dictionary.
d) That can't be Sue. She's abroad.
e) I may/might come to your party.
f) You mustn't drop litter in the street.
g) You don't have to wait.
h) You should stay/ought to stay in bed today.

Grammar 19

1 a) *must have dropped*
b) could/may/might have missed
c) could/was able to
d) should have told
e) didn't have/need to
f) can't have taken
g) may/might not have
h) needn't have
i) have/need to buy
j) shouldn't have

2 a) *have studied so late*
b) you able to stop him
c) have to/need to work hard
d) have lost his way
e) have hurt yourself
f) have told me
g) have enjoyed it
h) have helped her
i) not to have left/to have stayed
j) have done it

3 a) *should have taken an umbrella*
b) must have left it on the bus
c) couldn't get through
d) should have bought her a present
e) can't eat/stand oranges
f) might have forgotten the address
g) ought to have studied harder
h) could have had fun

Grammar 20

1 a) *asked*
b) had
c) had
d) said she didn't want me to
e) can't have stolen
f) had
g) you'd better
h) would be
i) have been
j) we'd remembered

2 1) 3   7) 3   13) 3
2) if   8) must   14) was
3) they   9) have   15) if
4) to   10) if   16) been
5) paint   11) can   17) us
6) to   12) have   18) 3

3 1) C   2) A   3) B   4) A
5) D   6) D   7) B   8) C
9) A   10) C   11) D   12) A
13) C   14) B   15) D

4 a) *don't have to*   e) must
b) mustn't   f) could
c) might have   g) had to
d) have to   h) should

5 a) *knew the answer, I would help you*
b) you run fast, you'll feel tired
c) was arrested by an off-duty policewoman
d) had left early, we wouldn't have missed the train
e) I hadn't eaten all the ice-cream
f) tell me where the bus station is
g) is being built by the local council
h) were you, I'd go to the doctor's
i) was broken (by someone) with/using a hammer
j) Amy to buy some milk

6 a) *have to go*
b) I were
c) my hair cut
d) have missed
e) was invented
f) have forgotten
g) had
h) must have worked
i) was given
j) needn't have

7 a) *having our house*
b) had his car
c) he'd
d) wouldn't take
e) tell me when
f) unless
g) wouldn't have
h) can't have
i) had to
j) asked

8 a) *written*
b) can't
c) where the train station was.
d) might have been
e) you have to
f) had to/must finish
g) must have opened
h) I were taller!
i) I have my car repaired
j) I'd scream

Grammar 21

1 a) *so that*
b) to
c) in order to
d) dressed, could/would
e) for
f) couldn't/wouldn't
g) can
h) could

2 a) *I went to the shops for some eggs.*
b) Nicola came here to have a meeting with the director.
c) We went on holiday for a rest.
d) Mike plays chess to relax.
e) I opened the window for some air.
f) Cristina went shopping for some new clothes.
g) I went to a private school to learn English.
h) Sam went to a specialist for treatment.

3 a) *left work early, he could go*
b) was rebuilt, make it
c) gave Jack her phone number, he could/would call
d) put on some suntan oil, I don't/won't get
e) hid the presents, nobody would/could see
f) had the party in a large hall, people would/could
g) arrived early, he could/would get
h) changed seats in the cinema, I could see
j) some sandwiches, wouldn't feel hungry
i) wore a funny hat, his friends would notice

Grammar 22

1 a) *such*   f) so much
b) so many   g) in the end
c) too   h) so much
d) so few   i) tall enough
e) so   j) so little

2 a) *so*   g) few
b) too   h) such
c) much   i) so
d) many   j) too
e) enough   k) so
f) little

3 a) *too*
b) as/because/since
c) so much
d) so many
e) so
f) so few
g) enough
h) so
i) so little
j) As/Since/Because

4 a) *I stayed at home and had a rest because I felt really tired.*
b) I didn't use that piece of string, because it wasn't long enough.
c) It was such a difficult question that I had to ask for help.
d) There were too few seats for all the guests.
e) There were too many guests and not enough seats.
f) We can't put that box in the car as there's too little space.
g) I've got too little time to do all my work.
h) I've got so much work that I can't go out.
i) She had so many children that she didn't know what to do.
j) The play was so good that the audience cheered.

5 a) *Sorry, but I haven't got enough time.*
b) Erica is not old enough to drive a car.
c) Paul has so many friends that he's always busy.

285

d) We had too little time to go sight-seeing.
e) It's so hot that I can't think!
f) There was so much snow that we couldn't travel.
g) It was such a long way that we decided to drive there.
h) As I'd run a long way, I felt exhausted./I'd run such a long way that I felt exhausted.

6 a) *slow to be in the running team.*
b) to the house, because/as it's not very far.
c) such a long film that we missed our last bus.
d) unhappy that she cried.
e) much money that he doesn't know what to do with it.
f) old enough to get married.
g) enough money to buy this bike.
h) enough plates I'm afraid.

Grammar 23

1 a) *however*
b) Although
c) Although
d) On the other hand
e) but
f) despite
g) In spite of
h) although

2 a) *Although*   e) still
b) but   f) although
c) However   g) Despite
d) even   h) spite

3 a) *the snow, we went out for a walk.*
b) some experts think prices will fall, others disagree.
c) losing at half-time, City won in the end.
d) it was hot, Diana wore her winter clothes.
e) but/, however, this summer it's rained all the time.
f) having a headache,/his headache, James still read until late.
g) but/, however, he (still) did well in the test.

Grammar 24

1 a) 4   b) 2   c) 7   d) 10
e) 6   f) 3   g) 9   h) 1
i) 5   j) 8

2 a) *Would you mind*
b) If I were you, I'd write
c) go
d) Could you
e) Would you like
f) I won't do it
g) Shall I help
h) Why don't you go
i) Could I borrow
j) should go

3 a) *I'll be back*
b) I'll have ice-cream

c) I think you should talk it over with your parents.
d) Shall I carry it?
e) How about going to the cinema?/Let's go to the cinema?/Why don't we go to the cinema?
f) Can I leave school early?
g) Could/Can you tell me how much it costs?
h) Would you like some lemonade?
i) Could you open the window?
j) No, I won't.

4 a) *you mind taking*
b) 'd rather have/'d prefer
c) can you wait
d) Can/May I leave
e) you turn off
f) How about going
g) won't talk
h) Shall I help
i) mind telling me
j) were you,

5 a) *should*
b) Can/Could/Would
c) Can/Could/Would
d) Will/Would
e) Let's
f) mind
g) rather
h) Can/Could/Would
i) Would
j) can/may

Grammar 25

1 a) *who*   e) that
b) whose   f) whose
c) who   g) whose
d) which

2 a) *whose*   e) whose
b) that   f) who
c) whose   g) who
d) who

3 a) D   b) N   c) N   d) D
e) N   f) N   g) D

4 a) *The book that John was reading was a bit frightening.*
b) ✓
c) In the end, our holiday was the best that we had ever had.
d) The dentist who I go to isn't very expensive.
e) The film which we saw last week was much better than this one.
f) ✓
g) ✓

5 a) *These are the boys I went on holiday with.*
b) This is the letter I've been waiting for.
c) That's the shop Sue bought her bike from.
d) That's the hotel I stayed at.
e) Tim is someone I hardly ever write to.
f) ✓
g) ✓
h) United were the best team (that) we played against.

6 a) *Friday was the last time that I saw Jim.*
b) The island that/which we visited was extremely beautiful.
c) The girl that/who I met was a friend of Philip's.
d) The meal that/which we ate wasn't very tasty.
e) Gina was the first person that/who I asked.
f) The book that/which I read didn't explain the problem.
g) The teacher that/who we usually have was away ill.
h) The friends that/who I met last night send you their love.

Grammar 26

1 a) *which*   f) that
b) What   g) whose
c) who   h) who
d) whose   i) which
e) that   j) who

2 a) *his* b) ✓ c) it d) she
e) it f) ✓ g) they

3 a) *The museum that we want to visit opens at 12.00.*
b) The boy whose bike was taken visited the police station.
c) The friend who met me at the airport carried my suitcase.
d) The meal that Tom cooked was delicious.
e) The friend who is staying with me comes from Paris.
f) The man whose wallet I found gave me a reward.
g) The shop in the centre that I go to is cheaper./The shop that I go to in the centre is cheaper.
h) The girl whose party I went to phoned me.
i) I know someone who likes you.

4 a) ✓   e) ✓
b) what   f) what/who
c) ✓   g) What
d) what   h) ✓

Grammar 27

1 a) *What time do you usually get up?*
b) What were you reading?
c) Why did you go there?
d) What have you done so far?
e) What do I have to do now?
f) How did you feel yesterday?
g) What are you doing?
h) Why have the lights gone out?/Why aren't the lights working?/Why isn't there any electricity?
i) Where did you leave your bike?/Where's your bike?
j) Who's coming to your party?

2 a) *Who lives next door?*
   b) Who do you play with?
   c) Who teaches you maths?/What does Mrs Dawson teach you?
   d) What do you (usually) eat for lunch?
   e) What frightens you?
   f) Who do you talk to most?
   g) Who do you sit next to in English?
   h) What helps you study?

3 a) *I haven't*   e) I didn't
   b) I am   f) I can't
   c) I did   g) I do
   d) I will   h) he isn't

Grammar 28

1 a) *I haven't*   f) they can
   b) I do   g) I won't
   c) I am   h) she hasn't
   d) she didn't   i) it is
   e) he has   j) she didn't

2 a) *Have we*   f) Is there
   b) Don't you   g) Has she
   c) Did she   h) Haven't you
   d) Don't you   i) Isn't there
   e) Is he   j) Did you

3 a) *aren't we*   f) don't they
   b) have you   g) do you
   c) aren't you   h) don't you
   d) will you   i) hasn't he
   e) isn't he   j) should I

4 a) *Paul doesn't like football, does he?*
   b) You've got a sister, haven't you?
   c) You haven't done your homework, have you?
   d) You sat next to Ellen, didn't you?
   e) The guests haven't arrived, have they?
   f) Your name is John, isn't it?
   g) Your name isn't John, is it?
   h) I didn't leave my wallet on the desk, did I?
   i) William hasn't got married, has he?
   j) This book is by Martin Aimless, isn't it?

5 a) *2*   b) 2   c) 2   d) 1
   e) 2   f) 2   g) 1   h) 2

6 a) *what the time is*
   b) what this means
   c) how much this costs
   d) what time the museum opens
   e) if/whether I'm in the right seat
   f) where Asham Street is
   g) if/whether this is Trafalgar Square
   h) when this bus leaves

Grammar 29

1 a) *there*   e) there, there
   b) It's   f) It's
   c) they're   g) their
   d) its   h) its

2 a) *There, It*   e) It
   b) It, it   f) There, it
   c) It, there   g) It, there, there
   d) It

3 a) *There is a small restaurant*
   b) It's strange that you went
   c) There's a big tree at the end of my
   d) It seems that Brian
   e) It's really cold
   f) It's a long way from here
   g) There aren't any/There are no batteries in your
   h) It appears that we're

Grammar 30

1 a) *at*   f) in
   b) on   g) over
   c) to   h) on
   d) in   i) on
   e) below   j) in

2 a) ✓   f) ✓
   b) in   g) on
   c) in   h) ✓
   d) at   i) in
   e) by/beside   j) over/through

3 a) *in*   f) inside
   b) on   g) on
   c) on   h) out
   d) in   i) on
   e) on   j) at

4 a) *in*   e) on
   b) at   f) to
   c) in   g) in
   d) in   h) over

5 a) *in*   e) opposite
   b) next to   f) near
   c) to   g) on
   d) inside   h) on

6 a) *at*   e) on/over
   b) over   f) on
   c) near   g) on
   d) under   h) in

Grammar 31

1 a) *in order to*   f) because
   b) too   g) Although
   c) they're   h) in
   d) whose   i) so
   e) for   j) In spite of

2 a) *but we decided*
   b) used to work
   c) such a
   d) the rain
   e) about spending
   f) There are
   g) don't/won't feel
   h) It's strange
   i) enough money
   j) you mind

3 1) *B*   2) C   3) C   4) a
   5) d   6) d   7) b   8) a
   9) d   10) b   11) c   12) b
   13) d   14) a   15) c

4 a) *on*   f) on
   b) beside   g) at
   c) to   h) opposite
   d) at   i) inside
   e) near   j) at

5 a) *Have you ever been to America?*
   b) *Has Andrew ever been to America?*
   c) Does Rita like rap music?
   d) Do you like rap music?
   e) Did you enjoy the film?
   f) Did Nigel enjoy the film?
   g) Are you going to London next summer?
   h) Is Maria going to London next summer?
   i) Can I borrow your mobile phone?
   j) Could you lend me your mobile phone?

6 a) *You've got*
   b) won't they
   c) Let's go
   d) 're not leaving
   e) haven't they
   f) can't you
   g) You weren't
   h) do you
   i) weren't they
   j) didn't forget

7 a) *read a book which she really*
   b) who visited me brought me a
   c) that I stayed in was cheaper than
   d) friend whose bike I borrowed wanted it
   e) to buy the vase (that) I saw in the
   f) who sings in the group has got
   g) I met a girl whose brother is in my
   h) that we're taking leaves
   i) who knocked at the door was selling
   j) which I saw with Luke was

8 1) ✓   7) she   13) he
   2) *who*   8) them   14) at
   3) to   9) much   15) ✓
   4) Then   10) you   16) it
   5) so   11) ✓   17) so
   6) who   12) that

Grammar 32

1 a) *one day*
   b) Nowadays
   c) This morning
   d) by
   e) the day after tomorrow
   f) During
   g) afterwards
   h) on

2 a) *we had/had had lunch, we went for a coffee*
   b) on time for lessons
   c) until 8.00
   d) three months ago
   e) at 12.00
   f) first of January
   g) day after tomorrow
   h) for three

3 a) *on*   e) At
   b) ago   f) nowadays
   c) later   g) in
   d) during   h) afterwards

4 a) *I go to the seaside in summer.*
   b) I've been at this school since 1997.
   c) George had a bath and then washed his hair.
   d) Dina was at my house until 10.00./Dina didn't leave my house until 10.00.
   e) The train arrived on time.
   f) I'll arrive by 2.00.
   g) Paul tried hard but in the end he gave up./he gave up in the end.
   h) I wasn't in time to say goodbye to Lisa.

5 a) *last*   e) one/some
   b) During   f) on
   c) After   g) afterwards
   d) for   h) at

Grammar 33

1 a) *How much*   e) much
   b) are   f) How many
   c) some   g) a
   d) some   h) was

2 a) *an*   e) many/–
   b) a   f) a
   c) some   g) some
   d) –   h) any/many

3 a) *give you some advice*
   b) any clean trousers
   c) There isn't much
   d) needs washing
   e) wasn't in the book

4 a) *some wood*
   b) There was
   c) any
   d) a chicken
   e) was very useful
   f) How many
   g) It's green
   h) they're on their way
   i) noise

5 a) *water*
   b) news
   c) glasses
   d) luggage
   e) eggs
   f) scissors
   g) loaf
   h) police officer/policeman/policewoman

Grammar 34

1 a) *Have you ever visited the United Kingdom?*
   b) On our trip, we visited Canterbury Cathedral.
   c) Love is a wonderful thing.
   d) Pets are not permitted in this hotel.
   e) A rabbit is a small wild furry animal with long ears./Rabbits are small wild furry animals with long ears.
   f) New York is in the United States of America.

2 a) –   b) a
   c) an, –   d) a, an
   e) a, –   f) –, –
   g) –, a

3 a) *is an*
   b) in a
   c) Parking is
   d) Fabio is at
   e) to the station on

Grammar 35

1 a) *the*   f) the, the
   b) the, the   g) a
   c) an, the   h) a
   d) An   i) a
   e) the, the   j) the, the

2 a) *plays the piano*
   b) help the
   c) bike is the
   d) is/has an appointment at the
   e) was about the life
   f) was scored by the

3 a) *The, the, the*   e) the, the, a
   b) the, –   f) the, a, the
   c) a, the   g) A, a, a
   d) the, the   h) the, the

Grammar 34 and 35 mixed

1 a) *The, a, –*   f) –, the, an, –
   b) –, the, a   g) –, the, a
   c) a, –, the   h) a, the, the
   d) the, a, a   i) the, the, the
   e) The, the, the j) a, the

2 a) *Could you get a loaf of bread from the baker's?*
   b) Milk is good for children.
   c) John is at work at the moment.
   d) We travelled to Hungary by car.
   e) Have you got a brother or sister?
   f) The war between the two countries was the longest in history.
   g) Who was the first astronaut who walked on the moon?
   h) The Nile is the longest river in the world.

3 a) *We travelled there on the train.*
   b) This one is the largest./This is the largest size.
   c) Clara is a (professional) singer.
   d) The unemployed often feel depressed.
   e) Anna is learning to play the guitar.
   f) Mike works in an office.
   g) Marie comes from France.
   h) David is still at work.

4 a) *A*   h) –   o) a
   b) a   i) a   p) an
   c) a   j) –   q) –
   d) –   k) the r) –
   e) –   l) a   s) a
   f) the   m) the t) –
   g) –   n) a

5 a) *Darrel was the*
   b) you have a dog at
   c) a chemistry

   d) The present (that/which) my friends
   e) is the capital of
   f) The first lesson tomorrow is
   g) the phone for you
   h) The film (that/which) we saw last night

6 a) 1 –   2 *The*
   b) 1 –   2 the
   c) 1 The   2 –
   d) 1 The   2 –
   e) 1 –   2 the
   f) 1 The   2 –
   g) 1 The   2 –
   h) 1 –   2 the

Grammar 36

1 a) *no*   d) Some
   b) each   e) either
   c) Not one   f) both tyres

2 a) *not one* d) all, each
   b) no   e) none
   c) All   f) either

3 a) *Every dog in the garden was barking.*
   b) Not a single person came to the meeting.
   c) None of my friends has got a car.
   d) Neither of these chairs is comfortable.
   e) There were no boys in the class.
   f) All we want to do is listen to a few CDs.
   g) Both books are interesting.

4 a) *None of these books is/are interesting.*
   b) All you have left is ten minutes.
   c) Neither of the hotels was/were suitable.
   d) Not a single person replied to my letter.
   e) Both Paul and his brother David are ill.
   f) All of the team played well.
   g) Every house in the street was searched (by the police).
   h) Some of the questions in the test were difficult/hard.

5 a) *1*   b) 2   c) 2   d) 1
   e) 1   f) 2   g) 2   h) 2

Grammar 37

1 a) *a large old green plastic bag*
   b) two square wooden tables
   c) a beautiful red silk dress
   d) a pair of antique silver jugs
   e) a small plastic bowl
   f) a long winding country road
   g) some dirty old football boots
   h) a long yellow cotton skirt
   i) a glass of cold freshly squeezed orange juice

2 a) *boiling*   f) fantastic
   b) gigantic   g) worried
   c) tired   h) warmer
   d) cool   i) bored
   e) exciting   j) interested

3 a) *The old couple lived happily together.*
b) You've worked hard.
c) Chris and Paul walk slowly.
d) Georgia plays the piano well.
e) Sue dances gracefully.
f) Kate isn't well/doesn't feel well.
g) Michael skates wonderfully.
h) Mary writes carefully.
i) Alex slept badly.
j) Ann completed the course successfully.

4 a) *happy*   f) fast
b) well   g) quite
c) hardly   h) hard
d) good   i) terrible
e) ill   j) extremely

5 a) *Peter has been working very <u>hard</u>.*
b) My sister bought me a <u>lovely blue woollen</u> sweater.
c) This book I'm reading is <u>excellent/extremely good</u>.
d) David felt <u>bad</u> because he'd shouted at his mother.
e) Everyone in the team played <u>well</u>.
f) Too much exercise can make you feel <u>tired</u>.
g) Paula felt <u>happy</u> when her exams were over.
h) Hans <u>has never arrived</u> late at school.
i) One boxer hit the other really <u>hard</u> right on the chin.
j) I'm not really <u>interested</u> in this car.

Grammar 38

1 a) *as tasty as*
b) the most interesting
c) oldest
d) than
e) worse
f) tallest
g) as hard as
h) worse
i) longer than
j) more quietly

2 a) *the longest*
b) less entertaining
c) faster than
d) the hottest
e) better than
f) just as tall as
g) more difficult
h) as large as
i) not as big as/just as big as/bigger than
j) the worst

3 a) *as good a runner as David (is)*
b) tallest (person) in the class
c) more than me/than I have
d) longer than Jane's (hair)
e) noisiest student in the school
f) as interesting as this one (is)
g) go faster than this/go any faster
h) eat as much as Andrew (did)

4 a) *just as, as*
b) the most
c) more/less, than, did
d) more
e) than, the
f) the least
g) just as, as
h) less, than

5 a) *biggest*   i) harder
b) greatest   j) –
c) –   k) fitter
d) –   l) –
e) –   m) –
f) fatter   n) –
g) smallest   o) wider
h) –

6 a) *talk more slowly*
b) isn't as frightening
c) the best cook
d) as fast as
e) less economical than
f) more exciting than
g) as hard as
h) is more interested
i) is older than
j) more than me

Grammar 39

1 a) *3*   b) 5   c) 8   d) 1
e) 4   f) 2   g) 6   h) 7

2 a) at   g) up
b) for   h) on
c) to   i) up
d) down   j) up
e) over   k) to
f) for   l) out

3 a) *didn't live up to*
b) drop in on
c) run out of
d) get on with
e) caught up with
f) looking forward to
g) keep up with
h) cut down on

4 a) *Brian takes after his mother.*
b) We've run out of food!
c) Mike and Tom don't get on well with each other.
d) Jean is very good at dealing with people.
e) The handlebars on my bike need seeing to.
f) Julia was very ill, but she's got over it now.
g) What exactly are you getting at?
h) Paul's new school didn't live up to his expectations.

5 a) *The central heating system needs seeing to.*
b) Let's drop in on Julia while we're here.
c) We're heading for Paris.
d) Our hotel room looks out onto/over the main road!
e) Two children started playing, and then the others joined in.

f) We called on my aunt on her birthday.
g) I'm afraid that we've run out of eggs.
h) Monica will call for you at 6.30.
i) Nobody understood what I was getting at.
j) I can't put up with so much air pollution.

Grammar 40

1 a) *wash*   e) try
b) look   f) fill
c) set   g) turned
d) called   h) dropped

2 a) *Turn the lights off when you leave the school.*
b) Jack turned up half-way through the lesson.
c) We can put you up for a week.
d) Marta is getting on well in her English class.
e) Lidia grew up in Uruguay.
f) How do you turn on the computer/turn the computer on?
g) Carol looked up the dates/looked the dates up in an encyclopedia.
h) Surfing is a great sport. When did you take it up?

3 a) *3*   b) 8   c) 1   d) 6
e) 4   f) 5   g) 7   h) 3

Grammar 41

1 a) *better*   e) best
b) each   f) for
c) hard   g) no
d) some   h) is

2 1) *d*   2) a   3) c   4) a
5) d   6) d   7) b   8) c
9) b   10) a   11) b   12) d
13) c   14) b   15) c

3 a) *of these*
b) until
c) smoking is allowed
d) some advice
e) as long as
f) since
g) classroom
h) on foot
i) any further
j) in time

4 a) *I can put you up.*
b) Carlos can't put up with the traffic any more.
c) Peter is getting on well at university.
d) I'll clear up the room if you do the washing up.
e) We're heading for Madrid.
f) Why don't you look up this word/look this word up in the dictionary?
g) Jane takes after her father.
h) Kelly's father is trying to give up smoking.

5
1) ✓   7) ago   13) after
2) *the*   8) much   14) after
3) it   9) the   15) up
4) a   10) more   16) once
5) was   11) one   17) the
6) ✓   12) ✓   18) ✓

6
a) *the*   f) –   k) the
b) –   g) lot   l) the
c) –   h) much   m) the
d) the   i) the   n) a
e) for   j) any   o) either

7
a) *a single*
b) no cheese
c) rich are
d) beautifully
e) the worst film
f) until

8
a) *much, than*   e) all, both
b) the, than   f) as, as
c) the, a   g) until, by
d) some, much   h) best, ever

9
a) *I'm really <u>interested</u> in travel.*
b) Kate's brother is <u>a doctor</u>.
c) I ate <u>some food</u> with Jack, and after that I went home.
d) <u>Milk</u> is good for you.
e) Can you give me <u>some advice</u>?
f) I've looked in the box. <u>Everything</u> is broken, I'm afraid.
g) They will have finished the new hospital <u>by</u> the end of May./They <u>won't have finished</u> the new hospital until the end of May.
h) There's <u>a police officer/ policeman/policewoman</u> waiting outside.
i) I come to class <u>on foot</u>.
j) Your hair <u>is</u> very beautiful.

Grammar 42

1
a) *Jim can't afford <u>to go</u> to the cinema twice a week.*
b) David wishes <u>to leave</u> the room.
c) ✓
d) I'd really like <u>to go</u> swimming on Saturday.
e) Emma pretended <u>to leave</u>, but waited outside.
f) ✓
g) My bike seems <u>to have</u> something wrong with it.
h) The director refused <u>to answer</u> Helen's phone call.

2
a) *loves*   f) continued
b) afford   g) bear
c) happen   h) offered
d) expected   i) pretended
e) learned   j) prefers

3
a) *to let me leave early*
b) singing/to sing for an hour without stopping
c) (that) you've passed the exam
d) to do well/that he'll do well
e) to do for the summer
f) clearing up my room

g) to go to the cinema with me
h) to get married
i) to see you later
j) to do this evening

4
a) *seems*   f) refused
b) hate   g) chose
c) want   h) like
d) asked   i) decided
e) hopes   j) agreed

5
a) *What do you intend to do?*
b) I can't bear getting up early!
c) I expect to see you in the morning.
d) Susan promised to be back at 6.00.
e) Pat learned to drive when he was young.
f) I offered to help Joe.
g) Ellen couldn't afford the ticket.
h) Tom refused to help.

Grammar 43

1
a) *to lock*   e) to open
b) to have   f) to take
c) talking   g) sky-diving
d) being   h) starting

2
a) *you fancy*
b) (that) he'd
c) I suggest/How about
d) keeps interrupting
e) Do/Would you mind
f) Imagine being
g) denied writing
h) can't help

3
a) *chose*   e) denied
b) afford   f) admitted
c) mind   g) decided
d) meant   h) fancy

4
a) *try*   e) denied
b) pretended   f) practise
c) expect   g) imagine
d) meant   h) refused

5
a) *forget*   e) kept
b) means   f) tried
c) admit   g) remember
d) stop   h) stand/bear

Grammar 44

1
a) *from*   e) about
b) to   f) for
c) for   g) on
d) to

2
a) *laughs at*
b) succeeds in
c) apologizes for
d) depends on
e) knows about
f) belongs to
g) reminds, of

3
a) *right about*
b) good at
c) famous for
d) interested in
e) annoyed with
f) kind to
g) frightened of

4
a) *Dick was bored with his work.*
b) This town reminds me of Glasgow.
c) Sara knows a lot about biology.
d) I'm looking for the art gallery.
e) I'm fond of cream cakes.
f) Sue is married to Adrian.
g) Dina is kind to animals.
h) Ugh! This cake tastes of rubber!
i) Lisa is jealous of you!
j) I feel excited about our new house!

5
a) *'m angry with*
b) ready
c) good at
d) felt upset about
e) dreamed about
f) rely on
g) bike to Jack
h) afraid of

6
a) *explain, to*
b) belonged to
c) depends on
d) paid for
e) apologized, for
f) remind, of
g) succeeded in
h) wait for

7
a) *4*   b) 6   c) 5   d) 2
e) 7   f) 1   g) 3

Grammar 45

1
a) *anyone*   f) Someone
b) anything   g) anything
c) nothing   h) No one
d) someone   i) anywhere
e) anything   j) somewhere

2
a) *do anything*
b) knows Mary better than I do
c) was late yesterday
d) nothing/no work
e) ask you something
f) here drinks
g) replied when I phoned/answered the phone
h) someone going to drive us there
i) I go I make friends
j) called for you this morning

3
a) *enjoy yourselves*
b) behave ourselves
c) hurt myself
d) express herself
e) introduce myself
f) blame yourself
g) talk, myself
h) cut himself

4
a) *There's something in the box.*
b) Everyone was dancing.
c) Something has annoyed/is annoying me.
d) There's nothing to eat./We've got nothing to eat.
e) There's no one in the office.
f) Everybody likes Julia.
g) You can have anything you like./Anything you like you can have.
h) Nowhere is better than home.

5 a) *Everybody/Everyone*
   b) something
   c) Something
   d) someone/somebody
   e) themselves
   f) One
   g) Everything
   h) Nothing
   i) yourself
   j) myself

6 a) *Someone spoke to me, but I can't remember their name.*
   b) Everything in the garden has been growing a lot lately.
   c) Carol didn't do anything/did nothing yesterday.
   d) There isn't anyone/There's no one waiting for you.
   e) Pete and Kate enjoyed themselves at the party.
   f) You fill in an application form, and then you wait for an answer./One fills in an application form, and then one waits for an answer.
   g) We need to do the shopping. There isn't anything in the fridge.

Grammar 46

1 a) *hers* e) theirs h) my
   b) her own f) your i) our
   c) yours g) his j) its
   d) mine

2 a) *Tell Monica it's Elena's turn, not hers.*
   b) Alice's younger brother's called Bill.
   c) Tim's sandwiches were tastier than ours.
   d) The film's beginning is good but its ending is weak.
   e) Are these keys yours or hers?
   f) Barbara fills in the patients' record cards at the doctor's.
   g) When it's raining, everybody's raincoats get wet.
   h) The manager's assistant reads all the customers' letters.
   i) Your sister's dog runs faster than ours.
   j) One's our teacher's car and the other's a visitor's.

3 a) *football boot, cheese sandwich*
   b) shop window, coat pocket
   c) garden gate, bicycle light
   d) department store, country cottage
   e) fire engine, rock singer
   f) post office, pencil sharpener
   g) football ground, school report
   h) shop assistant, railway station

4 a) *my sister's*
   b) are Sam's
   c) friend of mine
   d) my favourite television
   e) are your teachers'

f) a tin opener
g) are our neighbours'
h) on the kitchen

5 a) *There are two bus stops near my house.*
   b) Our cat sleeps all day in its bed.
   c) Have you met Jane's sister?
   d) Creatures like these live at the bottom of the sea.
   e) This book is mine.
   f) Those are two friends of my father's.
   g) Everybody's drawings were better than ours.
   h) Are these gloves yours or mine?/Are these your gloves or mine?
   i) The house stands on its own at the end of the street.
   j) I noticed these shoes in a shop window.

Grammar 47

1 a) *instead of* e) except
   b) either f) since
   c) also g) both
   d) such as h) yet

2 a) *Debra visited the castle and the museum, too.*
   b) Everyone was on time except Jill.
   c) I said it was raining but, in fact, it isn't!
   d) Karen couldn't play tennis, since she'd hurt her leg.
   e) In my view, smoking is bad for you.
   f) I ate the chocolate cake as well as the apple pie.
   g) Daniel played in goal instead of his brother.
   h) In conclusion, I'd like to thank the head teacher, Ann Coles.

3 1) c 2) b 3) a 4) d
   5) d 6) c 7) b 8) d
   9) a 10) b

4 a) *except* e) instead
   b) as well as this f) actually
   c) Personally g) such as
   d) both h) either

5 a) 5 b) 9 c) 3 d) 7
   e) 1 f) 4 g) 10 h) 2
   i) 8 j) 6

Grammar 48

1 a) *1* b) 2 c) 2 d) 2
   e) 3 f) 1

2 a) *We're meeting Uncle David on Tuesday evening at eight.*
   b) Last February I met Mrs Wilkinson for the first time.
   c) Tim lives in the south of France near Cannes.
   d) We saw a great film at the ABC called 'The Remains of the Day'.
   e) We went to a party at Mrs Harrisons' house on New Year's Eve.

f) Julia's reading 'A Portrait of a Lady' by Henry James.

3 a) *'First of all, who is going to carry the suitcase?' asked Emilie.*
   b) Kate said she'd be on time, but I didn't believe her.
   c) James said that he'd missed the train, got lost, and been arrested.
   d) When the bell rang, our teacher stood up and said, 'Stop writing, please.'
   e) 'On the other hand, we could go to the cinema, couldn't we?' said David.
   f) 'Good morning,' said Tina. 'How do you feel today?'
   g) If I were you, I'd ask for some help, or perhaps start again.
   h) The old stadium was eventually demolished: very few people went there, and it was becoming dangerous.

Grammar 49

1 a) *deciding* g) their
   b) swimming h) beautiful
   c) photo i) receipt
   d) question j) beginning
   e) ✓ k) psychiatrist
   f) known l) successful

2 a) *phone, received*
   b) whistle, field
   c) successfully, physics
   d) know, knife
   e) thief, leaving
   f) question, listening
   g) beginning, view
   h) columns, beautifully

3 a) *controlling* g) upsetting
   b) thickening h) hooking
   c) gripping i) writing
   d) choosing j) improving
   e) flying k) swimming
   f) making l) riding

4 Dear Becky,
   I'm sorry that I haven't written to you for so long. I'm afraid I've been very busy at school, and I haven't had much time for writing letters. Last week I finished my examinations, so now I'm getting ready to go on holiday.
   I was wondering whether you would like to come to stay for a few days? You can meet my friends, and we could all go swimming. The weather is really good now here in Italy, and I'm sure you will enjoy yourself.
   Best wishes,
   Silvia

5 a) *tomorrow*
   b) Wednesday
   c) advertisement
   d) neighbour
   e) through
   f) grateful
   g) necessary

h) disappointed
i) weather/whether
j) remember
k) library
l) answer

6 a) *debt*   j) autum**n**
  b) ex**h**ibition   k) ans**w**er
  c) hig**h**   l) daug**h**ter
  d) **k**nife   m) hal**f**
  e) lam**b**   n) ligh**t**
  f) **p**sychologist o) sal**m**on
  g) recei**p**t   p) **w**hole
  h) w**h**at   q) would
  i) ya**ch**t   r) **w**riting

Grammar 50

1 a) *4* b) 1 c) 9 d) 3
  e) 7 f) 2 g) 6 h) 5
  i) 8

2 a) *stare*   f) quite
  b) practise   g) aloud
  c) thorough   h) too
  d) advice   i) latter
  e) fare   j) loose

3 a) *3* b) – c) 3 d) –
  e) 3 f) 3 g) – h) 3
  i) – j) 3 k) 3 l) –
  m) – n) – o) –

4 Dear Silvia,
Thanks for your letter and your invitation to Italy! I've never travelled abroad before, and I'm really looking forward to staying with you and your family. I've spoken to my parents and they've agreed. They say they're going to phone soon to discuss the arrangements.
I've decided to have some Italian lessons so that I can practise when I come to Italy. I'd like you to write some simple sentences for me.
Please note my new address. We moved last week and now I've got a much bigger bedroom.
Best wishes,
Becky

5 a) *vegetable*   g) interesting
  b) language   h) biscuit
  c) queue   i) ceiling
  d) receive   j) different
  e) people   k) knowledge
  f) beautiful   l) independent

6 a) *eight* h) none
  b) bean   i) piece
  c) check   j) pair
  d) flower   k) write
  e) whole   l) rows
  f) muscle   m) so
  g) know   n) stair

Grammar 51

1 a) *hers*   e) anything
  b) to help   f) spending
  c) in   g) at
  d) as   h) anything

2 1) *b*   2) d   3) d   4) a
  5) c   6) b   7) a   8) d
  9) c   10) b 11) b 12) d
  13) a 14) c 15) c

3 a) *except Jeff*
  b) one knows
  c) the twins'
  d) refused to carry
  e) rely on
  f) a friend of
  g) began/started snowing
  h) closing

4 1) ✓   7) been   13) they
  2) *that* 8) got   14) ✓
  3) take 9) ✓   15) have
  4) me   10) for   16) with
  5) it   11) or   17) it
  6) for 12) it

5 a) *for*   i) forgotten
  b) her   j) even
  c) of   k) something
  d) no one/nobody l) Either
  e) begun/started m) kept
  f) hers   n) saw
  g) seemed   o) Someone
  h) with

6 Dear David,
It was great to hear from you after so long. I enjoyed hearing all your news. I didn't realize that you'd spent a year abroad. You must have had a really good time in Greece. I've decided to go there next summer. Perhaps we could go together.
I've had a fantastic year at college. The work is harder than the work we did at school, but it's more interesting. I'm studying Business Administration and Computer Science at the moment. I've also made lots of new friends.
I'm thinking of coming to Bristol for a few days to visit my sister. Would you like to meet? You could show me the sights and we could talk about our old schooldays.
Why don't you give me a ring and we could discuss it. It would be wonderful to see you again.
Best wishes,
Ellen

7 a) *Instead of*   f) as well
  b) every single   g) yours
  c) in fact   h) herself
  d) In conclusion i) on, in
  e) of my, mine   j) even

Vocabulary answers

Vocabulary 2

1. a) *uninteresting*
   b) disadvantage
   c) unfortunately
   d) impatient
   e) disappears
   f) unemployed
   g) disagree
   h) misunderstanding

2. a) *overslept*   e) rewrite
   b) underwear   f) overcooked
   c) overcoat   g) renew
   d) outplayed   h) underpaid

3. a) *friendship*
   b) foreigner
   c) childhood
   d) stewardess
   e) teenager
   f) spoonful
   g) neighbourhood
   h) handful
   i) machinery
   j) booklet

4. a) *inhabitants*
   b) boredom
   c) building
   d) accommodation
   e) refusal
   f) actor
   g) employee
   h) imagination
   i) cooker
   j) advertisement

5. a) *shortness*   f) thoroughness
   b) friendliness   g) happiness
   c) darkness   h) silliness
   d) loneliness   i) thinness
   e) tiredness   j) sickness

6. a) *heroic*   e) dangerous
   b) musical   f) foolish
   c) homeless   g) rainy
   d) motherly

Vocabulary 3

1. a) *tired*   f) confusing
   b) disappointing   g) exhausting
   c) frightening   h) interested
   d) embarrassed   i) surprised
   e) bored   j) annoying

2. a) *unlikely*   f) dislike
   b) shortage   g) sleepy
   c) impossible   h) unusual
   d) photography   i) cheerful
   e) useful   j) kindness

3. a) *unusually*
   b) surprisingly
   c) Interestingly
   d) successfully
   e) beautifully
   f) thoroughly
   g) awfully
   h) unsuccessfully
   i) unnecessarily
   j) obviously

4. a) *uncomfortable*
   b) independent
   c) reusable
   d) disappointment
   e) relationship
   f) unselfish
   g) unhealthy
   h) uncontrollable
   i) unshrinkable
   j) inexperienced

5. a) *receipt*   e) Marriage
   b) politician   f) application
   c) depth   g) knowledge
   d) patience   h) explanation

6. a) *theft*   e) angry
   b) belief   f) bravery
   c) suspicion   g) vanity
   d) length   h) ability

Vocabulary 4

1. a) *Have*   f) give   k) have
   b) do   g) take   l) take
   c) have   h) make   m) give
   d) make   i) do   n) take
   e) give   j) do   o) make

2. a) *4*   b) 8   c) 5
   d) 1   e) 10   f) 3
   g) 6   h) 9   i) 2
   j) 7

3. a) *protect, skin*
   b) clear, space
   c) appear, screen
   d) return, call
   e) rent, flat
   f) fight, suvival
   g) take, minute
   h) control, behaviour

4. a) ~~especially~~   f) ~~highly~~
   b) ~~properly~~   g) ~~perfectly~~
   c) ~~completely~~   h) ~~largely~~
   d) ~~greatly~~   i) ~~deeply~~
   e) ~~really~~   j) ~~strongly~~

5. a) *bank account*
   b) bargain price
   c) space shuttle

   d) sea floor
   e) student loan
   f) meat dish
   g) stomach ache

6. a) *afford to*   f) teach me how to
   b) likely to   g) slow to
   c) hard to   h) forget to
   d) hope to   i) designed to
   e) try not to   j) willing to

Vocabulary 5

1. a) *high*   d) pass   g) in
   b) spare   e) tell   h) lose
   c) time   f) on

2. a) *made*   e) burst   h) paid
   b) had   f) told   i) caught
   c) took   g) got   j) lost
   d) spent

3. a) *mess*   e) mad
   b) breath   f) temper
   c) alone   g) secret
   d) difference   h) leaf

4. a) *a bird*   e) a pig
   b) a bat   f) a picture
   c) life   g) rain
   d) a cucumber   h) houses

5. a) *life*   e) time
   b) soul   f) sound
   c) wide   g) down
   d) round   h) then

6. a) *have an early night*
   b) get ready
   c) take a day off
   d) have fun
   e) have nothing to do
   f) take it easy

Vocabulary 6

1. a) *footpath*   e) haircut
   b) paper clip   f) sunglasses
   c) shoelace   g) headache
   d) timetable   h) lamp post

2. a) *science fiction*
   b) walking stick
   c) school report
   d) alarm clock
   e) air-conditioning
   f) birthday party
   g) central heating
   h) washing machine

3. a) *bottle top*
   b) shop window
   c) bicycle pump

d) school entrance
e) bathroom mirror
f) television screen
g) pocket money
h) door handle

4 a) *hairdrier*
b) dishwasher
c) stain remover
d) fire extinguisher
e) pencil sharpener
f) bottle opener
g) lawn mower
h) food mixer
i) water heater
j) coffee maker

5 a) *day-dreamer*
b) shopkeeper
c) sunbather
d) babysitter
e) weightlifter
f) fire-fighter
g) bank manager
h) holidaymaker

6 a) *income*   f) upbringing
b) upset   g) outdoors
c) roundabout   h) outskirts
d) downstairs   i) Underground
e) overcoat   j) downpour

Vocabulary 7

1 a) *second-hand*
b) can't afford it
c) pay you back
d) save up
e) in debt
f) annual income
g) in a sale
h) be well-off

2 a) *pocket money*
b) cash desk
c) cut price
d) bookshop
e) department store
f) shop assistant
g) credit card
h) carrier bag

3 a) *earns*   e) by cheque
b) wages   f) receipt
c) borrowed   g) change
d) cash   h) owe

4 a) 6 b) 5 c) 7 d) 2 e) 4 f) 1
g) 8 h) 3

5 a) *packet*   e) box
b) tube   f) bar
c) tin   g) bunch
d) carton   h) loaf

6 1) *C*   2) A   3) D   4) C
5) B   6) D   7) A   8) D
9) A   10) B   11) C   12) A
13) C   14) B   15) D

Vocabulary 8

1 a) *cushion*   e) curtains
b) socket   f) carpet
c) radiator   g) drawer
d) pillow   h) sofa

2 a) *4* b) 5   c) 6   d) 1
e) 3 f) 2   g) 8   h) 7

3 a) *glass* – window
b) cloth – towel
c) door – gate
d) ground – floor
e) library – bookcase
f) wall – fence
g) fireplace – chimney
h) stair – step

4 a) *at home*   f) cupboard
b) stairs   g) at, in
c) wash-basin   h) a bath
d) ceiling   i) housework
e) cook, cooker   j) cellar

5 a) *bedroom*   f) dishwasher
b) armchair   g) keyhole
c) wash-basin   h) ashtray
d) dustbin   i) downstairs
e) flowerbed   j) bookcase

6 a) *put*   d) takes   g) looks
b) move   e) turn   h) drop
c) get   f) finish

Vocabulary 9

1 a) *angry*   f) bored
b) embarrassed g) cheerful
c) polite   h) bad-tempered
d) lazy   i) upset
e) sensible   j) nervous

2 a) *smile*   e) cry
b) nod   f) cheer
c) complain   g) shake his head
d) shout   h) whistle

3 a) *unreliable*
b) impatient
c) uninterested
d) dishonest
e) unfriendly
f) inexperienced
g) impolite
h) unhelpful
i) inconsiderate
j) unco-operative

4 a) *disappointed* e) ashamed
b) annoyed   f) exhausted
c) terrified   g) jealous
d) glad   h) fascinating

5 a) *longing for*   e) fancy
b) give up   f) fed up with
c) put me off   g) are fond of
d) get on my   h) let me down
   nerves

6 a) *mood*   f) heart
b) Thanks   g) conscience
c) trouble   h) temper
d) voice   i) hand
e) tears   j) death

7 Positive   Negative
Kind   *Unpleasant*
cheerful   lazy
clever   tense
generous   mean
relaxed   miserable
hard-working   stupid

Vocabulary 10

1 a) *husband*   f) single
b) couple   g) friendship
c) children   h) elder
d) twin   i) engaged
e) alike   j) housewife

2 a) *relations/relatives*
b) acquaintance
c) greeting
d) engagement
e) celebration
f) marriage
g) resemblance
h) death

3 a) *adults*   e) old
b) dead   f) young
c) wedding   g) relatives
d) daughter   h) birthday

4 a) *6* b) 9   c) 10 d) 8
e) 1 f) 7   g) 5   h) 2
i) 3 j) 4

5 a) *5* b) 4   c) 7   d) 1
e) 8 f) 6   g) 2   h) 3

6 a) *in*   e) after
b) away   f) out
c) on and off g) against
d) on   h) over

7 a) *grandparents* f) nephew
b) uncle   g) niece
c) aunt   h) only child
d) stepson   i) foreigner
e) sister-in-law j) stranger

Vocabulary 11

1 a) *waist*   e) shoulder
b) wrist   f) ankle
c) thumb   g) toes
d) nails   h) forehead

2 1) *C*   2) B   3) B   4) A
5) D   6) C   7) D   8) B
9) A   10) B   11) D   12) C
13) A   14) D   15) C

3 a) *fit*   e) suit
   b) dress up   f) disguise
   c) wear   g) put on
   d) look   h) go with

4 a) *sleeve* d) cap   g) blouse
   b) dress   e) shorts   h) sock
   c) suit   f) skirt

5 a) *tongue* e) arms   i) hand
   b) hair   f) heart   j) eye
   c) face   g) head
   d) foot   h) leg

6 a) cheek   h) shoulder
   b) chin   i) elbow
   c) neck   j) wrist
   d) bust   k) hip
   e) waist   l) bottom
   f) thigh   m) ankle
   g) knee   n) foot

Vocabulary 12

1 a) *crashed*   e) flooded
   b) injured   f) blocked
   c) collapsed   g) sank
   d) exploded   h) trapped

2 a) *prescription* e) pain
   b) temperature   f) chemist's
   c) get over   g) flu
   d) heal   h) sore throat

3 a) *bandage*   e) ward
   b) hospital   f) surgeon
   c) patient   g) blood
   d) operation   h) ambulance

4 a) *traffic jam*
   b) air pollution
   c) power failure
   d) parking ticket
   e) train strike
   f) car park
   g) bus stop
   h) rush hour
   i) water shortage
   j) city centre

5 a) *6*   b) 10   c) 2   d) 8
   e) 3   f) 5   g) 7   h) 1
   i) 9   j) 4

6 a) *3*   b) 6   c) 5   d) 2
   e) 4   f) 8   g) 1   h) 7

7 a) *3*   b) 9   c) 2   d) 6
   e) 5   f) 1   g) 8   h) 4
   i) 7

Vocabulary 13

1 1) *C*   2) D   3) A   4) D
   5) B   6) B   7) A   8) C
   9) A   10) D   11) C   12) B
   13) B   14) D   15) A

2 a) *down*   d) in   g) after
   b) off   e) for
   c) up   f) out

3 a) *information* e) reservation
   b) runway   f) cancellation
   c) departure   g) airport
   d) landing   h) takeoff

4 a) *7*   b) 3   c) 10   d) 8
   e) 1   f) 4   g) 9   h) 2
   i) 6   j) 5

5 a) *ancient*   f) suntanned
   b) seasick   g) reasonable
   c) popular   h) exhausted
   d) relaxing   i) warm
   e) local   j) open

6 a) *resort*   f) station
   b) breakfast   g) stop
   c) walk   h) village
   d) holiday   i) hostel
   e) ticket   j) cards

Vocabulary 14

1 a) *beat*   f) going
   b) applauded   g) drew
   c) enter for   h) spends
   d) holding   i) enjoy
   e) performed   j) missed

2 a) *spectators* f) group
   b) athletes   g) audience
   c) fans   h) viewers
   d) team   i) cast
   e) members   j) competitors

3 a) *prize*   f) ticket
   b) medal   g) exhibition
   c) queue   h) rod
   d) tyre   i) line
   e) whistle   j) screen

4 a) *knock* d) live   g) stand
   b) turn   e) go   h) drop
   c) join   f) make

5 a) *8*   b) 5   c) 7   d) 2
   e) 6   f) 3   g) 4   h) 1

6 1) *B*   2) C   3) B   4) A
   5) D   6) D   7) A   8) B
   9) A   10) C   11) D   12) C
   13) B   14) A   15) D

Vocabulary 15

1 1) *B*   2) D   3) C   4) A
   5) C   6) D   7) A   8) B
   9) B   10) C   11) D   12) A
   13) C   14) D   15) A

2 a) *square*   e) footpath
   b) countryside   f) view
   c) beach   g) Parking
   d) ground   h) country

3 a) *station*   f) part
   b) junction   g) place
   c) hall   h) traffic
   d) block   i) zone
   e) crossing   j) centre

4 a) *rural*   e) international
   b) neighbouring   f) local
   c) isolated   g) crowded
   d) capital   h) urban

5 a) *playground*   e) footpath
   b) crossroads   f) roadside
   c) roundabout   g) outskirts
   d) car park   h) footbridge

6 a) *castle*
   b) caravan
   c) semi-detached house
   d) bungalow
   e) bridge
   f) terraced house
   g) cottage
   h) tower

Vocabulary 16

1 a) *roll*   f) recipe
   b) course   g) tasty
   c) meal   h) cook
   d) cans   i) spoon
   e) frozen

2 a) *roast*   f) Peel
   b) mix   g) fry
   c) chop   h) Grate
   d) bake   i) Squeeze
   e) add   j) Boil

3 a) *salt*   e) chips
   b) fork   f) vinegar
   c) bacon   g) saucer
   d) butter   h) biscuits

4 a) *slice*   e) loaf
   b) bar   f) glass
   c) jar   g) pinch
   d) cup   h) carton/glass

5 a) *grape*   e) pie
   b) onion   f) plum
   c) lettuce   g) cheese
   d) lamb   h) chop

6 a) *menu*   d) takeaway
   b) bill   e) book
   c) dessert   f) tip

7 a) *a*
   b) some
   c) a
   d) –
   e) a
   f) a
   g) a
   h) –
   i) –
   j) some

8 a) lettuce   h) asparagus
   b) broccoli   i) courgette
   c) cauliflower j) celery
   d) pepper   k) cabbage
   e) leek   l) bean
   f) onion   m) carrot
   g) mushroom   n) aubergine

Vocabulary 17

1 a) *pass*   f) wages
   b) job   g) aloud
   c) teach   h) application
   d) studying   i) earns
   e) marks   j) office

2 a) *heart*   e) rules
   b) phone   f) date
   c) practice   g) time
   d) work   h) business

3 a) *look*   e) pick
   b) take   f) write
   c) get   g) hand
   d) keep   h) stand

4 a) *education*   f) employer
   b) unemployed   g) timetable
   c) carelessly   h) income
   d) successful   i) knowledge
   e) qualifications j) employees

5 a) 7   b) 10   c) 1   d) 9
   e) 6   f) 3   g) 5   h) 2
   i) 8   j) 4

6 1) *D*   2) B   3) B   4) A
   5) C   6) D   7) B   8) B
   9) A   10) B   11) D   12) D
   13) C   14) B   15) A

Vocabulary 18

1 a) *weather*   f) heatwave
   b) lightning   g) storm
   c) fog   h) cool
   d) shower   i) soaked
   e) season   j) snow

2 a) *swan*   f) mosquito
   b) goat   g) rabbit
   c) crab   h) giraffe
   d) butterfly   i) spider
   e) lizard   j) puppy

3 a) *branch*   e) thorn
   b) berry   f) bark
   c) root   g) blossom
   d) leaf   h) trunk

4 a) 8   b) 4   c) 7   d) 2
   e) 1   f) 8   g) 5   h) 3

5 1) *a*   2) c   3) d   4) c
   5) a   6) b   7) b   8) c
   9) d   10) b   11) a   12) d
   13) b   14) d   15) c

6 a) *protect, destroy*
   b) prevent, let
   c) clean up, pollute
   d) plant, cut down
   e) recycle, throw (them) away

7 a) *city, country*
   b) hills, mountains
   c) river, stream
   d) paths, tracks

   e) weeds, crops
   f) village, town
   g) fence, hedge
   h) farm, cottage

Vocabulary 19

1 a) *cell phone*   e) engine
   b) petrol   f) light
   c) electric   g) nails
   d) tyre   h) plumber

2 a) *answering machine*
   b) mobile phone
   c) sewing machine
   d) vacuum cleaner
   e) camera
   f) dishwasher
   g) photocopier

3 a) *ring*   e) plug   h) go
   b) blow   f) cut   i) warm
   c) wear   g) turn   j) run
   d) break

4 a) hard disk
   b) memory
   c) icon
   d) cursor
   e) print out
   f) button
   g) website
   h) modem
   i) highlight

5 a) *car*   e) frying pan
   b) electric   f) saw
      toothbrush   g) gun
   c) ladder   h) cello
   d) oven

6 a) *handle*   e) key
   b) battery   f) lock
   c) socket   g) plug
   d) switch   h) wire

7 a) *pump*   f) scissors
   b) tin-opener   g) thermometer
   c) lawnmower   h) binoculars
   d) razor   i) compass
   e) hairdrier   j) iron

Vocabulary 20

1 a) *needle*   f) string
   b) glue   g) scissors
   c) penknife   h) buttons
   d) rubber band   i) shoelace
   e) paper clip   j) ribbon

2 a) *notice*   f) file
   b) notepad   g) ruler
   c) correction   h) sharpener
      fluid   i) stamp
   d) diary   j) dictionary
   e) envelope

3 a) *hook*   e) curtains
   b) tablecloth   f) broom
   c) plant   g) doormat
   d) dustbin   h) fireplace

4 a) *comb*   f) toothpaste
   b) gown   g) alarm
   c) mirror   h) towel
   d) table   i) pillow
   e) slippers   j) hanger

5 a) *pedestrian crossing*
   b) lamp post
   c) pavement
   d) hedge
   e) gate
   f) kerb
   g) street sign
   h) subway

Vocabulary 21

1 a) *employer*   f) officer
   b) owner   g) painter
   c) mechanic   h) cashier
   d) manager   i) waiter
   e) teacher   j) postman

2 a) *gardener*   f) carpenter
   b) guide   g) electrician
   c) plumber   h) optician
   d) photographer   i) vet
   e) dentist   j) hairdresser

3 a) *member*   f) employee
   b) partner   g) supporter
   c) flatmate   h) team-mate
   d) guest   i) assistant
   e) host

4 a) *coward*   f) expert
   b) miser   g) fool
   c) optimist   h) genius
   d) celebrity   i) pessimist
   e) favourite   j) liar

5 a) *crew*   f) trio
   b) society   g) group
   c) staff   h) audience
   d) queue   i) team
   e) crowd   j) cast

6 a) *inhabitants*   f) scientist
   b) politician   g) criminal
   c) citizen   h) musician
   d) guitarist   i) lawyer
   e) survivor   j) opponent